Herschell Gordon Lewis, Godfather of Gore

ALSO BY RANDY PALMER

*Paul Blaisdell, Monster Maker:
A Biography of the B Movie Makeup
and Special Effects Artist*
(McFarland, 1997)

Herschell Gordon Lewis, Godfather of Gore:
The Films

by
RANDY PALMER

Foreword by HERSCHELL GORDON LEWIS
Foreword by DAVID F. FRIEDMAN

McFarland & Company, Inc., Publishers
Jefferson, North Carolina, and London

The present work is a reprint of the illustrated case bound edition of Herschell Gordon Lewis, Godfather of Gore: The Films, *first published in 2000 by McFarland.*

LIBRARY OF CONGRESS CATALOGUING-IN-PUBLICATION DATA

Palmer, Randy, 1953–
Herschell Gordon Lewis, godfather of gore : the films / by Randy Palmer ; foreword by Herschell Gordon Lewis ; foreword by David F. Friedman.
p. cm.
Includes filmography and index.

ISBN-13: 978-0-7864-2850-2
ISBN-10: 0-7864-2850-3 (softcover : 50# alkaline paper) ∞

1. Lewis, Herschell Gordon, 1926– . I. Title.
PN1998.3.L4682P35 2006 791.43'2233'092 — dc21 99-88929

British Library cataloguing data are available

©2000 Randy Palmer. All rights reserved

No part of this book may be reproduced or transmitted in any form or by any means, electronic or mechanical, including photocopying or recording, or by any information storage and retrieval system, without permission in writing from the publisher.

Cover images from promotional material for the film *A Taste of Blood* (1968)

Manufactured in the United States of America

*McFarland & Company, Inc., Publishers
Box 611, Jefferson, North Carolina 28640
www.mcfarlandpub.com*

To Charles and Jimmy

For bloody great times at the Savoy
and the Lee Highway Drive-In

Acknowledgments

I am deeply indebted to Herschell Gordon Lewis, who gave freely of his time over the years to repeatedly answer the same fool questions I asked every time I spoke to him. (Hey, I was forgetful!)

Special thanks to Charles Perry, who led me to the Quiet Room and provided the kind of help I needed when I needed it the most. (Are all quiet rooms padded like that one, CP?)

Thanks also to Patricia Miller (who knows a monster when she sees one), David F. Friedman, the Ranch Drive-In (long gone, but fondly remembered), Hungry Mother in association with Trash, Inc., and Taryn (who roused me from a fever-induced stupor on the Night of the Living Drive-In with a glass of Alka-Seltzer, and who was there when it counted the most).

A very special thanks to my eternal Lewis compatriots Geof O'Keefe and Bobby Liebling, who risked potentially lethal beatings by suburban Maryland rednecks just so we could get to the Ranch Drive-In Theatre in order to participate in the HGL festivities every Halloween. ("Electric In-Car Heaters! Free Coffee & Do-Nuts to Survivors!") We made it out alive.

Unless otherwise specified in the text, all quotations attributed to Herschell Gordon Lewis are either from interviews of Mr. Lewis conducted by the author, or from personal correspondence between Mr. Lewis and the author.

Contents

Acknowledgments	vii
Foreword by Herschell Gordon Lewis	1
Foreword by David F. Friedman	3
Preface	5
1. A Scar Is Born	7
2. Sexploitation Ain't No Dirty Word	11
3. Primed for Profit	15
4. Lucky Strikes	21
5. Sin 'n' Skin	27
6. A Slip of the Tongue	38
7. How Did It Play in Peoria?	60
8. A Little Southern Hospitality Never Hurt Anyone … Much	66
9. Canvassing for Corpuscles	83
10. Moonshine Monsters	97
11. 100 Percent Weird	104
12. Whatever Flips Your Wig	109
13. Sex-O-Rama	116
14. Gouts of Blood	121
15. Hellraiser	132
16. California Cowpoke	141
17. Here Comes Mr. Wizard	144
18. What a Bunch of Yahoos!	157
19. Gore Smorgasbord	160
20. Life After Gore	172
Filmography	183
Index	187

Foreword
by Herschell Gordon Lewis

Writing an introduction to another author's book about me is something like writing my own obituary. It isn't a comfortable task.

But Randy Palmer has accomplished what biographers of other people, ranging from Michael Jackson to Ronald Reagan, haven't been able to match: he combines fact with humor, whimsy with judgment, all without damage.

I have to admit that Randy has remembered, discovered, unearthed, or found somewhere episodes and events I had forgotten. So I can't accuse him of lack of scholarship ... not that scholarship pertains to the body of work he and I both regard with sardonic realism.

Nor can I accuse him of misinterpreting what I meant to convey, movie by movie. He seems to have a better handle on that than I did.

The facts are unassailable, incontrovertible, and, from a cinematic point of view, laughable: Dave Friedman and I produced and directed a movie that forever changed the course of motion picture history.

From there on, historians differ. Some accuse us of corrupting movie morality. Sorry, kids, movie morality was thoroughly corrupted before we got there. Others heap accolades on our stooping shoulders for opening wide the gates of realism in films. Sorry, kids, the one noun that can't apply to *Blood Feast* is "realism." It was as far-out a chunk of fantasy as anyone could ever conjure up.

What *Blood Feast* did was inaugurate a new genre of film — movies that didn't depend on star names or expensive effects or tons of studio hype–dollars to get themselves booked in theatres.

Oh, certainly low-budget films existed long, long before *Blood Feast*. Certainly there were films that didn't depend on star names, and films released (make that "excreted") without studio hype.

But not in one piece.

Two remarkable phenomena attend the collection of gore movies I made so long ago. First, it's remarkable that you're reading these words. After all, a logical question is, "Who the hell is this guy?" Actually, my professional "position" is considerably stronger in a profession whose requirements, talents, and applications are entirely different from moviemaking. That you bought or borrowed this book is ... well, it's amazing.

Second, here we have a gaggle of movies that in their entirety don't represent one-tenth the budget of a single major studio horror film. Yet they exist. People rent them on video every day. Some of them are available on DVD. In fact, theatres still play them, years and years after the original sins were committed! And how many of the big budget extravaganzas, made in that same era, still show anywhere? The longevity of *Blood Feast* and *Two Thousand Maniacs!* and *The Wizard of Gore* and *The Gore-Gore Girls* and *A Taste of Blood* and even two of my least favorite embarrassments, *Color Me Blood Red* and *The Gruesome Twosome* ... well, it's amazing.

So here we all are, many decades later. I still get phone calls asking if I'm interested in making *Blood Feast Part 2*. (My standard answer: "I have the script ready. Put your financing together and then call me." It effectively ends those negotiations.)

Randy, dear fellow, thank you for this book. Thank you for bringing back lost memories. Thank you for the permanence a book superimposes on any life or circumstance, no matter how trivial or insignificant that life or circumstance might be.

It occurs to me that all of us associated with these watershed pictures had a rollicking good time making them. No, no, we didn't realize that we were establishing our tiny beachhead in the history of filmmaking. But what the heck — it makes reminiscing that much sweeter, doesn't it?

What is so delightful is that Randy Palmer's text is absolutely in sync with my own irreverence. Even if I hadn't been the subject of his writing, I'd have enjoyed reading this. And I can't think of any greater compliment to bestow on an author.

— H. G. L., *Fort Lauderdale, Florida*
Fall 1999

Foreword
by David F. Friedman

One of the more auspicious days in my long, happy life occurred in 1959, when a gentleman introducing himself as Herschell Lewis called my office in Chicago, asking for an appointment to discuss the possibility of our firm distributing a feature film he was about to produce. The firm, Modern Film Distributors, was a small but relatively successful independent states-rights movie middleman, primarily serving theaters and drive-ins in the midwestern states, and occasionally handling a picture nationwide. I was, at age 35, one of the two partners owning the company.

"Sure," I said. "When would you like to meet?"

"I can be there in 20 minutes. I'm just up on the Near North."

"Come on over then."

Herschell has always been prompt. He walked in, smiling, tall, confident, conservatively well-dressed, impressive in grooming and mien. We sat, sipping soft drinks I'd offered, making introductory small talk. The guy was sharp as a straight razor. His wit was quick, his vocabulary on par with Roget's.

He told me about himself and his movie. He was in the business of making commercial and industrial films, an enterprise that flourished in Chicago at the time. As he related the story line of his feature project, I realized he knew what the independent film trade was all about. Anticipating the Big Question, he told me he had all the financing in place and didn't need any advance or guarantee from a distributor. That was the first time I'd ever heard that from a producer. That's what made this a truly auspicious day.

I've been in the motion picture business since "film" was a two-syllable word. In the 50-plus years I spent in this great racket, I had some great mentors: Jerry Pickman at Paramount, Kroger Babb, Dan Sonney, Russ Meyer and, more than all the others, Herschell Gordon Lewis.

While I had a basic education in the technical aspects of filmmaking, courtesy of the U.S. Army Signal Corps during WWII, Herschell honed that knowledge into a high school graduate level of competence. But more importantly, he made of me a semi-cultured individual who knew of Bizet and Borodin, Smetana and Sibelius, Lear and Laertes, Iago and Iolanthe. I, in turn, taught him carny slang and how to figure a house-nut, sliding-scale film deal.

A typical Herschellism: when asked by an impecunious crew member for the loan of five dollars until payday, Herschell would reply, "Like Polonius, I would neither a borrower nor a lender be." The supplicant, totally unable to fathom this quote, would quietly wander back to work, pondering for the rest of the day's shoot what had been said.

From that propitious day in 1959 until Herschell and I went our separate ways in 1964, our association was one of creative energy, mutual respect, consummate camaraderie, and joyous memories. The filmic output of those years, discussed in the following pages, continue to be shown in various mediums of transmission all over the world.

Whatever success I had in writing and producing movies after our split, I owe primarily to drinking at the fantastic fount of knowledge that flowed from the mind and mouth of Herschell Gordon Lewis.

— D. F. F., *Anniston, Alabama*
Fall 1999

Preface

Just think: Had Herschell Gordon Lewis not made a minor motion picture entitled *Blood Feast* in the early 1960s, it's doubtful that film fans of the new millennium would be reading about him. Lewis might have been remembered merely as a director of sleazy nudist-camp flicks — if at all. His crowning achievement might have been (gulp) *Daughter of the Sun*!

Not that that would have bothered Lewis. He'd be the first to admit that tucking a movie under your belt, especially one like *Daughter of the Sun*, or *She-Devils on Wheels*, or even *Blood Feast*, is not exactly in the same ballpark as solving the equations that apply to nuclear fission. (Of course, one may well respond that it is infinitely preferable to be held accountable for *Blood Feast* than for nuclear fission.)

But the completion of a feature film is no trivial matter. Hollywood is a land of missed opportunities, and there are hundreds upon hundreds of film projects that, for one reason or another, are formulated, planned, discussed, schematized, and even filmed — but never see the light of a projector bulb. Titles are announced and re-announced day after day in trade papers. Few announced titles actually get made. That Herschell Gordon Lewis was able to see through to completion a respectable number of feature-length projects over the course of a minor-league cinema career is a testament to his fortitude and determination. While some Hollywood moguls barely bat an eyelid at investing truckfuls of greenbacks in pictures that never get past the pre-production stage, the economics of independent film production virtually dictated that Lewis's films be finished and marketed on time and within budget. Once several thousand dollars had been committed to a Lewis project, the film had to be brought to a successful conclusion, if only because that several thousand dollars generally represented about a third of his budget! Independent producers like Roger Corman, Hammer Films, and American International Pictures could not afford to be wasteful. If money was spent, film was exposed. Sometimes the final product came close to making little or no sense (e.g., Corman's *The Terror*, Hammer's *Blood from the Mummy's Tomb*, Lewis's *Monster A' Go-Go*), but it was imperative to get the final product into theaters, sense and nonsense be damned. (And for pictures with titles like those, how much did it matter anyway?)

Herschell Lewis will readily admit that his oeuvre, for the most part, leaves much to be desired. He enjoys the attention and adulation of modern "gorror" fans, but he puts such accolades in perspective. His is an interesting story, even if it is merely a footnote to motion picture history.

— R. P.

CHAPTER 1

A Scar Is Born

> I've often referred to *Blood Feast* as a Walt Whitman poem. It's no good, but it was the first of its type.
>
> —*Herschell Gordon Lewis*

Hollywood is schlock-full of producers and directors with pumped-up egos who think of themselves as auteurs whose work must be considered alongside the best of Fritz Lang, Alfred Hitchcock, Howard Hawks, and Orson Welles. In actuality, these filmmakers are more like any other independent exploitation-minded individuals, anxious to see a quick return on their investment while making a pretense of redefining cinema art. In the muddled morass of executive story conferences, deal-making, plotline pitches and the like, filmmaker Herschell Gordon Lewis is like a cool breeze on a sweltering summer day. Listen to his personal tales of cinematic censure and you have to smile, even laugh. Of course, he can make you cringe as well, if you look at some of his pictures; and whether you're cringing at the blood and guts or the sheer technical incompetence on display doesn't matter, because in spite of everything, Herschell Gordon Lewis's stature as a schlock showman is secure. You have to admire his inherent honesty. He's never pretended to be something other than what he is. He *knows* his movies are trash, and he'll be among the first to admit it with a twinkle in his eye. It's difficult to think that *this* is the man who gave the world mashed torsos, shredded limbs, dangling eyeballs, and the genre's very first on-screen scalping. *This* guy? The nice-looking gentleman with the pleasant voice and warm handshake? *He* invented the spiked barrel roll? Unbelievable.

A glance at Lewis's checkered cinematic checklist shows a preponderance of two kinds of motion pictures: soft-core sex — especially of the "nudist" variety that dominated the sexploitation industry in the early 1960s — and hard-core horror. With titles like *Bell, Bare and Beautiful* and *Blood Orgy*, what else could one expect?

Like any savvy showman, Lewis had an instinct for movie trends, an ability to charm investors, and the determination to compete with the big boys on the block. When smaller independent companies like American International and Fanfare began reeling in the bucks with "anti-establishment" entertainment like *Hell's Angels on Wheels*, *The Trip*, and *Riot on Sunset Strip*, Herschell Gordon Lewis put his "gorror" movies on the back burner and concentrated on pictures with titles like *Just for the Hell of It* and *She-Devils on Wheels*. When the biker subgenre burned itself out at the end of the '60s, HG went back to making the kind of picture he knew best — the kind destined to bring him infamy over the years — the hard-core gore picture. As time went on, Lewis's horror films became ever more violent — so much so that, by the early 1970s, he had begun to parody his own product. His last horror effort, *The Gore-Gore Girls* (released as *Blood Orgy* in some regions), mixed guffaws with grue, leaving audiences unsure whether to laugh or vomit. When the killer cuts off a go-go dancer's nipples, for example, the gory effect is diluted by a close-up which shows the wicked wounds spurting not blood, but milk — and in two flavors, no less.

It is Lewis's belief that modern producers and directors are in a sense mechanical moviemakers who would never think to include such outrageous moments of silliness in their work. "Today's motion pictures are made on something like a production-line basis," claims Lewis, "and it gets worse every year." Undoubtedly the filmmaker is thinking of series pictures like *Friday the 13th*, *Nightmare on Elm Street*, or *Halloween* — even *Rocky*. Although there are moments of inspiration in these films, for the most part they are hackneyed productions using connect-the-dot scenarios that are patterned after the most successful title of the series — usually the first. As an independent filmmaker in the 1960s, Lewis followed patterns, but only in the sense that he was making a certain kind of film: specifically, the gore film. There was never any thought of producing a *Blood Feast Part 2*, only of making a follow-up that was similar in style. Thus, there are no sequels in the Lewis canon. In fact, it wasn't until the reign of shocker sequels in the 1980s that the director was approached by an established company to make a new "gorror" film. Significantly (though hardly surprising), that pitch was for *Blood Feast Part 2*.

Although Herschell Gordon Lewis used to call Chicago home, he was actually born in Pittsburgh on June 15, 1926. His father passed away when Herschell was only six, and the family later moved to the Windy City. Lewis remained in Chicago throughout his high school years and afterward enrolled in Northwestern University, eventually receiving a master's degree in journalism and a Ph.D. in psychology.

In his youth Lewis was a bona fide film fan whose tastes ran the gamut from comedies to creepies, but he never gave serious thought to becoming a filmmaker until much later. His journalism degree earned him a position at Mississippi State, where he taught graduate courses in mass communication — specifically, advertising. He also taught English, journalism, and humanities. At the time, Lewis thought teaching was where it was at. But while "it" may have been there, big money was not. As it happened, he was approached by a friend with the idea of producing advertising material for a 32-store retail chain. Unfortunately, the offer came at a time when HG still had a teaching contract. He eventually let that contract expire to jump on the advertising bandwagon, but found the wagon had left without him: His friend had bailed out of the business.

Lewis began scouring publications like *Advertising Age* and answering ads. He eventually received offers from two interested parties: The Cotton Council of Memphis, who needed a public relations director, and a Pennsylvania radio station, WCOJ in Coatesville, who needed a morning DJ for their 6:00 to 9:00 time slot. WCOJ wanted their morning man to double as the company's advertising executive, selling blocks of advertising time in the afternoons. Lewis opted to go with WCOJ and thereby moved into the fringes of the entertainment industry.

As soon as Herschell saw his first WCOJ paycheck he began searching for another job, and eventually ended up at WRAC in Racine, Wisconsin, where he was made station manager. There he gained the kind of hands-on experience in production and advertising that would come in handy in his later career as a professional in the exploitation field.

From radio, Lewis segued into television. In the early 1950s he relocated to Oklahoma to take advantage of opportunities at WKY-TV, where he quickly jumped on the vertical track and worked his way up to producer-director. Eventually a schoolmate from Northwestern invited him back to Chicago, where he found work at one of the city's numerous advertising agencies which specialized in television spots; but it wasn't long before he put together his own film-production company.

As Lewis has frequently pointed out, the climate of film production in the early 1960s was such that an independent filmmaker — especially one whose creativity was necessarily held in check by budgetary constraints — was forced to become an innovator, or perish as a producer of motion pictures. Several years earlier the two men responsible for creating American International Pictures, James H. Nicholson and Samuel Z. Arkoff, had put up their collective stake to throw the Hollywood dice, knowing full well they were loaded (the dice, that is). Gambling on their ability to beat the odds with fresh concepts and unique production techniques — not the least of which was convincing exhibitors to commit to playing pictures that had only been campaigned, not actually made — Nicholson and Arkoff managed to infiltrate Hollywood's backyard while the major companies weren't paying attention. (They were preoccupied with the threat of television, which they saw as the great usurper of cinema success.)

Things were different for Herschell Gordon Lewis. For one thing, although he would soon acquire a partner who knew something about film technique and advertising, it was no longer the early '50s, and he was not operating out of Hollywood. Where AIP established itself mainly by concentrating on the self-styled "teen terror" picture (*I Was a Teenage Werewolf*, *Invasion of the Saucer Men*, *Dragstrip Riot*), and Hammer made inroads with their blood-engorged color updates of legitimate horror classics (*The Curse of Frankenstein*, *Horror of Dracula*, *The Mummy*), Lewis had neither the funding nor the staffing to compete in these areas. Chicago was an industrial-film city. There hadn't been a feature film made there in over forty years. "We had to work harder at making our product unique," Lewis recalled. Compared with such majors as 20th Century–Fox and Warner Bros., the future Godfather of Gore lamented, "the independent film producer hasn't the cash resources to release a film nationally." This meant that Lewis would never be able to compete on the basis of timing. Because of the minimal number of film prints available to the average low-budget independent producer, his films could only be released regionally or sequentially. "A major company might come out with 700 prints of a feature and saturate the country overnight," Lewis explained. "They would play the picture to death everywhere and then throw away the film prints that had been chopped to bits through repeated use, using the rest for B- and C-runs as they might come up." HG could not do that. At best, an independent producer might have just 30 or 40 prints to work with, and in some cases fewer than that. The most successful of Herschell's early sin-'n'-skin pictures, *The Adventures of Lucky Pierre*, had to earn its profits piecemeal, because only 11 prints of the movie were made. "Those prints were used over and over, until they were absolutely shredded," noted Lewis.

Although as a director HG was to gain notoriety as the originator of the gory horror, or "gorror," film, his first few pictures had nothing to do with fear, though they were rife with fantasy — sexual fantasy. It was Herschell's assertion that the road to success for the independent producer of the 1960s was paved with sex and horror — two surefire ingredients that makers of low-budget pictures returned to again and again. At one time this had been true for the Western as well, but until Clint Eastwood and Sergio Leone reinvented that genre with their "spaghetti westerns" of the 1960s, tales of the Wild West were box-office poison. Because of the exploitation angles inherent to films of the sex and scare genres, it was much easier for producers to secure financial backing for pictures that pandered to those tastes.

Lewis believed that the only way he could achieve real success in the film business was to "make a picture that was either so loaded with sex or so loaded with horror" that it would virtually demand to be noticed. However, making a picture "loaded with sex" meant making what was then known as a "stag" film — pornographic pap that could only play at adult theaters in major metropolitan areas. Prior to the implementation of the Motion Picture Association of America's rating standards, such films were labeled "adults-only" fare. Later on, of course, they were rated X (when producers bothered submitting them for ratings) or went out with self-imposed triple-X ratings. Lewis's alternative — making a film "loaded with horror" — meant a bigger, better chance at marketability. Marketability, of course, would translate into more film rentals and ultimately more money in the producer's pocket. In retrospect it was not a difficult choice to make.

Thus, eventually, was born the idea for *Blood Feast*.

CHAPTER 2

Sexploitation Ain't No Dirty Word

> There was a time when putting Paul Newman's name on a theater marquee would have guaranteed instant box office success. Today it means nothing. Pictures like *Raiders of the Lost Ark* would have succeeded if "Joe Glutz" had been the star.
>
> — *Herschell Gordon Lewis*

Hollywood's "star system" was rapidly becoming a thing of the past when H. G. Lewis acquired his first Mitchell camera—and lucky for him. American International rarely featured players of any real stature in their assembly-line product, although some of the AIP producers, such as Alex Gordon, often got old-timers (a euphemism for has-beens) to appear in their pictures. Lewis took note of this phenomenon and asked himself whether anyone would have gone to see *The She-Creature* just because Tom Conway was in it. The obvious answer was no. People weren't buying tickets to *The She-Creature* because they wanted to see Tom Conway; they were buying tickets because of AIP's outlandish advertising campaign. The same thing was true of the Hammer films made before Christopher Lee and Peter Cushing became important names in the fantasy film field. (Although Cushing had been a popular British television actor, he was not well known outside Britain at the time of Hammer's twin breakthrough productions, *The Curse of Frankenstein* and *Horror of Dracula*.)

"We couldn't come out and say Paul Newman is in our pictures," Lewis admitted unapologetically. "We could never get someone of that stature to work for us for the salaries we paid! I had Bill Kerwin in my pictures! But who was going to go see a Bill Kerwin movie?" Although he sounds as if he's playing down his own product, Lewis made an important observation here: "This is what the independents superimposed on the film industry," he pointed out, "the intention to campaign rather than to star."

Although there certainly was room to better understand the workings of the industry and learn the lessons of filmmaking technique, when H. G. Lewis began his professional motion picture career he already had a solid grasp of the basics of the film business. For one thing, Lewis was a fan of cinema in general, going out to see whatever was popular whenever he could. The only genre of film that Lewis didn't follow was, oddly enough, the horror film. "I had never been a real horror movie fan," Lewis confessed. "I like entertainment of a much lighter weight in nature, but that's my own constitutional requirement. My favorite film is *King Solomon's Mines*—for reasons I can't even begin to tell you. *The African Queen* is another one. I regard it as a superior piece of filmmaking, as most people do."

Lewis was more interested in directors than in film genres. He liked Hitchcock's pictures, as well as many of the films made by Howard Hawks and Robert Wise. He also thought one of the most promising young directors of the '60s was Peter Bogdanovich. "I thought originally that Peter Bogdanovich was the find of the century," Herschell added. "But it turned out he was a hack, just like I am! Really, only Alfred Hitchcock had consistency, and ultimately he became a parody of himself."

Herschell did more than simply watch motion pictures; he studied them, assimilating the basics of the craft by proxy. It certainly wasn't a substitute for experience, of course, but Lewis's background in teaching gave him an edge when it came to absorbing technical information.

Given that HG looks at film production as a "mechanized" kind of art, it shouldn't come as much of a surprise to learn that Lewis never went to film school, or studied in the shadow of masters such as Hitchcock and Peckinpah, or toiled for years in 16mm before embarking on his first feature. He boldly claimed, "When I decided to try my hand at feature film production, I brought together a group of people that were my friends, to start. They weren't [friends] by the time we finished the unholy enterprise! Like most first-time filmmakers, I thought I knew everything about film because I knew how to aim and fire a camera. I knew how to load a camera, I knew how to cut for opticals, I knew how to mix a multiple sound track. What else is there!? To this day I have never met a person in the commercial film business who does not think that he or she — or *it* — can make a feature. They think that every successful film producer is just some lucky guy who happens by accident to overcome his innate lack of IQ and figure out a way to bilk the public of millions of dollars by slapping together a feature film. And that's my point — that making a feature is a mechanical job. *But*— and this is the significant point — making a feature that someone will go to see is *not* a mechanical job."

Here's a case in point: Popular horror-fantasy writer Stephen King believed he knew enough about filmmaking technique to direct his own movie. His novels had been turned into motion pictures; he had written screenplays for motion pictures; he had hung around movie sets often and played minor parts in pictures other directors made based on his stories and novels. Because his name added boffo to the box office — especially in the 1980s, when King adaptations were at a peak — it wasn't difficult for King to convince someone that he could direct an adaptation of his own short story, "Trucks." With a cast and crew handpicked for him by the producers, King stepped up to the plate to direct his first feature, which was retitled *Maximum Overdrive*. (The film was remade — or more correctly, the story was re-adapted — and released as *Trucks* in 1999.) Unfortunately, although King understood the mechanics of putting together a motion picture, he made a film that nobody cared to see. Obviously, being Stephen King couldn't guarantee the final product would be a satisfying motion picture experience.

Of course, some of H. G. Lewis's own movies are barely watchable. *Blood Feast* is extremely crude in execution. *The Gruesome Twosome* is rushed and padded and, most unforgivably, unexciting. *A Taste of Blood* is simply boring. To Lewis's credit, however, when he wasn't at the mercy of a minuscule budget or ultra-tight deadline, he could make entertaining pictures. *Two Thousand Maniacs!* is enjoyable (assuming you're either a splatter fan or just a bit twisted), and *The Gore-Gore Girls* is amusing at the same time that it is stomach-churning. Conversely, *The Wizard of Gore*, with its nonsensical interludes of characters wandering back and forth between surrealistic sequences of blood and guts, is merely puzzling.

Lewis is among the first to concede that most of his movies aren't very good. He readily acknowledges their crudities and laughs at their inconsistencies along with the next person. As a down-to-earth individual, HG is engaging and witty, and while he doesn't mind making appearances at horror movie conventions around the country, he knows his celebrity status is to be taken with a grain of salt — or a clot of blood, as the case may be.

In Chicago, Lewis was involved in producing industrial pictures — usually short instructional efforts used by blue-collar and government employers to educate their workforce. "I had been shooting commercial films using one of the few studios that had 35mm equipment," Lewis recalled. "These were industrial films, public relations spots, some television commercials, and sales films. They were made for the government, for the Air Force, and so forth. I made a half-hour film in 35mm for the Post Office that was pure propaganda to show off some of the new equipment they had put into place. I also made films for companies like the Link Belt Company, the content of which I've long since forgotten, but I do recall these were made to show potential buyers some rather technical information. The point is, these things weren't for general consumption." Obviously. With titles like *Lift Safely*, these projects certainly weren't bound to get anyone too excited; and even diehard Herschell Gordon Lewis collectors aren't interested in these industrial shorts. (Had HG directed one of those *Signal 30*–type highway safety "scare" films routinely shown in high school classes, gorehounds might have had something worth collecting.)

In the late 1950s, Lewis bought a half interest in a film studio owned by a man named Martin Schmidhofer. Since neither of them was interested in calling the outfit Lewis and Schmidhofer Films, it became known as Lewis and Martin Films. (Think of the confusion that might have erupted had HG decided to call the company Martin and Lewis!) Lewis picked up a few technical tips from Schmidhofer, who was essentially a cameraman. Eventually, Schmidhofer moved to Florida to pursue a career as a newsreel photographer, and Lewis closed down the company.

Herschell had been making money with Lewis and Martin Films, but as a creative individual he longed to do something that was personally more rewarding. One day a friend of his innocently asked, "How do you make any money in your business?" Without giving it much thought, Lewis answered simply, "The only way to make real money in the film business is to shoot a feature." When the friend then asked, "So why don't you shoot a feature?" Lewis fell silent. He had no answer.

The reason Herschell Lewis hadn't made a feature film up to that point was that he hadn't been thinking in terms of making features. "The money had never been available to do one," said HG, "so I had never seriously considered the idea." When Schmidhofer left, Lewis was finally goaded into action. He figured the time was ripe to move on to bigger — and hopefully better — things. He began scouting around the Chicago area for chumps — er, investors — who were willing to take a chance on his filmmaking talents.

Obviously, a person situated in a production center like Los Angeles enjoys an advantage over those wanting to make films who live in areas where films are seldom made. Not only are the creative forces already in place in film production centers, but so are most of the potential investors who have the income required to back a feature film. If you live in New York, you invest in theater or while away your time (and money) along Wall Street; if you live in Washington, you invest in election campaigns; and if you live in LA, you invest in motion pictures. The equation is relatively simple; it's the monetary factors that become stumbling blocks on the road to independent filmmaking. Depending on the numbers available, you make independent features in the manner of Orson Welles, Howard Hawks, Roger Corman, Ed Wood — or H. G. Lewis.

There's really much more to it than that, of course. Independent filmmaking didn't spring suddenly into existence in the 1950s; but it was during the decade of atomic radiation mutations (giant ants, killer shrews, amazing colossal men, et al.), scares of "Reds under the beds," juvenile delinquency, and rock-and-roll that independent film production really took off. Every week hardtop and drive-in theaters across America played movies with titles like *Hot Rod Girl*, *Teenage Zombies*, *The Monster That Challenged the World*, *Terror from the Year 5000*, and *The Blob*.

Independent producers were soon making enough money with these low-budget quickies that even the major companies began making and distributing them. *The Deadly Mantis*, *The Leech Woman*, *The Incredible Shrinking Man*, and *The Alligator People* were all movies backed by major companies like Universal, 20th Century–Fox and Warner Bros.

It was in this kind of climate, in the twilight of the '50s, that Herschell Gordon Lewis found himself struggling to gain acceptance as one more independent voice in the exploitation sweepstakes. Traditionally, Cinefantastique — whether constructed around elements of horror, fantasy, or science-fiction — was a guaranteed moneymaker. Genre productions were not considered high-risk ventures. Rarely did these movies become box-office smashes (although that would happen with increasing frequency as the years passed, culminating in the 1970s with blockbusters like *The Exorcist*, *Jaws*, and *Halloween*), but they could be counted on to make a tidy profit — and sometimes a huge profit if things "clicked" just right, as had happened with Herman Cohen's 1956 production, *I Was a Teenage Werewolf*.

For the specialist filmmaker, however, there was an alternative to horror and sci-fi — another genre that was also a tried and true moneymaker: the "sexploitation" picture. These low-profile titles were mostly soft-core products that played in burlesque houses between live striptease acts. (How times have changed. The striptease has become a kind of lost adult "art," replaced by live sex shows featuring exhibitionistic performers who engage in a variety of copulatory gymnastics to appease masses of salivating voyeurs.) Only 16mm "loops" — designed for projection in secluded booths in "adults only" bookstores, where customers paid 25 or 50 cents to watch a portion of the film — contained the sort of hard-core images associated with triple-X-rated films today.

Lewis wasn't interested in making hard-core loops, but he did think a sexy, soft-core feature produced for a minimum investment was a viable project for someone like himself. He already owned the necessary photographic equipment; all he really needed was enough money to begin shooting. Well, that and a couple of other necessities — like a script, some actors, and perhaps a director.

Chapter 3

Primed for Profit

> We brought half the cast to the premiere, we set up interviews, we had press luncheons. It was pretty much like introducing the Edsel automobile: We had all this hoopla but then nothing much to follow it up.
>
> — Herschell Gordon Lewis

Once he had determined his filmmaking agenda, Herschell moved forward rapidly. With the number of personal and professional contacts he had in the Chicago area, putting together a group of investors was a challenging endeavor, but certainly not an impossible one. Altogether, Lewis managed to raise about $100,000. With this bankroll he formed Mid-Continent Films, the entity that gave birth to his premiere film production, *The Prime Time* (1960). It was the first feature film made in Chicago in over forty years.

The $100,000 figure may seem high when one considers that AIP was making films like *Voodoo Woman* and *The Undead* with recognizable cast names for not much more than half that amount, but as Lewis readily admits, some stupendous errors were made that inflated the budget of the film beyond all expectations. What should have required an expenditure of $30,000 or $35,000 ended up costing Mid-Continent almost its entire bankroll.

For the kind of picture Lewis intended to make, it wasn't necessary to use Screen Actors Guild (SAG) members — but he did. Neither did he have to hire a union crew — but he did that, too. It wasn't really necessary to pay someone else to write the picture — but he thought he should. And it certainly wasn't imperative to pay another person to direct — but he did that as well. As later events would show, H. G. Lewis was perfectly capable of authoring a professional script and directing his own features. Lewis would eventually use amateur actors in his pictures — sometimes even friends and acquaintances. Sure, he would have gotten better results with top-rank professionals, but as HG often pointed out, that would have made little difference in terms of the amount of money to be made. Lewis never considered himself an amateur; he was merely trying to make a buck. But at the beginning of his filmmaking career, Herschell became a victim of his own ignorance. And, as he also admits, ego occasionally got in his way as well. If not for these two limiting factors, *The Prime Time* could have been completed with a lot less hassle on a significantly smaller budget.

One of Herschell's comrades, Fred Niles (who, like HG, ran a commercial film studio in the Chicago area), introduced him to a writer named Robert Abel. Niles said Abel had written screenplays for a variety of successful features. Abel himself claimed authorship of the 1959 monster film *The Giant Behemoth* (a.k.a. *Behemoth the Sea Monster*), though the on-screen titles credited the screenplay to the director, Eugene Lourie. (In fact Lourie co-authored the screenplay with Daniel Hyatt, but Hyatt received no screen credit.) The truth of the matter seems to be that the script was based on a *story* composed by Abel and fellow writer Allen Adler. Although he took Abel at his word, Lewis checked out the film years later and discovered that it had in fact been written by Lourie. With years of filmmaking experience under his belt by that time, this hardly surprised him. Hollywood had been overrun with egocentrics anxious to perpetuate their own myths for years; why should the independent scene be any different?

The (bogus) *Behemoth* claim, coupled with Fred Niles's recommendation, lured Lewis into hiring Abel to pen the script for *The Prime Time*. The finished work was serviceable—just. Lewis thought Abel's script wasn't very good, but to his surprise he was alone in his judgment; everyone else in the Mid-Continent investment group thought they had a winner on their hands. As the solitary dissenter, Lewis let his first-time film jitters get the better of him and ended up accepting Abel's work anyway. The story was plain and simple—*too* plain and simple, as it turned out. Herschell described the plot this way: "It was about a young man who was in love with a girl who got herself in trouble. In getting her out of trouble he had a certain amount of adventure, all of which was relatively harmless, and they both emerged sadder and wiser at the picture's conclusion." Pressed for further story details, Lewis responded, "Believe me when I tell you that I have just *elaborated* on the plot!"

With script in hand, Lewis began the search for a director. "I didn't know any better," he admitted, "so I hired Gordon Weisenborn to direct the picture." Following Hollywood tradition, he then held auditions to select a cast. "That went on for weeks," Lewis groaned. "I don't think there was an out-of-work actor in Chicago or around Chicago who didn't audition for us." In the end Mid-Continent had a cast composed mainly of stage actors; "not the ideal situation," noted Lewis. Scoring parts in the picture were Jo Ann LeCompte, Frank Roche, James Brooks, Betty Senter—and Karen Black as the "Painted Woman." With the components now in place, the countdown to principal photography could finally get underway.

Years later Lewis would acknowledge, "I made two horrendous errors on *The Prime Time*. First, I settled for a screenplay which I *knew* wasn't any good, and second, I let other people take final control of the budget away from me." These mistakes cost Lewis dearly, running *The Prime Time* over schedule and over budget. Not only that, but there were also problems with Fred Niles's studio, which processed the film footage. "I was unhappy with the way the film had been handled at the Niles studio," Lewis complained. "I felt that it was a tour de force for his billing department. We ended up with a film that cost far more than it should have, was only moderately entertaining, and which had absolutely no exploitation factor to it at all." One generally profits from mistakes, but not in this instance.

Inexperience was to blame for some of the production's shortcomings, of course, but there was another problem as well: ego. Lewis wanted his first feature to *look* like a Hollywood product. For him, that meant using a union crew and casting with SAG members, paying an experienced writer to compose the script, and hiring a director rather than directing the picture himself.

Lewis also hired a professional cinematographer, Andrew M. Costikyan, and a professional film editor, Elsie Kerbin, to work on *The Prime Time*. When filming and editing were completed, Lewis took the movie to Erwin Joseph, a film distributor in Chicago who knew just about everyone in the business. He ran a company called Modern Film Distributors. Lewis described Joseph as "an old-time, hard-boiled independent operator whose principal claim to fame was distributing a film called *Mom and Dad* which had been made long before. He also handled *Reefer Madness* [the anti-marijuana picture that became a cult favorite on college campuses in the 1970s] and some of the early independent pictures that were regarded at one time as somewhat racy." Joseph expressed interest in *The Prime Time* and ended up offering Mid-Continent Films a states' rights distribution deal in exchange for a $100,000 guarantee. Lewis was hoping to get more money from Joseph's company, since his original investors had put up almost a hundred grand to start with; but that was all Joseph was prepared to offer. Somewhat reluctantly, Lewis agreed to the terms, "and from that point on it was straight downhill," he complained. One positive event emerged from Lewis's brief association with Joseph's company, however, for it was at the Modern Film Distributors office that Lewis met his future filmmaking partner, David Friedman. The two found an instant rapport. Though Friedman would not be involved in the making of *The Prime Time*, his previous experience in the film business (he had worked at Paramount Pictures as a film publicist) would prove invaluable later on, when Lewis began directing horror films.

Herschell hired a New York advertising agency that specialized in designing film campaigns to work up the promotional materials for *The Prime Time*— another move that cost the investors in Mid-Continent. "They charged a lung and a half to make up a campaign for our picture," Lewis sighed. It was an expensive lesson to learn, but at least HG decided he and his partners would design their own campaigns for future films — if there were any. "For independent filmmakers we really went first class on that first feature," Lewis said. "We had a beautiful film score that we spent a *lot* of money on, although I later came to realize that is not the way to do it. It makes you look good while you're doing it — spending the money, that is — and it looks good to have a big crew, it looks good to have lots of 'gophers'— but what doesn't look good is people sitting in the theater later on saying 'so what!'"

The Prime Time had its world premiere in Madison, Wisconsin. (It was known in some locations as *Hell Kitten*.) To get people talking about the picture, Herschell transported members of the cast to the premiere "at tremendous expense," he recalled. Press luncheons and interviews were arranged, and while the ballyhoo got people talking, they were talking about how *bad* the movie was. Even HG knew early on that *The Prime Time* was a bust. "I was in the minority in thinking it wasn't much of a film," Lewis said. Conversely, the Mid-Continent investors were proud to have been involved in the production of an actual feature film, and their opinions of the picture were doubtless clouded by their own egos and by financial considerations. The primary *Prime Time* problem was its story line, or lack of one. "*The Prime Time* had very little guts to it," said Lewis. (Herschell would see to it that his future films had plenty of guts.)

Erwin Joseph expected the film would do better outside Wisconsin, especially if it was paired with a second feature to create a double bill. He acquired the rights to a picture called *Carnival Story*, a major release starring Steve Forrest that had flopped at the box office when it debuted in 1954. Lewis and Joseph designed a special ad campaign built around the two features as a double-feature package, but that strategy didn't work either. "The combination just didn't excite anyone," said Lewis.

Before the investors in Mid-Continent Films realized their picture wasn't going to make any money, they were feeling very *up*. The $100,000 guarantee from Modern Film Distributors was (supposedly) in effect, and there was even some money left over in the company coffers. "None of the danger signals were showing yet," Lewis remembered, "and in fact Erwin Joseph attended a screening of *The Prime Time* and began telling everyone within earshot how successful it was going to be. We were all on a high based on actually having completed a feature film. That we were able to do it seemed a miracle in itself." With all the happy faces showing, and because they had not blown all of Mid-Continent's capital, a decision was made to produce a follow-up feature. The leftover funds were used to purchase a half-finished script from a fellow named Jim McGinn, who had co-written the story inside of three weeks with help from a friend known as Seymour Zolotareff. According to HG, this script had all the components that *The Prime Time* lacked: "It had a strong plotline about the rise and fall of someone on the order of Hugh Hefner," Lewis explained. "In fact, McGinn had actually worked for Hefner, which is where he got the idea for the plot. It wasn't really designed to show anything other than an arrogant personality in the publishing field. It was not planned as a nudie." The picture was called *Living Venus*.

This time Lewis decided to direct the picture himself, but he was still spending money to bring in a union crew. "At the time I felt that a feature could not get playdates unless it was made with union people," Lewis said. "That was part of the naïveté I inherited going into feature film production." During the shooting of the new film Lewis formed the opinion that union crews (or at least this particular ensemble) were "foot-draggers." Having had experience loading and unloading film during his industrial film production days, Herschell knew unloading a camera shouldn't take longer than 30 seconds, yet his union cameraman was taking a full five minutes to do it — and at 5:25 in the afternoon, when the production would be forced into overtime at 5:30. "That was a frustrating experience," Lewis grumbled. But another learning experience, as well.

It didn't take long for HG to come to the conclusion that the unions involved in the picture-making business were interested only in protecting their members' positions — never mind the producer's. "That applies to Chrysler Motors, it applies to TWA, it applies to a symphony orchestra that will miss half a season," Lewis reasoned. "In this kind of case, a film production unit will take the position of having as many of its people employed whether or not they are really needed. That's just my opinion, but it's an opinion that has remained unchanged over the years." Significantly, *Living Venus* was the second and last picture Lewis made with a union workforce. In the future he allowed his basic business acumen to dictate picture-making policy. "I learned that it is possible to shoot a film more effectively using a much smaller crew, because the crew becomes dedicated to the project at hand," Lewis said. "If people want to work, they don't care whether everybody on the film is part of the Screen Actors Guild or whether you have a Guild contract."

Using SAG members at least insured an acting troupe made up of motion picture professionals. The cast of *Living Venus* included Harvey Korman (whose appearances on television's *Carol Burnett Show* won him widespread acclaim in the 1960s and '70s) and comedian Billy Falbo, who would go on to star in Lewis's first full-fledged nudie-cutie picture, *The Adventures of Lucky Pierre*. Chicago actress Karen Black (who costarred opposite Bruce Dern in Alfred Hitchcock's final film, *Family Plot*) had already worked for Herschell in *The Prime Time*. At the time these thespians were working for Herschell Gordon Lewis, nobody knew who they were. Moreover, no one cared. "Karen Black cost us a lot of money due to her poutiness," Lewis claimed, "and her part wasn't even that large." (That might be because Lewis agreed to cut a nude scene involving the actress after her agent requested that it be removed in exchange for monetary compensation.)

In later pictures Lewis shied away from employing union actors, with the result that the overall quality of acting fell off significantly. *Blood Feast*, for instance, is loaded with embarrassingly atrocious histrionics. But for H. G. Lewis, an actor's ability to realistically play a role was never an issue—and not because he didn't like good acting. Lewis enjoyed thespian talent as much as any film fan, but that's not what he was selling. Audiences who came to a Herschell Gordon Lewis movie were not interested in insightful characterizations and bold dramatics; they were after naughty jokes and naked flesh, and later on, violence and viscera.

Living Venus, a black-and-white production, clocked in at just under 75 minutes. It was released shortly after *The Prime Time* in 1960. An interesting actor who turned up in the film was Bill Kerwin, who was new to the movie business but destined to become an important part of Lewis's "stock company." Acting under the name William Kerwin, and later Thomas Wood, he would go on to star in Lewis's first two "gorror" outings, *Blood Feast* and *Two Thousand Maniacs!* As Herschell delighted in pointing out, Kerwin was actually a better actor than some of the SAG members who played in *The Prime Time* and *Living Venus*. (In later years the actor was also known as Rooney Kerwin.) Kerwin took on the film's featured part, the high-flying publisher Jack Norwall.

As *Living Venus* was being readied for its first run, the box-office results of *The Prime Time* were tallied, and Lewis and Erwin Joseph were shocked to learn that the picture was losing money. In fact, it became such a financial disaster that Modern Film Distributors was forced to default on its deal with Mid-Continent. Even worse, Erwin Joseph later died in the midst of litigation involving the original $100,000 guarantee. "I felt awful about it, because I was actually opposed to the litigation," revealed Lewis. "I was opposed to it because I was the producer on *The Prime Time* and I had approved procedures I shouldn't, so I felt largely responsible [for its financial loss]."

Lewis acknowledged that part of the problem stemmed from his responding to the call of his own ego. "What I had done I'd done out of ignorance and to some extent out of ego," he allowed, "because I had been trying to ape procedures the major film companies used. In essence I was taking a 'big shot' approach and it didn't work." Lewis himself turned out to be the film's biggest loser, because he was the biggest investor in Mid-Continent. "When Erwin Joseph had the gall to go and die, it effectively sealed his fate for all eternity — but it also sealed mine for at least a couple of years afterward, since all of my money was tied up in *The Prime Time* and *Living Venus*," Lewis said.

Things would get worse before they got any better. Although a few of the investors in Mid-Continent knew who Erwin Joseph was, he was really a peripheral figure. It was Lewis who represented the company to its investors, so it was to Lewis that the investors turned for the status of their investments. Unsurprisingly, there were some hard feelings in evidence. "I couldn't really blame the investors for feeling it was I who had caused them to lose money, because obviously, if they hadn't known me, they wouldn't have lost their money," Lewis admitted. No one was wounded more than Herschell, who had sold off his own studio to raise capital for *The Prime Time*. Now with no money and no Mid-Continent Films, Lewis was forced to abandon his future film plans, at least temporarily.

To help put his house back in order, Herschell took a job with a company called United Film and Recording Studios (UFRS), which was run by a man named Bill Klein. Klein had mixed the sound on *Living Venus*. Like Herschell's first professional film venture, Lewis and Martin Films, UFRS made commercials and industrial pictures, but the company's equipment was terribly antiquated. Lewis joked, "Klein was an old-fashioned guy with an old-fashioned studio and *very* old-fashioned equipment. But he was a decent fellow." Decent enough to welcome Lewis to UFRS at a time when HG had few other opportunities available to him in the business. During his stint at UFRS, Herschell became the company producer and occasional cameraman, working on a variety of commercials made to order for a wide range of clients. Although the hours and the salary were par for the course, fate intervened to pay off a unique dividend. As Lewis recalled, "It was while I was at United Film and Recording Studio that something happened which would change my history dramatically."

Chapter 4

Lucky Strikes

> In one scene I told the girl to stretch, but she thought I said "scratch," so she reached around and started scratching her rear end.
>
> — *Herschell Gordon Lewis*

When Herschell Lewis accepted the offer from Bill Klein to become a producer at United Film and Recording Studio, he was merely trying to keep a foot in the door of the film business. Lewis's primary income at the time was derived from composing advertising copy by the hour for a company known as the Morlock Advertising Agency. Lewis recalled, "Morlock was very conservative, very tightly run. I often wonder where I would have been if it hadn't been for Morlock, because [that job] kept me from reaching a point of panic. Every dime I had was gone because of the failure of *The Prime Time* and *Living Venus*. The future seemed bleak in that my film studio was gone, Mid-Continent Films was gone, Erwin Joseph was gone — along with that $100,000 guarantee — and it looked like there was going to be a long, long rebuilding process." But Fate intervened — this time in the guise of David Friedman, who unexpectedly turned up on Lewis's doorstep with an especially fortuitous opportunity. Friedman said something to HG that was destined to have an impact on both men's futures: "Al Sack says if we can make a one-reel nudie he'll pay us a thousand bucks for the Dallas exchange area."

Lewis replied in all innocence, "What's a one-reel nudie?"

The way Friedman explained it, the adult film market was undergoing change at the grassroots level. Viewers had grown tired of watching the same old scratchy, badly focused, black-and-white claptrap that adult film producers had been dishing out over the past few years. Naked flesh required pictorial perspicuity. In other words, the era of the cheap stag flick was over. Modern audiences demanded modern sexcapades lighted with clarity and color.

Friedman showed Herschell a short film he had imported from Holland. The action took place in a nudist camp. There wasn't much of a plot in evidence, but there was plenty of skin. HG figured it wouldn't be too difficult to come up with something similar for the American market. "At the time, nudist pictures were considered extraordinarily daring," said Lewis. "They had very nominal playoffs, usually at borderline theaters which couldn't compete for first-run films, and occasionally at drive-ins either at the tail end of the season or at the very beginning. Obviously, we knew where our potential audience was, and it was up to us to take advantage of that market."

To make a one-reeler that would run about twelve minutes required a thousand feet of color film stock. Before Lewis and Friedman got their hands on it, an incident took place that would dramatically alter the future course of events. It started innocuously enough, during a meeting with a man by the name of Jack Curtin at the United Film and Recording Studio. "Actually my office was UFRS's screening room," Lewis revealed. "Whenever they screened a film in there I had to duck my head so there would be no shadow on the screen!" A small office, to be sure, but nevertheless an office in a professional film studio.

Curtin was a New Yorker who represented a film processing laboratory called Color Service Laboratory, located at the time on 45th Street in Manhattan. Curtin had produced one or two independent features himself, and he enjoyed making the rounds of various film companies and shooting the bull with other independent filmmakers.

Curtin knew Lewis as the force behind *The Prime Time* and *Living Venus*, but liked him anyway. During the course of their meeting, Curtin asked Lewis what he was working on. Although there were no plans for any other pictures beyond the one-reeler HG and David Friedman were supposed to make for Al Sack, he didn't dare admit as much. According to Lewis, "When someone in the film business asks, 'What are you making?' you must provide an answer. There is no such response as 'Nothing'; at least not while you have one shred of ego and pride left in you." True to this principle, Lewis played up his partnership with Friedman and Sack and the Dallas exchange area. He then suggested, "Since this is being made in color, maybe we can do business with Color Service Laboratory."

Lewis's panache impressed Curtin, and Curtin proposed a counteroffer. Instead of making a one-reel nudie for Al Sack, why not make an entire 75-minute feature for Color Service Laboratories? CSL was looking for original features to increase their own revenue, and the company was willing to postpone laboratory costs for 90 days after Lewis turned in an answer print (the first print made from the film negative). The deal sounded almost too good to be true, but if CSL was willing to defer the lab costs as Curtin promised, Lewis figured they could be paid out of accumulated film rentals once the film was in release.

Herschell contacted Dave Friedman and relayed the CSL offer, urging him to come along for the ride. Friedman agreed. At this point Erwin Joseph had not yet died, and Friedman got in touch with him to discuss a monetary advance for the project. Joseph hadn't enough money on hand—he was still smarting from the losses incurred by *Living Venus* and *The Prime Time*—but he managed to scrape together roughly $12,000 from a group of faceless investors who wanted to get into the picture business (it seemed there was always someone, somewhere, with enough capital who wanted to get into the business). That paltry sum became the entire budget for the first Friedman-Lewis collaboration, *The Adventures of Lucky Pierre*.

Herschell was living in the Chicago suburb of Highland Park, and his house became in effect the production office for *Lucky Pierre*. Friedman and his wife, Carol, would drive to Highland Park, and Carol visited with Herschell's wife while the men hovered over a typewriter, pounding out story line for their picture. They managed to finish the entire script over a single weekend—which sounds amazing until you realize that Roger Corman occasionally completed an entire *film* in just a handful of days. (Corman's most famous black comedy, *The Little Shop of Horrors*, was completed inside of three nights and two days.)

Lewis and Friedman shot *Lucky Pierre* in four days on a budget, according to Friedman, of $7,500. Economizing to the max, they purchased 8,000 feet of film stock — just enough to make a short feature film. Principal photography was matched so tightly to the amount of raw stock on hand that once all the scene slates had been cut off there wasn't enough footage left over to make a preview trailer. The filmmakers were forced to duplicate footage from portions of the finished picture for the trailer. "That's what I call false economy," Herschell joked. "But then, everything about *Lucky Pierre* was short and sweet." So short and sweet that there actually was no film crew other than Lewis and Friedman. The actors had to work their own clapper boards, because with Lewis running the camera and Friedman recording the sound, there was no one else to work the clapper. Lewis told the cast members to hold the board in front of their face, announce the scene number, slap the stick closed, toss it aside, and begin acting. It was a cheap idea, but it worked. And who would ever know? (Until now, that is.)

Erwin Joseph made more than money available to Lewis and Friedman; he also supplied facilities for location shooting — specifically, the Aurora drive-in theater, which he owned. Lewis spent a full day shooting on the Aurora acreage, and some of the film was shot at Lewis's own house in Highland Park. Herschell's old sound recording engineer, Bill Klein, got into the act as well, making arrangements to shoot at the United Film and Recording Studio building. A number of scenes were also shot outdoors in secluded, wooded areas. Given that Chicago is officially known as the Windy City, and that *The Adventures of Lucky Pierre* was being made in mid–October, it won't come as much of a surprise to learn that Lewis's female cast members were none too pleased to be filming out of doors. Even HG admitted, "Those girls were so cold their nipples were turning *purple!*"

Lucky Pierre was made at a time when it was considered morally inappropriate for a woman to remove her brassiere, but Lewis wasn't really breaking any new taboos. The first professionally distributed nudie was Russ Meyer's *The Immoral Mr. Teas* (1959). However, Meyer filmed that picture using 16mm film, and most theaters were not equipped to project 16mm; Hollywood productions were photographed in 35mm. So although *The Immoral Mr. Teas* was technically the first nudie movie, *The Adventures of Lucky Pierre* was the first 35mm nudie. "In that respect I suppose *Lucky Pierre* had a pioneer overtone," reflected Lewis, "but in my view the category was originated by a fellow named Walter Bibo, who shot a picture in the late 1950s [1957] called *Garden of Eden*. He made it in Tampa [Florida]. *Garden of Eden* made an *enormous* amount of money, but Bibo wasted most of it on court cases involving that picture. It ran into censorship problems; it was banned from city to city. Bibo felt that the American Sunbathing Association was on a par with the American Medical Association, so he tried to fight for the right to show his picture. So in a sense he paved the way for the rest of us to make that kind of picture."

Since *The Adventures of Lucky Pierre* was produced without the benefit of a cast professionally experienced in the making of adult film fare, Friedman and Lewis were forced to conduct a search for young, reasonably attractive women who could be convinced to take their clothes off in front of a camera. It was not an easy mission. Herschell recalled, "We had seven of the *ugliest* girls ever to appear in a nudie. That was not by choice; it's just that it was not respectable in those days for women to disrobe on camera." He eventually tracked down a girl who had once worked in a burlesque show, so at least there was someone in the cast who knew how to undress with an air of eroticism. Friedman ran into so many girls who said "no" to baring their breasts for the movie that he was forced to start looking at out-of-state talent, eventually settling for a bank teller from Minnesota who was willing to peel for the picture.

The final cast was composed almost entirely of spunky amateurs, and it showed. There were two exceptions: Billy Falbo, who everyone agreed was wonderful as Mr. Lucky himself, Pierre; and Bill Kerwin, who received screen credit as William Kerwin. (By the time he took a major part in Lewis's seminal *Blood Feast*, Kerwin would adopt the stage name Thomas Wood.)

Quality of acting was almost always in question in a Herschell Gordon Lewis picture, but never more so than in *Lucky Pierre*. Lewis recalled, "In one scene where I told a girl to stretch, she thought I said 'scratch,' so she reached around and started scratching her rear end." With no extra film (or money, or time) available for reshoots, Lewis ended up retaining the blooper in the final cut. Rather than let his audience laugh at the film, however, he forced them to laugh *with* it by adding a sandpaper-type scratch effect to the soundtrack. Lewis noted, "We really couldn't make a mistake with *Lucky Pierre* because there were no rules to violate."

The picture consisted mainly of episodic comedy routines, or a series of "blackouts"—the kind of thing that was popular in vaudeville's heyday, and that television's *Rowan and Martin's Laugh-In* brought back into vogue in the late 1960s. Each comedic episode ended with a pair of dice being tossed and turning up snake-eyes. As HG noted, there wasn't much in the way of a plotline. There would be a "wipe" effect and the film would move on to the next vignette. Since Lewis and Friedman didn't want to spend money unnecessarily, instead of using laboratory facilities to create the wipe effects, they used "shirt-board wipes." Lewis explained, "We actually used the cardboard that used to come inside a new shirt. We wiped it across the camera lens!" Roger Corman, eat your heart out.

Lewis edited the film on a Movieola borrowed from Bill Klein. Without the benefit of precise technical training, some people would hesitate to attempt such a delicate task. Not so, Herschell Gordon Lewis. "The technical aspects of filmmaking never held any terrors for me," he said. Lewis had learned almost everything he knew about films and filmmaking technique from Martin Schmidhofer. In fact, Lewis thought that, compared to making a one-minute commercial, doing a feature was duck soup. "There was nothing to it!" he laughed.

Audiences warmed to *Lucky Pierre*. Lewis credits much of the movie's success to Billy Falbo, the Chicago nightclub performer who took on the title role. With his rubbery face and features that suggested the perennial loser, Falbo won over viewers without even trying. According to Lewis, Falbo had great comic timing. He got along tremendously well with the rest of the cast and crew, and his jovial antics generated a positive behind-the-scenes mood that carried over onto the screen. "Billy Falbo deserves much of the credit for making *Lucky Pierre* a success," Lewis said admiringly.

When the picture had completed shooting and Lewis moved into the editing process, he and Friedman began scouting around for someone to score it. Lewis's friend Larry Wellington brought in a musician named Kenny Soderblom, who turned up at the recording session with over a dozen wind instruments, ranging from a soprano flute to a bass saxophone—all of which he played himself. "I swear Soderblom was the most talented musician I ever met," said Lewis. Together, Soderblom and Wellington wrote a lighthearted score that helped infuse the picture with an innocent sort of charm. It was a bit difficult to record the sound because the filmmakers were forced to rely on an ancient piece of equipment known as a variable density sound mixer. The mixer was so old the company that made it had retired it from their production line prior to World War II. Fortunately, *The Adventures of Lucky Pierre* was a three-track picture, comprising only voice, music, and effects—about as basic as you can get. For this kind of production, Klein's equipment sufficed.

Friedman and Lewis worked up their own advertising campaign for *Lucky Pierre*. With catchlines like "A Pinch of Pepper ... a Nip of Ginger ... a Dash of Mustard ... in as Spicy a Dish of Adult Cinema as you'll ever taste," they were able to target their primary audience—and hit the bullseye. They took their promotional materials, along with the finished film, to a Chicago theater owner named Tom Dowd. Dowd owned the Capri Theater, which usually ran fairly offbeat pictures: independent and foreign-language (subtitled) "art" films, straightforward sexploitation, and so-called nudist-camp pictures. He booked *The Adventures of Lucky Pierre* into the Capri on a percentage basis.

After the twin disasters of *The Prime Time* and *Living Venus*, Herschell felt his luck was due for a change. As it happened, *Lucky Pierre* was indeed lucky. It was held over at the Capri, running for an unprecedented nine weeks and becoming the highest grossing picture in the theater's history. Lewis and Friedman were able to recoup their investment, earn back the film's entire negative cost, and net a respectable profit—all from that one movie house. The film's performance at the Capri also foreshadowed what it would do subsequently in its region-by-region release.

The Adventures of Lucky Pierre would probably only be rated PG-13 today, but in 1961 it was "The film they said could not be shown." (Actually, that was part of Herschell's promotional campaign.) "Audiences flocked to see it," Lewis noted, "and it played and played and played, until some of the prints were absolutely shredded to bits." The 11 prints that had been struck of the movie meant that eventually the picture would be unplayable due to celluloid wear and tear. That didn't stop Lewis, though. Years afterward, when Herschell received a desperate telephone call from a friend named Eddie Ross who needed a movie—*any* movie—to fill a playdate for his Plaza Theater in Chicago, the only product Lewis had on hand was a beat-up copy of *Lucky Pierre*. Ross complained, "I can't show that picture again; I've already shown it six times!"

But Ross was in a jam. "The worst thing that can happen to a theater owner is to experience a miss-out," Lewis said. "A miss-out occurs when a film has been booked and people begin to arrive at the theater, but no one has delivered a print of the picture yet." With nowhere else to

turn, Ross relented: "Okay, send over *Lucky Pierre*." The lone print sitting in Herschell's office was a "junker," a copy so badly worn out — with torn sprocket holes, editing tape, scratches, burns, etc. — it was no longer considered projectible. Lewis sent it to Ross's theater in a taxi, and the next day Ross called Lewis to congratulate him.

"Congratulate me for what?" Herschell wanted to know.

"Your picture *Lucky Pierre* has set another house record."

Lewis was surprised. "Oh, really?"

"Yes," Ross affirmed. "It broke eleven times when we showed it. And *that* is a house record."

Herschell Gordon Lewis, circa 1972, in the Chicago business office of Lewis Motion Picture Enterprises.

CHAPTER 5

Sin 'n' Skin

> Virginia Bell had, as her primary asset, a 48-inch bosom. She was also three months pregnant, and I could only hope, while we were shooting the picture, that she wouldn't trip and fall on me.
>
> — *Herschell Gordon Lewis*

The popularity of *The Adventures of Lucky Pierre* was a sign of good times to come, but its box-office returns were held in check by the film's own minuscule budget. Because Lewis and Friedman could only pay to process a tiny quantity of film prints for distribution to movie exhibitors, there could only be a handful of bookings at any given time. That meant Lewis and Friedman were going to have to be patient to realize long-term profits from the picture. *Very* patient. Although *The Adventures of Lucky Pierre* was doing well at the box office, film rental fees were not paid on a weekly basis, but had a tendency to come in sporadically, especially for independent producers who lacked the clout of a major studio. Exacerbating the situation was the regional playoff route the film was forced to take. It was a long, arduous process. Money would be coming in, but not quickly enough to finance an immediate follow-up. How to strike while the iron was hot?

Then, Friedman and Lewis had a brainstorm. They knew they could save money if they made their next film in black and white. The problem was that the nature of the nudie film business virtually demanded the use of color film stock. An unusual compromise was reached. Herschell explained, "We knew our potential audience, and we knew that the people who would go to see this movie wouldn't care if the plotline was in black and white. What they wanted to see were bare bodies in color!" The result was a picture photographed partly in black and white and partly in color: *Daughter of the Sun*.

Making a nudist-camp picture meant journeying to an exotic locale where nature camps dotted the landscape like rainbow-colored seashells along the beach. It meant going to south Florida. Just outside the Miami area was a secluded private nudist resort known as Spartan Tropical Gardens, which is where Lewis and Friedman shot the color sequences for *Daughter of the Sun*. Their "star" was a young girl named Rusty Allen who was supposed to be "the most beautiful girl in the world" — at least according to the movie's advertising campaign. Lewis himself claimed Rusty was so good-looking "she made everyone around her look like a dog!" Significantly, Rusty was not an actress; nor was she a citizen of Spartan Tropical Gardens. Rusty Allen was actually a cigarette girl working at a Miami night

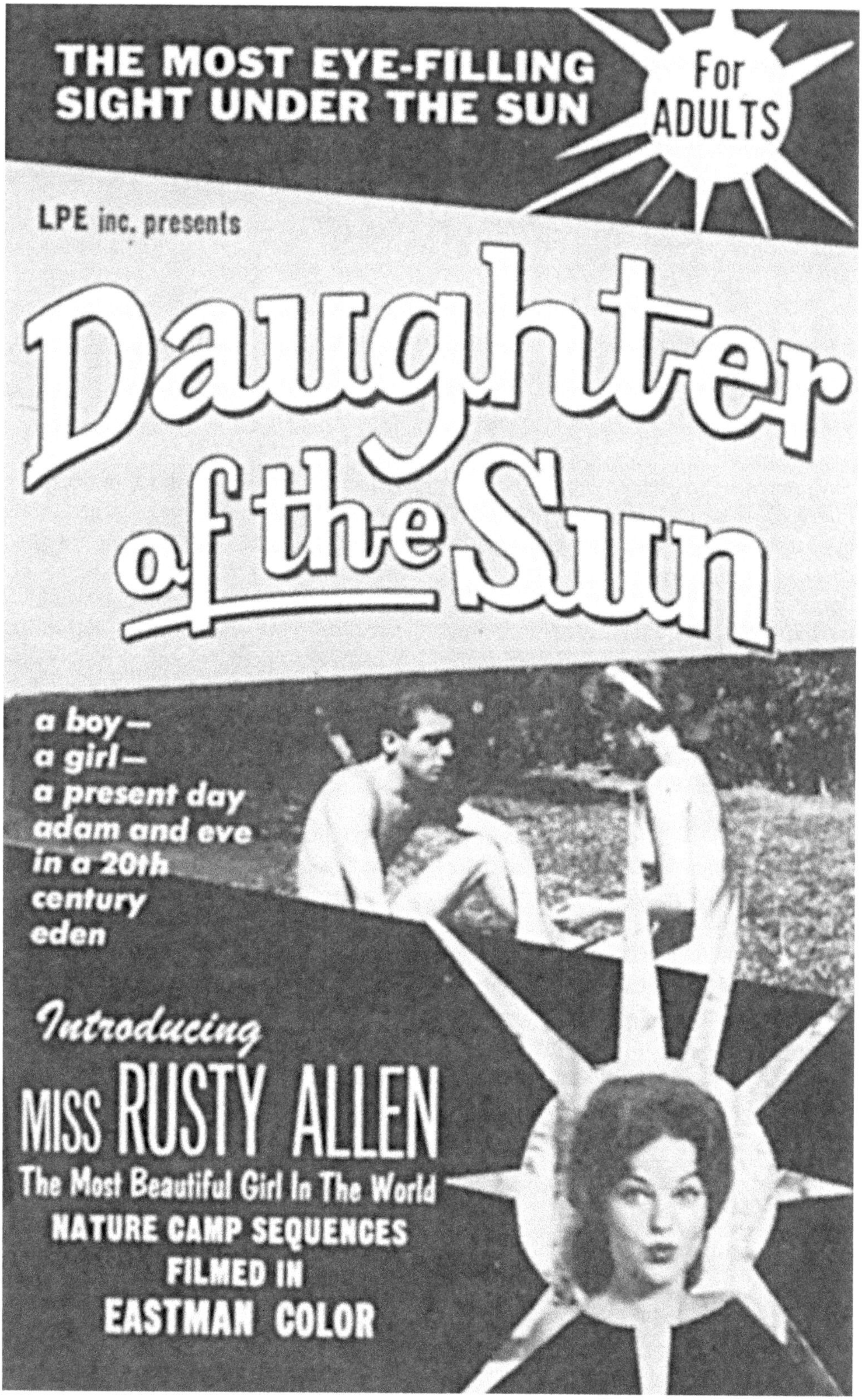

THE MOST EYE-FILLING SIGHT UNDER THE SUN

For ADULTS

LPE inc. presents

Daughter of the Sun

a boy —
a girl —
a present day
adam and eve
in a 20th
century
eden

Introducing

MISS RUSTY ALLEN

The Most Beautiful Girl In The World

**NATURE CAMP SEQUENCES
FILMED IN
EASTMAN COLOR**

spot known as Tony Sweet's. Lewis met her at the restaurant during a preliminary jaunt to Florida to scout production locations. Rusty was more than willing to appear in the buff once Lewis explained that she would be performing in the title role. She would *be* the *Daughter of the Sun*. With stars in her eyes and dollar signs in her head, Rusty eagerly turned the other cheek, leaving her cigarette career behind for her behind career.

After completing the color sequences at Spartan, Lewis and Friedman cranked up their black-and-white cameras at a variety of other Miami locations. Not a single frame of film was exposed on a studio floor, as the filmmakers preferred to shoot in natural locations to give the picture a semblance of "size." The trade-off, of course, was suffering the pitfalls of location sound, with handheld boom microphones picking up all sorts of unwanted noise. It was the kind of low-budget situation H. G. Lewis was learning to live with. Besides, *Daughter of the Sun* was not the kind of picture that required studio sound. Who in the world was going to care whether or not a nudist-camp picture had state-of-the-art sound synchronization?

After all the footage was cut together, Lewis decided the picture was, in a word, peculiar. Part of the problem originated with Bill Johnson, a fellow Chicagoan who once had a stake in Lewis and Martin Films. Lewis was under the impression that Johnson was pretty knowledgeable when it came to film editing technique, so he turned over all the footage from *Daughter of the Sun* to Johnson to edit. This turned into another costly learning experience for the young filmmaker. Somehow Johnson misplaced part of the film footage and ended up splicing together a sequence consisting entirely of actor-reaction shots. The action(s) to which the characters were supposed to be responding couldn't be found, and Lewis ended up releasing the picture with the botched segment intact. Since the director never received any complaints from exhibitors or viewers, it's entirely possible that audiences really *didn't* care about those black-and-white plot points, after all.

As if to prove the point, several years later HG received a phone call from a distributor who wanted a print of *Daughter of the Sun* to play in some second-run theater bookings in North Carolina. Because of the picture's black-and-white and color segmentation, the processing lab had always shipped the two types of footage separately. Lewis had to assemble the film in its proper running sequence himself. When he told his North Carolina contact this, the distributor responded, "That's not necessary, I know how the picture goes. I can put it together myself."

Lewis shipped out the film components and thought no more about it. *Daughter of the Sun* was considered somewhat unusual not only because it was filmed in monochrome as well as color, but also because it was one of the first independent productions to feature a significant amount of action before the main title crawl. (The practice later became quite common.) Six months after the playdates the footage was returned. Lewis projected the film in his office and watched in stupefied silence. It had been

Opposite: Before blood 'n' guts came sin 'n' skin. Lewis's ***Daughter of the Sun*** (1962) interlaced black-and-white dramatics and color nudist camp footage for an unusual effect. "LPE Inc." was the abbreviation for "Lucky Pierre Enterprises."

Apropos of the title, there was more sunning than sinning in *Daughter of the Sun*, but adult audiences didn't seem to mind so long as there was plenty of skin on display. Rusty Allen takes center stage in this group shot.

assembled into a totally incoherent mess. All the color segments had been spliced together into one big chunk, and the black-and-white segments were likewise in another chunk. No one had bothered putting the segments in their proper running order. HG phoned the distributor and asked what had happened.

"What do you mean?" came the response.

"Didn't anyone object when you screened the picture this way?" Lewis wanted to know.

"No."

"Well, didn't you think it was kind of odd that about twenty minutes before it's over, it says 'The End'?"

The distributor said earnestly, "Well, you had all kinds of things going on before the front titles, so I didn't think it was so odd to have things going on after the end titles." As Lewis noted, this kind of reasoning speaks for itself. "It's certainly an indication of what one can get away with in the picture business," he allowed. "People just didn't comment that the film said *The End* when it wasn't yet over, or that the plotline went rushing ahead making no sense whatsoever." Lewis recut the film into its proper sequence, but he was never really convinced that he had needed to bother.

Although *Daughter of the Sun* hadn't the box-office legs of *The Adventures of Lucky Pierre*, it was still a profitable venture. The film clocked in at just 68 minutes—short even by nudie standards. Lewis released it under the auspices of "Lucky Pierre Enterprises, Inc.," hopeful that a bit of *Pierre*'s luck would rub off on *Daughter*. Neither Lewis nor David Friedman attached their real names to the project, however. The credits listed the producer as "Davis Freeman"; the director was "Lewis H. Gordon."

Daughter of the Sun and *The Adventures of Lucky Pierre* helped compensate for the twin disasters of *The Prime Time* and *Living Venus*. Word soon spread through the industry that there was an up-and-coming independent filmmaker named Herschell Gordon Lewis who appeared to know what he was doing. (Or was it Lewis H. Gordon?) More calls began to come in: What was Herschell going to film next? Was there a new picture ready yet for marketing? How soon could a follow-up be delivered? The queries weren't coming from HG's friends, either; he was getting input from hard-boiled businessmen who were interested in making a buck and knew and appreciated what motion pictures could do for them.

There began a series of projects for other people—movies made to order—along the line of *Daughter of the Sun*. Through the smallish fraternity of the independents of the '60s, word spread quickly that Herschell Gordon Lewis was someone with the ability to make movies that made money. For a while Lewis and Friedman toyed with the idea of making a sequel to *Lucky Pierre*, but the project never gelled, primarily because comedian Billy Falbo let greed get the better of him. Everyone who had worked on the first film knew the part of Pierre could only be played by Falbo if a sequel were to be made—and Falbo knew it, too. Aware of how much money the first film generated, he astutely demanded a profit percentage if Lewis were serious about making *Lucky Pierre Part Two*. The fact that he was represented by one of the biggest talent agencies around—the William Morris company—didn't help matters. Since Lewis and Friedman were not about to give anyone a percentage of the profits, *Pierre Two* came up snake eyes and died.

The filmmakers reprised their *Daughter of the Sun* formula in several made-to-order pictures for theater owner Tom Dowd. *Nature's Playmates* (1962) and *Goldilocks and the Three Bares* (1963, also shown under the title *Goldilocks' Three Chicks*) were basic by-the-numbers affairs that relied on bouncing buns to titillate ticket buyers. *Goldilocks* was a light-hearted romp produced by Dowd and David Friedman (operating under cover as Davis Freeman), and directed by Lewis. The cast featured some rather interesting names. Joey Maxim, a stand-up comedian, appeared as himself. In nudie roles were Toni Toomey, Maria Stinger, and Delores Mooney — and one has to wonder what their real names were. Letting it all hang out in one of the featured male roles was Mal Arnold, who would achieve notoriety as the mad Egyptian caterer of Herschell's later film, *Blood Feast*. (This is a scary thought in itself.) Racking up another Lewis credit was Bill Kerwin, also destined for stardom (of a sort) in *Blood Feast*. Lastly, and most significantly, the girl who would receive credit for devising *Blood Feast*'s screenplay, Allison Louise Downe, was featured in the film's starring role as Alison Edwards. (Downe would continue to work with H. G. Lewis throughout his career, both in front of and behind the camera. On different pictures she was credited as A. Louise Downe, Allison Louise Downe, or Louise Downe.)

Downe also appeared in *Nature's Playmates* in the role of Diana. Written by Bentley Williams, produced by Tom Dowd and David Friedman (once again as Davis Freeman) and directed by H. G. Lewis (taking credit as Lewis H. Gordon), the film ran just over an hour. Other names featured in *Nature's Playmates* were Al Glick, Judy Parsons (who also appeared in *Goldilocks and the Three Bares*), Shirley Gresham, Amy O'Donnell, and one of the most prominent double-barreled burlesque queens, Doris Wishman. (Surprisingly, Doris did not appear in any other H. G. Lewis nudies.)

One of the most offbeat projects Lewis worked on was *Sin, Suffer and Repent*, which became a 1965 release. It was not a picture made for Tom Dowd like the other nudies discussed here; it was a "fix-up job" for a fellow HG knew in Toledo, Ohio. Herschell recalled, "A friend of mine who was a film distributor in Toledo had bought a British picture about venereal disease. It was one of those old *Mom and Dad* type of films, where you have lectures directed at the audience. You break into [the story] and give a 'live' lecture. He knew that a VD picture couldn't *possibly* do any business, so what he did was buy a copy of the *Birth of a Baby* film and splice them together."

Let's pause for a moment here for some social commentary and background. The medical film footage lifted from *Birth of a Baby* was incorporated into a number of early sexploitation features as a way to get full frontal nudity past state censors — no matter in how bad taste it might be. It was used even as late as 1969, when American International spliced it into a "mature" educational offering entitled *Helga*. It seems unbelievable that there was an audience who enjoyed watching this sort of thing — but then those same people are probably wondering how on earth a bunch of horror movie addicts could want to see movies in which scenes of brutality and gore are the main attraction.

Lewis continued, "Obviously, the insertion of a scene of the birth of a child into the middle of a picture about venereal diseases didn't make a lot of sense. So I got together with this fellow and we took the British film and cut out some of the VD stuff, and shot some new footage of a girl on a gurney being rolled down the aisle of a hospital. The girl is pregnant; there's a huge bulge under the sheet. The hospital never did understand quite what we were shooting, or why! And neither did I. Anyway, he cut that into the film just before the birth scene." And Lewis swears that's all he had to do with *Sin, Suffer and Repent!* (Believe it or not, the Ohioan actually made money with this thing.)

The last black-and-white picture Lewis made was *Scum of the Earth* (1963), a film sometimes seen under the title *The Devil's Camera*. "That was another picture that we shot in Miami," recalled Lewis. "It isn't a bad film by any means, but because it was made in black and white its playoff was very limited." The film is notable mainly for its casting of Allison Louise Downe in a starring role opposite Bill Kerwin, who adopted a new name for this performance: Thomas Sweetwood. (Perhaps he was so embarrassed by the picture that he decided his pseudonym had better have a pseudonym.) Also in the cast was Sandra Sinclair, destined for death in *Blood Feast*. And Mal Arnold was back as well. It might have been the nuances of Mal's *Scum of the Earth* performance that convinced Lewis he would make a terrific Egyptian caterer. But it's doubtful.

"*Scum of the Earth* was made at a time when more and more independent features were being made in color," Lewis pointed out. "It managed to turn a profit, but in retrospect I realize we should have made that film in color. It was really a minor film, which is one reason I opted to shoot it in black and white." In fact, *Scum of the Earth* was *so* minor a project, the only reason it was made at all was that Herschell got cold one day in his Chicago office.

"I hated cold weather," Lewis admitted, "and whenever it became too cold, I would look for reasons to shoot a picture. That's how *Scum of the Earth* got made. Dave Friedman and I had a pattern, in fact. Every year when it got cold, we'd do another picture in Miami." The integrity of the film artist at work.

In taking advantage of situations and opportunities that afforded reasons to take a southerly sojourn, Lewis would sometimes embark on a bona fide movie project of his own, as he did with *Scum of the Earth*. He would also accept the most miserable, minor-league work, as long as it justified an excursion to sun country, as happened with *The Magic Land of Mother Goose* (1967). "*Mother Goose* was simply a camera job," said Lewis. "It was a film that was made for someone else, and the producer needed someone who knew how to operate a camera. So I agreed to be the camera operator on that picture." The only other detail Herschell could furnish about *The Magic Land of Mother Goose* was that it afforded him one more opportunity to soak up some Florida sunshine. Oh, the drudgery, the drudgery.

Although he was queried over and over again by potential partners, Herschell felt it unwise to let his own production information get out: what a film cost to make, what its profit margin was—the kind of details that could be potentially damaging to a relatively fresh face on the film scene. Although both Lewis and Friedman were proud that they had been able to make features so cheaply, they didn't want others privy to such "sacred" information. Rather than alienate potential investors, exhibitors, distributors, and others in the business end of the industry by refusing to divulge facts and figures of this nature, Lewis pretended to be forthcoming, but supplied the same piece of *non*-information every time he was asked what a picture cost to make: "We brought that one in for under $400,000." The only thing he didn't tell them was that *all* his films were brought in for *way* under $400,000 — sometimes even under $40,000! On the other hand, Friedman often admitted up front what a picture had cost to make. It became a kind of ticking time-bomb for the duo, especially when Friedman neglected to inform Herschell he'd already admitted what it cost to make something like *Daughter of the Sun*. "I would approach a potential backer and suggest that if they wanted us to make a feature for them, we would need 'X' number of dollars," recalled Lewis, "and they would get this look of shocked bewilderment on their faces. 'What do you mean? We know what it costs you to make these things. Dave already told us!'" A silent partner Friedman was not.

One of Friedman's New York business associates, Adolf Herman, put together a film script of his own, but he wanted somebody to make the picture for him. Since Lewis and Friedman were hot news on the independent scene at that time, Herman wanted to get them involved. But when Lewis sat down to read Herman's script, he groaned. "If it had a plot," he said years later, "I don't remember it." Lewis often referred to it as a "torn T-shirt picture." In other words it was a story that contained a lot of mindless violence and a certain amount of philosophizing — mostly in one-syllable words, as it turned out.

Nevertheless, Lewis and Friedman decided to make the picture for Herman. The script could be rewritten, anonymously if necessary. Once the deal was finalized Lewis purchased the necessary film stock and hired a crew. By this time, he and Friedman were known as honest filmmakers because they paid their cast and crew members on time. "As anyone who has ever worked on independent features can verify," revealed HG, "you can show up for shooting one day and find nobody else there. You might find a hotel maid stripping the beds, saying, 'I don't know where they went.'" Lewis and Friedman bent over backward to make sure that didn't happen on their pictures, and they managed to build a reputation as people who paid their bills in full and on time. Friedman always carried a checkbook, and when an actor was finished with his lines for the day he was paid then and there. It might have put a momentary dent in their collective pocketbook, but it was a method that insured future cooperation. Whenever Lewis needed someone to work on a film, folks made themselves available without a second thought.

With film locations secured, a hand-picked crew in place, and raw film stock loaded in his Mitchell camera, Lewis was ready to begin shooting Adolf Herman's movie. There was one small hang-up: The production money from Adolf's company had not yet arrived. Four days before filming was slated to begin, Friedman journeyed to New York to get a check from Adolf personally. He returned, long-faced and empty-handed, that same evening. "Adolf can't put his deal together," Friedman reported. Still, there was an alternative. A fellow named Stanford Kohlberg was also interested in the film business, and he had money at the ready. If they could convince Kohlberg to finance the project, Lewis and Friedman wouldn't lose anything on their investment. "Okay, let's see what he says," Herschell said.

Kohlberg agreed to get the ball rolling by committing his own funds to the production — as long as the picture was another nudie. Since Herschell didn't really like Herman's "torn T-shirt" concept anyway, Kohlberg's stipulation came as a kind of reprieve. With a check for $10,000 in hand to get them started, Lewis and Friedman sat down over the weekend and wrote a sex-comedy with the oddball title, *Boin-n-g!* The title was representative of a sound effect used throughout the film as a laugh-getter. (Use your own imagination here.)

It some ways the story that came out of Lewis and Friedman's weekend workshop was autobiographical, because it concerned two fellows who make nudie movies. It was certainly anecdotal. Lewis tailored the script to fit the locations that had already been lined up for Adolf Herman's ill-fated production; and cast members who previously had worked in several of the earlier nudie films, such as Larry Aberman (credited on-screen as Lawrence J. Aberwood) and Bill Kerwin, signed on to take part in it.

Everything went smoothly during the five-day shoot, excepting a single sequence shot with an Arriflex camera instead of the standard Mitchell. A mechanical glitch caused the movie film to move through the Arriflex at only 12 frames per second (fps), so the action appeared speeded-up when it was developed. (Standard motion picture film is recorded and projected at 24 fps.) Typically, rather than toss out what had been shot with the Arriflex — as usual, there wasn't time or money available for reshoots — Lewis kept it in the film's final cut and dubbed in a speeded-up version of "Stars and Stripes" on the soundtrack. "The finished picture was extraordinarily good for that kind of film," judged Lewis.

Friedman, who had known Kohlberg for some time, urged Lewis to keep an eye on the record books during their involvement, because he thought Kohlberg's history of film rentals was not always on the up-and-up. Almost immediately Friedman found himself at odds with Kohlberg over the rights to territorial distribution deals on *Boin-n-g!* Kohlberg claimed that if someone offered to pay $15,000 to play *Boin-n-g!* in a particular territory, they'd pay $20,000. Both Friedman and Lewis knew from their previous experience that Kohlberg was right — to a point. It's really a matter of give and take, just as when a customer negotiates with the dealer on the purchase price of a new automobile. The dealer starts high so he can come down; the buyer offers low so she can increase her offer. As HG pointed out, however, if someone agrees to your $20,000 asking price and you then raise it to $25,000, you had better be a good reader of the other person's psyche — otherwise you're liable to lose the deal to your own greed. Lewis added, "My opinion of Stan Kohlberg was that Kohlberg was never a master of psychology. He was street-smart, but he wasn't the kind of partner who would wear well with me." Lewis didn't say anything right away because they were all making money. (Or at least it *appeared* they were making money. Later on they would discover the existence of some monetary subterfuge.)

After *Boin-n-g!* was completed and making its regional rounds, Lewis was approached by Eli Jackson and Leroy Griffith, a couple of theater owners who specialized in booking burlesque performers and nudie films together as part of a combination package. During the time Lewis was active in the nudie-cutie genre there was an entire network of theaters that combined live shows and film. HG's visitors were at the forefront of this movement. Like many others who had been conferring with Lewis and Friedman, Jackson and Griffith thought the time was right to get into film production themselves. And like everyone else, they had their own ideas about what constituted a good story line. Eli Jackson, in fact, was married to a burlesque performer named Virginia Bell, and his idea was to build an entire picture around her. Herschell remembered, "I had never heard of Virginia Bell, but other people assured me that she was a big star in the burlesque circuit. Eli and Leroy wanted to shoot this film in a hurry, and the reason was that Virginia Bell was pregnant. I guess it was her first pregnancy because no one was sure that she would emerge from it and still be able to perform in burlesque. These fellows wanted to capture her on film before she lost her figure."

While Herschell began hammering out a script—ultimately titled *Bell, Bare and Beautiful*—David Friedman made a telephone call to Stan Kohlberg to see if he was interested in putting up the money to do another feature. In fact Kohlberg was sitting on the other end of the line counting receipts from the first bookings of *Boin-n-g!* Impressed with the numbers that film was generating, he greeted Friedman's proposal with an enthusiastic "Absolutely!" With Kohlberg's blessing (and money), Lewis and Friedman would be making another picture back-to-back with *Bell, Bare and Beautiful*.

Lewis was more than appreciative that Friedman had been able to get the funding for another production in gear, but he rebelled against the idea of doing yet another nudie movie. Besides the picture they were getting ready to make for Griffith and Jackson, they had already done *Daughter of the Sun*, *The Adventures of Lucky Pierre*, *Goldilocks and the Three Bares*, *Nature's Playmates*, and *Boin-n-g!* Tom Dowd, the first theater owner to show *Lucky Pierre*, had also gotten into the production business and had made several nudie-cutie pictures of his own. Lewis reminded his partner, "Everywhere we go in the industry just about every exhibitor is talking about making one of these pictures. There are only a certain number of ways to show naked girls playing volleyball. Let's do something *different*." On reflection Friedman agreed: There were too many nudist-camp pictures and sex comedies. Profits were sure to fall off significantly before much longer. Perhaps the time was right to begin thinking about other kinds of pictures they could do. (As it happened, Herschell was way off the mark in his assessment of the nudie industry. These films continued to make money for many more years. David Friedman produced a number of them after he and Lewis went their separate ways. Ultimately, hard-core pornography killed the nudie-cuties, but that's another story for another time.)

H. G. Lewis's key point was that their next film should be something that the major film studios could not or would not make. "We eventually narrowed our choices down to two," Lewis said. "We could either do a film that was so loaded with sex as to be almost unfilmable, or we could do a picture that was so loaded with horror as to be equally unfilmable. And since there was an overabundance of nudie pictures, we opted for the horror angle. We decided our picture would be the ultimate grotesque horror film." With that goal in mind, horror-film history was about to be made.

The filmmakers returned to Miami to work on *Bell, Bare and Beautiful*, photographing much of the picture at Spartan Tropical Gardens, where Lewis had filmed *Daughter of the Sun* and *Nature's Playmates*. The film had a more interesting plotline than the run-of-the-mill nudist-camp extravaganzas and nudie-cuties that Lewis and Friedman had been making for the past few years. A young millionaire becomes obsessed with a beautiful, unknown woman, whom he repeatedly dreams about. An investigation reveals that she is a real person — a big-breasted stripper who spends most of her time at a local nudist camp. And that's about as interesting as *Bell, Bare and Beautiful* ever became, because the rest of the picture was taken up with footage at the old Spartan stamping-ground. At least Herschell succeeded in delivering what Eli Jackson wanted: plenty of nudity with his wife, Virginia Bell, hanging out all over the place.

A few scenes that didn't involve any nudity were shot at Leroy Griffith's home in Miami Beach, and more footage was shot at the Miami studio where the television series *Flipper* was being made. The studio's head honchos insisted that Lewis's company work only at night, after the *Flipper* crew had departed for the day. They also had to make certain to put everything back in its place before the crew returned the following day. "We became the 'Draculas' of filmmaking there," Lewis quipped. It was an exhausting time for everyone involved: Production personnel often worked around the clock to meet deadlines, including one 40-hour stretch without a break. "It was not a pleasant experience," Lewis noted. In addition, Virginia Bell had a burlesque booking coming up, putting the filmmakers under even more pressure.

Once again adopting their Lewis H. Gordon and Davis Freeman personas, Lewis and Friedman went through the motions on *Bell, Bare and Beautiful*, but they were spending nearly every spare moment thinking, planning, writing, and talking about their upcoming horror movie. As time permitted, Lewis began writing the script based on ideas supplied by Allison Louise Downe. That script, of course, was to eventually bear the title *Blood Feast*.

It was decided to create a new corporate identity for the upcoming production. Stan Kohlberg brought in his own partner, Sid Reich, an accountant from New York. The new company was christened the Jacqueline-Kay Corporation. Lewis and Friedman were the operating partners in this company; Kohlberg and Reich were the silent partners. (Although a lot of money would pour soon into the company coffers, a rift eventually developed among the parties, causing the premature collapse of Jacqueline-Kay.)

To capitalize on selected locations, the filmmakers were scheduled to move into production on *Blood Feast* immediately following the completion of the Virginia Bell film — so the script was a mere *fourteen* pages long at completion! "It was thinly scripted," admitted Lewis with masterful understatement. Louise Downe, by now one of the regulars on Lewis's crew, came up with the idea of using Ishtar, the supposed "Egyptian Goddess of Blood" (actually the Babylonian Earth-mother goddess), as the central plot device, and Lewis awarded her screenwriting credit because he liked her idea so much.

In reality the script was developed by a number of people. Parts of it were left unwritten, and once filming actually got underway dialogue often was concocted on the spot. It was not a situation conducive to quality filmmaking — but then, H. G. Lewis never pretended to be making a quality product. "*Blood Feast* was so cheap to make, I never tell anyone what it really cost," the director stressed. For a movie that was eventually described as "thoroughly revolting grade-Z horror garbage," it was destined to become an incredible moneymaker for everyone involved.

CHAPTER 6

A Slip of the Tongue

> We needed fake blood, and we needed gallons of it. I hated the kind of blood that was available, because in every major film I had seen, the blood never looked right. So we ended up manufacturing our own. We also needed a kind of blood that could be ingested, that our actors could spit out. So the main component in our stage blood became Kaopectate.
>
> — *Herschell Gordon Lewis*

H. G. Lewis had returned to Spartan Tropical Gardens to film most of *Bell, Bare and Beautiful*, and it was in and around Miami that *Blood Feast* was made. Lewis's stock crew, headed up by Bill Kerwin, adored the Miami of the early 1960s. Lewis made most of his early pictures there, before the drug culture of the 1960s and '70s blossomed into the crack epidemic of the '80s, turning the downtown area into a drugged-out, crime-ridden dump. "We were in love with Miami back then," Lewis reminisced. "We shot more film there than anybody."

But in 1963 there was still an air of innocence in the atmosphere. H. G. Lewis would be the first producer-director to shatter the allure of the retirement oasis with his shocking and hard-hitting style of horror-in-overdrive filmmaking. The intelligent, soft-spoken Lewis seemed wholly at odds with the images his 35mm camera recorded. It's as if the style of guerrilla gore-fare for which he became known required a fictionalized persona behind it: Most people just couldn't believe that a picture like *Blood Feast* could have been made by a rational human being. The filmmaker must be some burly, Neolithic sort; seriously cracked, possibly even dangerous. Put a real knife in his hand instead of a rubber-bladed prop and see how fast you'd regret it.

It took a long time for Lewis to resurface in the industry after his final fling with film fear in 1972; but when he did, fans discovered an intelligent, articulate, smartly-dressed and witty individual—not at all what some had anticipated after seeing such warped wonders as *The Wizard of Gore* and *Two Thousand Maniacs!* Even Herschell himself admitted, "I get crank letters to this day about my pictures from people who can't understand at all that something like *Blood Feast* could be made by civilized people."

Once the fans realized that Lewis wasn't quite as loony as his work might suggest, the filmmaker found himself in demand at fantasy film conventions, and publications that had loathed him before lionized him now. Nevertheless, most mainstream critics disparaged Lewis and his films at every opportunity. Even writers and editors of genre publications such as *Famous Monsters of Filmland* and the late, lamented *Castle of Frankenstein* refused to run articles about his films.

When Lewis was just beginning his horror film career, no one, least of all he himself, had any idea that his reinvention of the gore score would have any impact on the genre as a whole. Had someone suggested that *Blood Feast* was destined to become a cult favorite, that gore-saturated horror movies would eventually become an international phenomenon, both Lewis and Friedman would have had a good laugh. *Blood Feast* a cult favorite? Gore going mainstream? Get real.

Before *Blood Feast* began filming, the company took some time to experiment with the gore effects they planned to use in the picture. Herschell was dissatisfied with the stage blood manufactured by professional supply companies and decided to try a more realistic concoction of his own. He recalled that the blood manufactured by Max Factor they had used briefly in *Living Venus* was too purple — but since that picture was made in black and white that didn't matter. *Blood Feast* would be in color, and the camera was going to record the bloodshed in nauseating close-up. Purple stage blood was out. Besides, the Max Factor blood was usually sold in small vials or bottles, and Lewis needed *gallons* of it.

He went to a place called Barfred Laboratories in Coral Gables, Florida, to compound his own brand of blood. Getting the proper color and consistency was essential, of course, but Lewis had another criterion for *Blood Feast* blood: It had to be safe to swallow, because there were scenes in the script that would require the actors to spit, gurgle, drool, and otherwise dribble the stuff from their mouths. Barfred Laboratories managed to come up with a formula that proved so successful that Herschell would use it for the rest of his bloody career.

As it happened, the over-the-counter diarrhea remedy known as Kaopectate formed the basis for Lewis's stage blood. Obviously Kaopectate could be tolerated by the digestive tract since that was what it was made for; but it also had good consistency. All that was needed was to alter the color, which Barfred did by adding red food coloring. The concoction ended up costing Lewis $7.50 a gallon. "Over the years we used lots and lots of that blood," said Lewis, "and as far as I know Barfred is still selling it. It was great blood, but it stained everything it touched. In retrospect maybe I should have claimed the formulation, but we were a bunch of cooperative fellows who were getting a kick out of doing this, and we were just delighted to have it. Anyway, it was really Barfred's formula, so although I was the contractor, they were the inventors." Too bad. Lewis might have made as much money selling digestible stage blood as he did making movies.

What was eventually to become the world's first gore film began inauspiciously, as a little script penned by H. G. Lewis and A. Louise Downe. And "script" may be an overstatement; the *Blood Feast* script was really just a lengthy outline. Skeletal as it was, however, it synopsized all the major action, the gore set pieces, and the critical turns of the plot. In addition to helping conceptualize the picture, Louise Downe also worked with Lewis on some of the gore effects. The company went into production knowing they would be creating a "gorror" movie. There was no reason to think they could offer much else to paying customers. Certainly, with the kind of resources at their disposal no one could honestly believe they were going to wow audiences with incredible set design, insightful characterization, and dazzling camera movements. With its chintzy shooting schedule (nine days) and anorexic budget ($24,500), the film still had to meet its early '60s competition. AIP had retired their 1950s "B-creatures" to concentrate on a series of Edgar Allan Poe adaptations (the term is used advisedly) starring recognizable genre names such as Vincent Price, Peter Lorre, and Boris Karloff. Hammer was producing their own series of Frankenstein and Dracula subjects featuring British beasties Christopher Lee and Peter Cushing. Herschell could only boast of Bill Kerwin, and who was going to go to a movie because Bill Kerwin was in it? (Even if Kerwin donned his Thomas Wood persona, who was going to go see a Thomas Wood picture?)

From the start, then, Herschell knew he had to bring something innovative to the motion picture screen that the major companies, as well as the successful new independents, could not or would not make. About the only thing Lewis's troupe could afford was theatrical stage blood and other low-tech makeup items such as nose putty, greasepaint, and mortician's wax. Not to forget the animal innards provided by local meatpacking plants. As Lewis would soon find out, there was gold in that thar gore.

The story line that meandered through the 14 pages of film script was certainly original for its day. The plot boiled down to these essentials: Fuad Ramses, a madman who runs an exotic catering service specializing in Egyptian cuisine, wants to resurrect an Egyptian goddess of blood called Ishtar. The resurrection ritual involves serving an authentic Egyptian feast created from an assortment of human body parts and organs, with blood substituting for Worcestershire sauce. Without the aid of volunteer organ donors Fuad has to wing it, so he begins to prey on defenseless young women he locates in conveniently isolated situations.

The Egyptian motif was Louise Downe's idea, and it was a good one, even if the "goddess of blood" wasn't authentic. Ancient Egyptian culture lent itself to imaginative interpretations for several reasons. First, Hollywood had already primed the public with tales of Egyptian curses, reincarnation, and living mummies in a variety of movies, including the classic Boris Karloff chiller, *The Mummy* (1932), and its so-so spin-offs, *The Mummy's Hand* (1940), *The Mummy's Tomb* (1942), *The Mummy's Ghost* (1944), and *The Mummy's Curse* (1944), through the grade-B buffoonery of *Abbott and Costello Meet the Mummy* (1955). Egyptian blood vengeance rites certainly were not unheard of, and the culture's surgical talents were formidable. During the mummification process—which involved removing organs from the carcass and stitching it back together—the brain was extracted, almost unbelievably, through the nose. (Lewis, of course, took the easy route and ripped it out of a smashed skull. To each his own.)

Structurally, *Blood Feast*'s screenplay anticipated the slasher film sequels of the 1980s following in the wake of *Halloween* and *Friday the 13th*. The plotline unraveled slowly and predictably, punctuated by episodes of blood and gore as victims were struck down one by one. The kill pattern invoked in *Blood Feast* worked just as well 15 years later, and in fact continues to work in today's films. "The theme of *Blood Feast* was one I felt lent itself to the kind of low-budget, intensive production that we were geared to make," Lewis commented. "Your ego goes out the window and you make a picture for the audience rather than for the satisfaction of self or the winning of an award."

Although Allison Louise Downe shared scriptwriting credit with Lewis, the story line was really devised by "a consortium of people," according to the director. "I would say the largest scriptwriter was circumstance, in that we would concoct dialogue on the spot," he elaborated. "We didn't have time to do much else." In fact, Lewis and his crew had arrived in Miami without a single word of the script written; but that was all right, because the filmmakers knew exactly what they intended to do. "Actually Louise Downe and I wrote *Blood Feast* together in tandem, taking turns on the typewriter," Lewis explained. "When one of us would write because the other had become exhausted from hitting the keys, the other would start fooling around with ideas for gore effects." It was a method that worked especially well because they could bounce ideas off one another, maintaining a pace and energy that would carry over into the film itself.

Except in the British Hammer productions of the late 1950s, such as *The Curse of Frankenstein* and *Horror of Dracula*, movie violence had remained relatively mild over the years. Lewis proposed to change that. He made a list of the kinds of effects he wanted to accentuate in *Blood Feast*. First, audiences would see people dying with their eyes open for the first time. "Everyone always died peacefully in movies," Lewis pointed out. "A gangster would gasp out his last message and close his eyes. Also, the skin seemed never to be broken in conventional films. We broke and *entered* the skin. Thirdly, nothing ever dripped. There were a whole bunch of taboos that we set out deliberately to violate in order to position our picture. I wanted it so that no exhibitor could say, 'Oh, I've seen that before, done better.'"

HG certainly made good on his promise. There had never been anything like *Blood Feast*. The picture was not a "whodunit," but a "howdunit." And the answer was, with cleavers, hatchets, knives, and numerous other sharp implements. The heavies in Herschell's movies never employed something as mundane as a pistol to do in their victims. HG admitted, "We couldn't match major studio production values, we didn't have name actors and actresses, and there was no special effect we could do, such as the exploding uniforms which Sam Peckinpah brought out later. What could we do to justify playing time for our movie? The answer was that we could provide effects, however crudely drawn, that nobody else *would* do."

There is a qualifier to keep in mind about those effects, however: Nobody else would do them *at that time*. The grotesque gore in HG's pictures—even some of the astoundingly sickening sights seen in his later *The Wizard of Gore* and *The Gore-Gore Girls*—was eventually surpassed by young filmmakers who turned out such super-gore products as *The Re-animator* and *Dead-Alive* (a.k.a. *Brain Dead*). In assessing Lewis's films, you have to keep in mind the time frame of their production to appreciate the impact *Blood Feast* had on the future of horror. "Sam Peckinpah's pictures, especially *The Wild Bunch* [1969], were criticized as overtly violent," Lewis pointed out, "but in many ways I felt that they were deficient compared to *Blood Feast* in 1963. Peckinpah's blood was much more watery than ours, for one thing! And even though he used the exploding uniforms, that was because Peckinpah shot people. We *dismembered* them. It's a very basic equation: When you dismember somebody it's going to be much more bloody and repulsive than if you simply shoot them." An apt observation.

Lewis acknowledges the efforts of other filmmakers who have taken crude gore effects to new heights; but, he maintains, "modern gore films have a kind of gray sameness to them. I can't tell *Friday the 13th Part 4* from *Halloween 5*. Even though the concept was standardized — my horror films were gore films, plain and simple — there are no two of them you could ever mistake for one another. And it was a deliberate intention that we never have two films that looked the same." Lewis was not just tooting his own horn, either; *Blood Feast* is as different from *Two Thousand Maniacs!* as *Color Me Blood Red* is from *The Gruesome Twosome*. He never recycled plots. And to his eternal credit, the story lines HG employed in these pictures were much more inventive than the "splatter films" of the 1970s and '80s.

Interestingly, his most ordinary yarn drove the action of his final effort, *The Gore-Gore Girls*, the plot of which can be reduced to this one-sentence synopsis: A maniac systematically kills off go-go dancers. Compare this synopsis to, say, *Friday the 13th* parts one through nine, in which a maniac systematically kills off teenagers. Or the *Nightmare on Elm Street* series, in which a disfigured maniac systematically kills off high school students. Or the *Halloween* series, in which a masked maniac systematically kills off young adults. Whereas modern filmmakers often seemed to rely on "cookie-cutter" scripts to grind out endless sequels to a popular original title, H. G. Lewis reinvented the gorror picture with each new release.

There were limitations, of course. No matter how inventive the script might be, a picture is going to suffer if its production budget is too small. In HG's case, budgets weren't small; they were microbic! Beyond the obvious monetary restrictions, *Blood Feast* is further hampered by what might be described as bad pretending. (It isn't good enough to be called bad acting.) It also suffers from some particularly poor day-for-night photography, frequent over-the-top dubbing (especially during the infamous "tongue scene"), and a threadbare music score. But none of this mattered to HG, who measured the importance of the film in terms of receipts versus cost. By that yardstick *Blood Feast* was a resounding success. Although he declined to reveal exact figures, Lewis did quip, "I don't think *Star Wars* made as much money as *Blood Feast*!" (In a candid moment he admitted that the film brought in at least a half million dollars, but Lewis forfeited ownership of *Blood Feast* in the late 1960s and remained unaware of whatever profits the picture garnered thereafter.)

Blood Feast kicks off in high gear, immediately delivering the kind of gory sequence that became Lewis's terror trademark. Lewis wasn't interested in generating suspense or mystery; he was aiming for anxiety. "*Blood Feast* is certainly no mystery," Lewis confirmed. "In the first three minutes it's quite apparent who the heavy is. It's absolutely beyond question that there's evil afoot." With surprising restraint (considering his previous experience making nudie pictures), Lewis focuses on a curvaceous beauty (Sandra Sinclair) drawing a bubble bath. As she relaxes in the tub, a voice on the radio warns of a dangerous killer on the loose. (It's HG's voice, incidentally. Why pay someone else to recite a mouthful of lines he could do himself?) The "beast" sneaks in and stabs "beauty" in the eye with a butcher knife. There is no spurting blood (early Lewis gore was very rudimentary) but the action pauses while the killer, Fuad Ramses, considers his prize: a mutilated eyeball hanging in tatters from the weapon. A reverse shot reveals the victim's bloody eye socket. The woman is already dead. (Presumably a stab through the eye will penetrate the brain and cause instant death. Such a presumption also means that HG didn't have to complicate the shooting with a struggle between killer and victim in a bathtub full of sudsy water.)

This might have been enough of a shock opening for filmmakers like William Castle or Terence Fisher; but Lewis was defining a new subgenre of horror here. Thus, merely stabbing out an eyeball wouldn't suffice; there had to be more. After Ramses ogles the orb, the camera follows as he pulls out a meat cleaver and begins hacking away at the body in the bath. The placement of the camera obscures the action until Fuad stands tall and proud and then makes off with the object of his demented desire. Lewis then cuts to a panning shot of the bathing ex-beauty, allowing us to see that the killer has hacked his way through flesh, gristle, muscle, and bone to amputate her leg. Lastly, the camera moves in for a forensic close-up of a ragged stump sticking out of the water, clumps of flesh hanging in bloody tatters and a broken-off thigh bone jutting up from the whole gory mess. Just to make sure that any dimwits in attendance don't misunderstand what has happened, HG follows with a close-up of the next day's front-page headline: LEGS CUT OFF! You can't get more pointed than that.

Funnily enough, Lewis doesn't recall lingering on the gore in *Blood Feast*, but there are numerous extraneous shots of blood-spattered bodies that the camera studies with cold, clinical detachment. Lewis judged, "The camera didn't linger in *Blood Feast* the way it did in, say, *The Gruesome Twosome* or *The Gore-Gore Girls*. I think that's because we were a little afraid of what we were doing. There was a certain primitivism to the plot and the effects." Most would agree with his last statement, but certainly not the first. HG's camera studied leg stumps, hearts, and heads emptied of brains the way the Discovery Channel studies the mating habits of insects — with macrophotographic close-ups.

Ramses' Exotic Catering restaurant is visited by Mrs. Fremont (Lyn Bolton), a socialite who wants to impress her status-conscious friends with a snazzy party given in honor of her daughter, Suzette (Connie Mason). Ramses suggests an authentic Egyptian feast — the kind that hasn't been served for over 5,000 years. Mrs. Fremont agrees and the wheels are set in motion to resurrect Ishtar, the Egyptian goddess of blood.

Mal Arnold was a local Miami actor who signed with Lewis to appear in *Bell, Bare and Beautiful* and *Blood Feast* back-to-back. Anxious to impress, he attacked the role of Fuad Ramses with relish. (Too bad he didn't try good acting.) Arnold vanished back into the woodwork after finishing his stint on *Blood Feast*. (Maybe he realized he wasn't all that good.) Representing the forces of good were Lewis stalwart Bill Kerwin (acting under the name Thomas Wood) as detective Pete Thornton, and Scott Hall, who landed the role of the police captain by chance. "The fellow we hired to play the police captain didn't show up when we were ready to begin shooting," said Lewis, "so we were stuck. I decided to draft in Scott, who was the oldest member of the crew and seemed right to play the police captain. He had been a friend of Dave [Friedman] who lived in Sarasota [Florida]." Hall was an old-time carnival man, a "carny" in the parlance of the thrill-ride industry. "One thing about carnies," noted Lewis. "They *work*. I'll take a carny any day."

Hall might have been a great carny, but he was probably the worst actor to appear in *Blood Feast*— and that's saying a mouthful. "Scott was not a consummate actor," Lewis acknowledged. "He had no acting background. He hadn't the vaguest idea of how to play a scene. Finally, when it became apparent that he could not act at *all*, my instructions to him were to shout his lines, to be angry all the time. We had no time to create a Marlon Brando. So he shouted his lines, which is an old acting trick that probably goes back to Shakespeare. It may be a reason why the film didn't win an Oscar, but that's the only penalty I've had to pay. Whether the audience thought he was an actor was not really a factor because no one ever walked out of *Blood Feast* because the police captain can't act."

Hall also had no sense of costume control. He constantly misplaced props. With such a small crew at his disposal Lewis had no one assigned to costumes, so each actor was expected to handle their own costuming chores. Everyone seemed to do all right except Scott Hall. As the crew began setting up to shoot scenes at the Syrian restaurant that stood in for Fuad Ramses' Exotic Catering, Hall announced that he couldn't find his hat. There was no time to search for a lost hat, so Herschell threw another hat to him and told Hall to use it instead.

In previous scenes Hall had been wearing a felt hat, but Herschell had just handed him a straw hat. For some reason, Hall thought it important to maintain consistency between hats. "This is a straw hat," Hall objected. "I had a felt hat before." (It was okay to fail at acting, but hats were another matter entirely.)

"Holding onto props was simply not in Scott Hall's realm of experience," Lewis said. "What was in his realm of experience was that once you've finished shooting your scene, you take off your coat and tie — and your hat!— roll up your sleeves, and help the crew wrap up the cables. That's why I liked people like Scott Hall." Hats be damned.

Not only did HG settle for players like Hall, he didn't mind using friends and associates that worked for next to nothing. Of course, you get what you pay for. "Whenever someone would come to me and ask if they could be in one of my films, I'd say, Certainly," Lewis admitted. "It was one way to save money, although we saved money in different ways. I would have everyone on the crew work on a flat rate. Everybody in the business knew how I worked, that I was anxious to get a film done in a hurry! They also knew that nobody was going to be exploited, and that I wouldn't say they were going to work 'about' two weeks if they were really going to work 'about' four weeks. So the actors in my pictures, whether they were professionals or not, or if they were friends or associates, worked 'flat.' You got X dollars and you either play that role, or handle that mike boom, or run the sound recorder. Sometimes you would play that role *and* handle that mike boom!"

A minor role in *Blood Feast* filled by an associate of Herschell's was that of Dr. Flanders, the lecturer who talks briefly about Egyptian blood sacrifice during the picture's heartrending flashback. Lewis settled on another old-time carny, Al Golden. Golden was what was known as a "book pitchman." As Lewis explained, "Years ago they would sell books in theaters during the intermission, with the suggestion that the books were full of lecherous pictures — which they weren't — and that's what this fellow used to do in the Gayety Theatre in North Miami." But there's a difference between a sales pitch

"Simon says ... fold arms!" says Bill Kerwin to self-professed actress Connie Mason, who responds, "Did I get it right?" The stars of *Blood Feast* on the "set" (actually the Suez Motel in Miami, Florida). Partially obscured on the wall behind Kerwin is a nameplate which reads "Ramses."

and bona fide acting (although H. G. Lewis might deny it!). As it happened, Al Golden kept stumbling over the word "identify" in the *Blood Feast* script. "He kept saying '*en*-dentify'," said Lewis. No matter how many times they ran through the speech, "identify" kept coming out "*en*-dentify." Finally HG gave up and recorded the narration anyway. He went back later during the editing stage and clipped the soundtrack so that it sounded as if Golden were saying "*eh*-dentify," which was at least a little better. "That was the kind of acting we had, though," Lewis commented.

Most of the victims in *Blood Feast* were actresses who had also appeared in *Bell, Bare and Beautiful*. This was a shortcut for Lewis, who thought it unnecessary to scout around for another bevy of beauties to perform in his horror picture. After all, the films would never play together, and there surely wouldn't be much cross-pollination of viewers (dirty old horror movie aficionados?), so why go to all that bother? The downside was that Lewis surrounded himself with a group of women whose primary show-business talent was knowing how to take off their clothes. Acting was a secondary consideration, if it was considered at all.

Numerous other shortcuts were taken throughout the filming. (The budget made shortcuts mandatory.) *Blood Feast* was finished in eight days. David Friedman turned up in a small role as a drunken sailor who walks a girl to her motel room door. "Of course, if that picture had been made ten years later, he wouldn't have staggered away, he would have entered the room with her," Lewis noted. Interestingly, despite Lewis's background as a maker of nudie pictures, he felt it important to uphold a sexual morality in *Blood Feast*. "There were simply no sexual overtones in *Blood Feast*," Lewis said matter-of-factly. By the 1970s and '80s, the so-called "splatter" films would consistently mix sex and death in a seesawing relationship. The *Friday the 13th* series, especially, linked violent death to sexual promiscuity. Female characters who had sexual intercourse in these pictures ended up getting penetrated all over again by a knife or similar phallic implement. (And the guys didn't fare much better.) Almost invariably, the only characters who survived were those who refrained from playing sexual games. In stark contrast, in the gorror film world of Herschell Gordon Lewis, no room was allocated to the sexual element.

With the film's minimal budget came minimal filmmaking equipment. Lewis employed a standard Mitchell camera with a sound-shield blimp for most scenes, and used handheld Arriflex and Eyemo cameras for cinema-verité effects. The Eyemo, a very old unit that had been used primarily in the 1930s for newsreel photography, was especially useful for shooting point-of-view shots, such as the barrel roll in *Two Thousand Maniacs!* but without a sound blimp, overdubbing was necessary. In addition, the Eyemo was a mechanical unit; it had to be hand-wound and exposed only 30 feet of film before running down. But it had its uses.

Sound recording was done on a MagnaCord machine employing a synchronized signal. The equipment was old when Herschell was using it; it's considered ancient now. The MagnaCord was one of the first magnetic synchronous recorders, running at 15 inches per second using quarter-inch tape. Lewis also owned an Ampex recorder, which weighed the equivalent of two full suitcases, or Connie Mason's makeup supplies. The crew relied on "shotgun" microphones instead of the more standard hanging mike. Lewis thought the hanging microphone (which was omnidirectional, as opposed to the unidirectional shotgun) was more trouble than it was worth. "I'm still puzzled to this day why some people continue to use them," Lewis remarked. "They involve re-lighting the set to avoid mike shadows, and there is always the risk that the mike is going to drop into the picture. The sound is just as good with a shotgun microphone, and you only have one crewman on the floor whose shadow can be controlled so it won't come into the frame. I think for some filmmakers it's a matter of being trapped into tradition. I imagine the success of some producers and directors like Stephen Spielberg and George Lucas comes from *not* being trapped in tradition."

Lewis often looked at other director's pictures, not only to keep tabs on what was going on in the business, but because he had been a lifelong movie fan. "I like every movie I've ever seen," he claimed, adding a qualifying afterthought: "except for anything with Barbra Streisand or Carol Channing or Mickey Rooney. Those are just my particular prejudices."

As a film watcher, Lewis saw nothing on the horror horizon to compare with *Blood Feast*, at least in terms of prolonged, unadulterated violence. "We had no tradition to forget," Lewis said, "because our only constraint was budget, and budget forces you to be an innovator. You don't have any decisions to make because they are already made for you by the budget. Someone says 'let's shoot that one more time.' Forget it — it's not a matter of how good the acting is, it's a matter of whether you can get by with what you've already shot. Sometimes when using the Mitchell camera, if we shot a hundred-foot take and somehow ruined it, we would open up the camera and take out that hundred feet of film and put it aside. I could not see paying to process film we were not going to use in the final cut. But we wouldn't throw it out either, because we could always use it for film leader." Every little bit counts.

Except for the minor irritations that accompany the production of any low-budget movie, the *Blood Feast* shoot progressed smoothly. The single major hurdle HG encountered was the hiring of an actress — and that term is used very loosely here — known as Connie Mason. She was a David Friedman discovery who was paid a total of $175 to star in *Blood Feast*. Connie had turned up in the pages of Hugh Hefner's *Playboy* magazine around the time that *Blood Feast* was going into production. (By the time the film was released she had become a Hefner favorite and was featured as the Playmate of the Month for June 1963. The film's promotional campaign seized on this fact and publicized Connie Mason as "*Playboy*'s Favorite Playmate." Publisher Hefner even devoted a small portion of his ongoing historical/pictorial series, "Sex in the Cinema," to *Blood Feast*. The magazine included a black-and-white photo of actor Jerome Eden brandishing a human heart, although how that ties into a series about sex in the movies is something that even Hugh Hefner probably couldn't explain.)

David Friedman was enraptured with Connie Mason and insisted she play the female lead in *Blood Feast* opposite Bill Kerwin. As good as Kerwin was — and he was undoubtedly the best actor Herschell ever had in his troupe — he made Connie Mason look that much worse. She couldn't act, she couldn't emote, she was stiff, and she read her lines off cue cards because she had so much difficulty memorizing the script. Lewis acknowledged, "It was hard not to laugh at Connie Mason. Many of the others in the cast and crew didn't have a lot of respect for her because she had such great difficulty learning her lines. In fact, she had a terrible time learning how to say *anything!* We wrote her lines on pieces of cardboard which were affixed to the shirt front of the person standing across from her. The camera couldn't see it, but she could. We were consistently taking lines away from her and giving them to other actors, even offscreen voices, just to get the picture finished. Oh, the wonderful world of make-do!"

Connie Mason may have been an embarrassment to her coworkers, but Lewis didn't care because he never took the actors in his movies seriously. As he would be quick to point out, he was not selling performances; he was selling horror, or, prior to *Blood Feast*, sex — or at least nudity. The actors weren't all that important. Lewis reiterated, "The role of the actor in a low-budget picture is a secondary consideration, especially if it's a specialty picture like *Blood Feast*, where the audience is concentrating on the gore more than the acting."

Connie Mason's best feature was her extraordinary good looks, making her a prime candidate to play the heroine-in-jeopardy. "She was good at posturing, which many models are," Lewis allowed. "She had approximately 78 teeth, making her a dental wonder. But she did have a lovely smile. She was the kind of girl who had a bone structure that would age gracefully. She was a female Tab Hunter. A more contemporary parallel would be Morgan Fairchild. I've seen Morgan in several films and there is a term we used to use for this kind of person: 'glossy female brute.' I think that's a marvelously apt term. 'Cardboard cutout' is another good one."

Nevertheless, Connie Mason had an important function in *Blood Feast*—standing around, sitting around, walking around, lying around, and looking good while she was doing it—and she fulfilled that function admirably. Lewis's opinion of the generic celluloid seductress is, unsurprisingly, totally facetious: "Some of these people seem so carefully put together that sometimes you wonder how much plastic surgery is underlying the beauty. The term 'glossy female brute' applies to people who spend half the day making up and the other half looking in a mirror to make certain it was done right. Connie was naturally beautiful. Dave was entranced by her because she had something to do with *Playboy*. But that was inconsequential, because I always felt that [*Playboy* models] were plastic people anyway. That mold she fit, but my biggest problem was that we were on a tight shooting schedule, and Connie Mason could not meet the schedule. She was never on time. Everybody else was on time, but not Connie. She was too busy making up!"

Apparently Ms. Mason had it in her head that, as a performer in a movie called *Blood Feast*, she was now a bona fide "star" and entitled to the sort of treatment historically afforded stars. HG recalled, "They almost threw us out of the motel where we were staying while filming, because Connie's room was such a disaster. Her makeup was all over the room. Rotted fruit was all over the room. She had a notion that actresses should be waited upon. I had come across that before, of course, but never to this extent. So we disabused her of that notion very quickly. Connie had never acted before; she just had a notion in her head of what an actress should be and should do. Unfortunately, Dave was so enchanted he kept treating her like the star she was not. I don't think Dave was enchanted on a romantic level, but he certainly saw something more to her than I did. What I interpreted as insecurity Dave regarded as charm. Connie was ornamental, but she was terribly awkward in her gestures, and that comes from not having any dramatic training. If she had spent five years with Lee Strasberg she would have had the kind of polish that would have given her enough confidence so that *maybe* her room would not have been the mess it was!"

Actually Lewis's problems with Connie Mason on the set of *Blood Feast* were marginal compared to what he would experience during the production of his second gore film, *Two Thousand Maniacs!* because her role in the earlier film was much smaller. "*Two Thousand Maniacs!* became a severe problem for us because the film was shot through with Connie Mason," explained Lewis. "In *Blood Feast* her part was not that substantial. She has a couple of scenes in her home, there are some scenes we shot in the Suez Motel, which is where we used to stay when we went to Miami to make pictures. We were known as 'those crazy film people' who always paid for their rooms!" David Friedman was the one who talked Herschell into featuring Connie opposite Bill Kerwin in *Two Thousand Maniacs!* to capitalize a second time on her *Playboy* appearances, and Lewis regretted every moment of it.

Herschell also maintained the opinion that the acting in his films, overall, really wasn't *that* bad. He never tried to disguise the fact that he put friends and business associates in front of the camera.

"They are certainly no worse than some actors I know," he commented. "As a matter of fact, some of my friends who have about as much acting talent as a half-wit oyster are more talented than actors such as Tab Hunter or Marilyn Monroe or Dorothy Lamour or Rod Taylor, or some others who parade around calling themselves actors." As is readily apparent, Lewis is nothing if not opinionated, and he has never shied away from sharing those opinions with anyone who might lend an ear (provided they can expect to get it back).

Lewis has worked with some well-known players. Harvey Korman was in *Living Venus*, Tim Holt made his final film appearance in *This Stuff'll Kill Ya*, Karen Black was part of *The Prime Time*, and Henny Youngman did his "take my wife" schtick in *The Gore-Gore Girls*. "These people can't act," insisted Lewis, "but there are people around who say they can. I saw an act once at the Shrine Circus where someone had trained cows to run in a circle. Big deal! But that's what these people are — trained animals! Herschell Gordon Lewis's Dancing Bears!" (If you're not shaking your head yet in disbelief, read on.)

Connie Mason is the only female character in *Blood Feast* to emerge intact physically and psychically. The others had their legs chopped off, hearts ripped out, or were otherwise mashed, maimed, or mutilated. Following the film's opening shock sequence ("LEGS CUT OFF!"), while the police are chasing their own tails, Fuad Ramses stalks his second victim: a young woman (Ashlyn Martin) rendezvousing with her lover (Gene Courtier) on a secluded beach. "That's the scene where the maniac rips the brains out of the girl's head," Lewis affirmed. "Ashlyn was another *Playboy* girl and she didn't have any brains to be ripped out, so we had to fake it." Good old Herschell.

The scene on the beach was filmed night-for-night. Using just two spotlights for illumination ensured that the surrounding beach area would remain dark — as it would at night, of course — but the obvious way in which the scene is lit calls attention to itself, accentuating the picture's low budget. Nevertheless, this is how Lewis recorded the scene. "We were always thin on lights," he acknowledged. "It was a mechanical problem that we lived with. I wanted to shoot night-for-night because you just can't get good dramatic footage using day-for-night photography; the polarizing filter blacks out people's faces and you can't get any reactions. The problem we had was in the amount of area we could light. We lit an area roughly fifteen feet square. We added the effect of a police car 'mars' light by putting a red filter over one of our master lights and swinging it back and forth!" (That's one even Roger Corman hadn't thought of.) Dramatically, it made sense that neither victim would be able to see the killer approaching until he was almost on top of them, but there is still that nagging question: *Where is all that light coming from?* Lewis reasoned, as he often did, that no one in the audience would actually care. If a ticket-buyer didn't walk out of *Blood Feast* because the police captain couldn't act, would he walk out because the beach scene was not realistically lighted? Of course not. Critics might care, but they aren't the ones buying tickets at the box office. Case, as they say, closed.

Filming took place just outside the Suez Motel. The Suez was across the street from another motel called the Colonial, which was usually packed wall-to-wall with New Yorkers. Each Saturday night the Suez offered some kind of entertainment for its guests — a live band, a movie, a magician, a singer, or something else.

While the film production team was there the manager of the Suez approached Lewis to see if it was possible for something to be filmed involving the motel so the guests could watch — and that would be their Saturday night entertainment. Lewis figured, *Why not?* The scene on the beach could be shot anywhere along the coast; why not shoot it as conveniently as possible, a mere 50 feet from their own rooms?

By Saturday night, word had spread across the street to the competing Colonial Motel, so Herschell had quite an audience in attendance for the beach blanket dingbat scene. "Everyone was hanging out of their balconies to get a better view," he recalled. "I had no problem with that, except it meant we had to aim our cameras in one direction only, toward the ocean, and we were picking up a lot of ocean noises. But we were able to get by."

In the beach scene, Fuad Ramses sneaks up on the young couple making out on the sand. This time he's after a brain. Too bad he picked this couple, though, because they both act brain-damaged before anything remotely brain-damaging happens. Although the young lady is concerned for their safety — who knows what kind of maniac might be out there creeping around in the dark with a big ol' meat cleaver? — her boyfriend Tony insists they continue to cuddle. (You know how guys are.) Sure enough, here comes Fuad with his meat cleaver. He knocks Tony unconscious and proceeds to have his way with the girl — which in this case means he chops open her skull and scoops out her brains. Although Lewis didn't photograph the impact of the blade hitting the scalp (like the "LEGS CUT OFF!" scene, the viewer only sees the weapon slicing through the air), he tried to make up for it by dwelling on the bloody brain Fuad cradles lovingly in his cupped hands.

Standing in for a mass of human brain tissue was — a mass of animal brain tissue. Typically, Lewis used sheep viscera in his horror pictures because he felt sheep organs most closely matched the size and appearance of human body parts. (How does he *know* this stuff?)

David Friedman wanted to include shots of a snake slithering around the body on the beach. It was a totally gratuitous and unnecessary idea — the kind of thing that helped define Herschell Lewis's outrageous brand of horror. "Dave had a thing for snakes," said Lewis, "and in the early planning stages of *Blood Feast* he disappeared for several hours and came back from the Miami Serpentarium with a huge boa constrictor. I hadn't thought of it before, but I felt that a snake, or the image of snakes, was implicitly 'evil,' so it was a fine idea to have the snake in the picture somewhere." Friedman kept the boa in a basket in his room at the Suez, and no one on the crew would go near it. (The motel management had no idea what was going on. If they had, they might have charged for an extra guest.)

After the individual shots of the beach murder were completed, Lewis recorded additional footage of the victim's body from several angles to make sure audiences would get a clear view of all the blood and gore. It was at this point that Friedman wanted to introduce the snake into the scene. Lewis recalled, "When we got to that part of the scene, Dave put the snake on the sand and it immediately scuttled off into the darkness! We got a little of it on film. I suddenly got this sinking feeling in my chest, and all I could think of was the next day's edition of the Miami *Herald* with a big headline that said, 'CHILD SQUEEZED TO DEATH BY BOA CONSTRICTOR; FILM CREW HELD!'" Fortunately for everyone, the police captain

A Slip of the Tongue 51

Top: Of Ashlyn Martin, the beach bunny in *Blood Feast* (1963), Herschell Gordon Lewis remarked, "She didn't have any brains to be ripped out, so we had to fake it." *Bottom:* Fuad Ramses (Mal Arnold) reaches for a gory component to add to the recipe of his *Blood Feast*. That's Ashlyn Martin in repose — the actress who paid to have her hair set just for this scene.

who couldn't act, Scott Hall, came to the rescue. "While the rest of us were standing around horror-stricken," Lewis said, "to his eternal credit Scott rushed after the snake and threw a cardboard box over it, and the snake stopped dead. Scott saved us! Dave got it back to the serpentarium in one piece and good working order — I *think*. At least nobody can say we didn't provide some entertainment that night for the people staying at the Suez. What's even funnier is that they thought this was all part of the act, or a joke, or that we had a trained snake or something. Unbelievable!"

Herschell would often remark about the professionalism — or lack of it — in some of the cast members that worked with him on *Blood Feast* and other pictures in later years. He commented, "That scene in which the brains were ripped out of the girl's head gave me additional insight into the psychology of the actress. We made light of what we were doing because we knew how briefly the candle of celebrity status would flicker for these people. But *they* didn't know. We had no track record — nor had anyone — in filming gore. When we tried to explain what we were doing, or planning to do, people visualized drama rather than actual physical effects. So the day we told this girl that her brains would be ripped out, which we did very candidly, so there would be no confusion about it later on, she went out and had her hair done! In fact I think she had it dyed, because her *hair* was going to be featured in a motion picture! It was really somewhat embarrassing to see the way these people showed up to be mangled and dismembered. In came this girl with this perfectly crafted hair, and all she did after two lines of dialogue was get her brains torn out! In fact, the young man she was with had several lines afterward where he explains to the police what he thinks may have happened, but she didn't have that part; all she did was go '*Arghh*' and fall over. Anyway, that poor girl spent the next three days trying to wash the stage blood and sheep's brains out of her hair."

Probably the most infamous of the gore sequences in *Blood Feast* is the tongue scene, if for no other reason than that the idea of yanking out someone's tongue seems even more grotesque than chopping off a leg or hacking out a brain (although that one does come close). "Imagine the pain you would feel having your tongue ripped out by its roots," Lewis suggested. As it happened, the young woman playing the victim in this scene, Astrid Olsen, was a Scandinavian model with — surprise!— *Playboy* connections. Like Connie Mason, Astrid was "discovered" by Friedman, who found her working at the Miami *Playboy* Club. Like the brainless beach bunny, Astrid had no qualms about getting herself gored up for the camera, because she looked upon this role as her big break into show business. Unfortunately, Astrid's boyfriend tagged along for the shoot, making a nuisance of himself at every available opportunity while Lewis and Friedman were trying to get the sequence in the can. "Astrid's whole part," described Lewis, "was walking drunkenly up the motel stairs and then having her tongue pulled out after she went inside. It made no difference to me who took these roles. Dave liked to cast, so it made a difference to him. I was only concerned whether her mouth was big enough to hold a sheep's tongue, along with the stage blood and other stuff we wanted to cram in it. As it turned out, her mouth was certainly big enough to hold one tongue and probably several others, besides her own, so she was adequate for the role."

Astrid's boyfriend became annoyed with Fuad himself, Mal Arnold, because he didn't like the way the actor was manhandling his lady — never mind that "manhandling" was part of the script. "I don't know *what* Astrid had told her boyfriend," Lewis said, "but he was rather disturbed by it. I said to her, 'Now Miss Olsen, this actor may get a little rough with you in this scene.' And she said, 'Ooh! I *like* a man who is rough!' I'll never forget that, because she said it in front of her boyfriend."

The sheep's tongue had been kept on ice during the shoot but had gotten a bit gamy by the time Herschell got around to filming the scene. In fact, it smelled so strongly that he decided it might be better not to put the tongue in the actress's mouth. Instead, HG shot a long sequence of Mal Arnold with his fingers jammed inside Astrid Olsen's mouth as the two struggled on the motel bed. The sheep tongue was doused with Pine-Sol to eliminate at least some of the stench, and Lewis then simply cut to a close-up of Arnold pulling the tongue *away* from, rather than out of, the victim's open mouth. Of course Lewis also inserted a gratuitous shot of Arnold holding the tongue aloft (it was so big he had to use two hands), but he also added a shot of what appears to be torn-up chunks of meat and at least a pint of stage blood, all dripping out of the dead girl's mouth. In reality Lewis used a concoction made up of clear gelatin, cranberry mix, and stage blood, which looked properly repulsive on screen. "Cranberry mix always looks horrible when you don't know what it is," said Lewis, revealing one of the tricks of his trade. "It looks good when you're eating it, but in the context of that scene it looks ghastly. I think audiences were less sickened by the tongue than they were when she turns her head and all this glop falls out the side. *That's* the part that sickens 'em."

Blood Feast also includes a flashback sequence depicting the "blood ritual of Ishtar," in which a young girl's heart is cut out of her chest. Jerome Eden was the actor holding the sacrificial knife, which had a removable point and could be held against the victim's chest to give the appearance that the blade was buried deep inside. Louise Downe and Herschell fashioned a cavity on the actress's chest using layers of ordinary wax covered with chicken skin. The pocket would even hold a shallow pool of stage blood. The end result looked quite realistic. Eden, holding a sheep's heart against the wax cavity, seemed to pull the bloody organ straight out of the open wound as the camera rolled. Friedman's boa constrictor made another appearance as Eden entered the frame holding the serpent over the girl's body. There was no reason to include the snake in this scene except that Friedman wanted to use it again. (If you're going to drive three hours to procure a snake for a movie, you're damn well going to make sure it was worth the time and effort.)

The least memorable effect in *Blood Feast* is seen during the flogging of a victim near the film's finale. Lewis rigged up a thin-stringed flogger for Mal Arnold to use in the shot, which was "goreographed" so that the victim was strapped vertically to the wall, her bare back exposed to the camera. "The flogger was so soft it was like getting hit with a sponge," Lewis claimed. Stage blood was added to the flogger so that it would leave a trail on the actress's skin, but Mal Arnold had horrible aim: he kept hitting the curtain next to the girl rather than the girl herself. Every time the actress whimpered from the "impact" of the whip, the audience laughed. Lewis admitted, "that was not one of our better

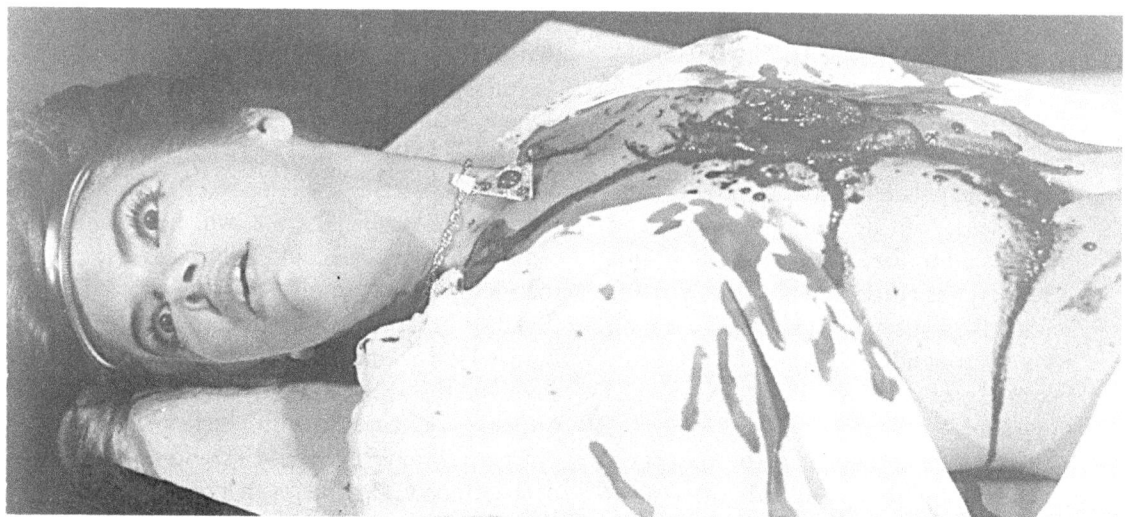

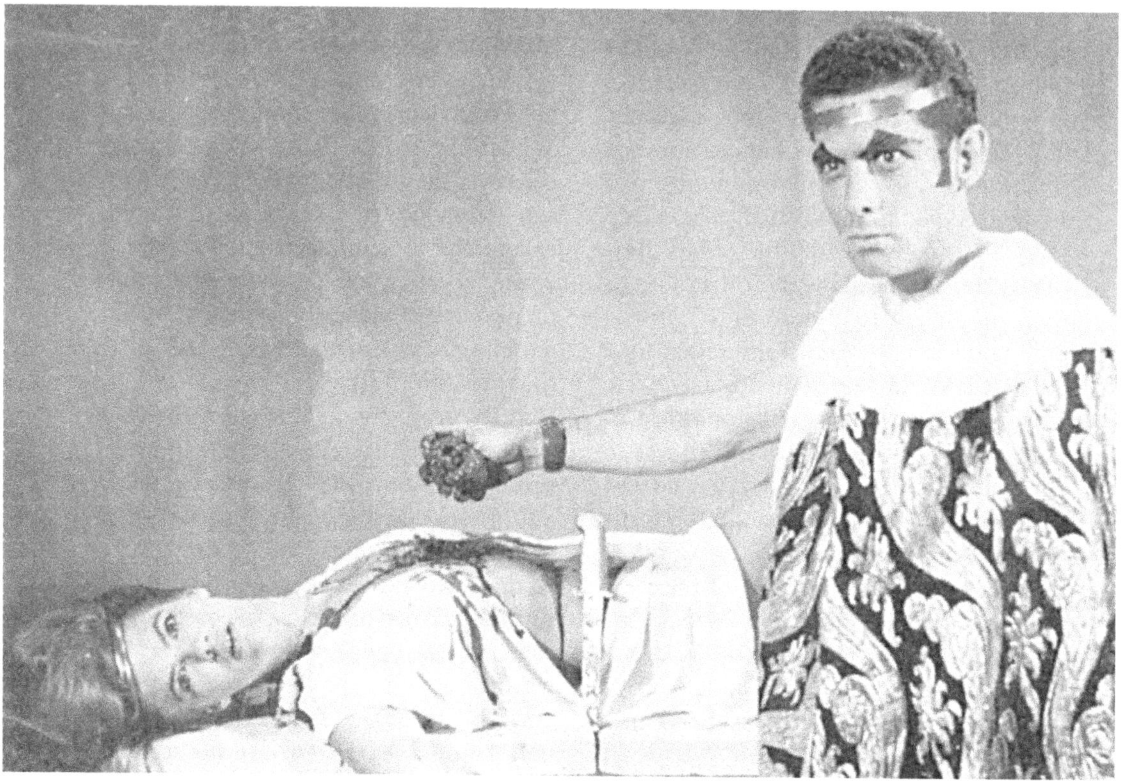

Top: Lewis and *Blood Feast* scriptwriter Allison Louise Downe both worked on the picture's gory makeup stunts. The effect here was created by applying successive layers of mortician's wax (a common item used for horror movie makeups) to the actress's chest to create a bowl-shaped wound which could hold a small quantity of stage blood. The sacrificial victim was played by Louise Kamp. *Bottom:* Frequent Lewis actor Jerome Eden was cast as the Egyptian High Priest who rips the heart from a human sacrifice (Louise Kamp) in a flashback scene in *Blood Feast.*

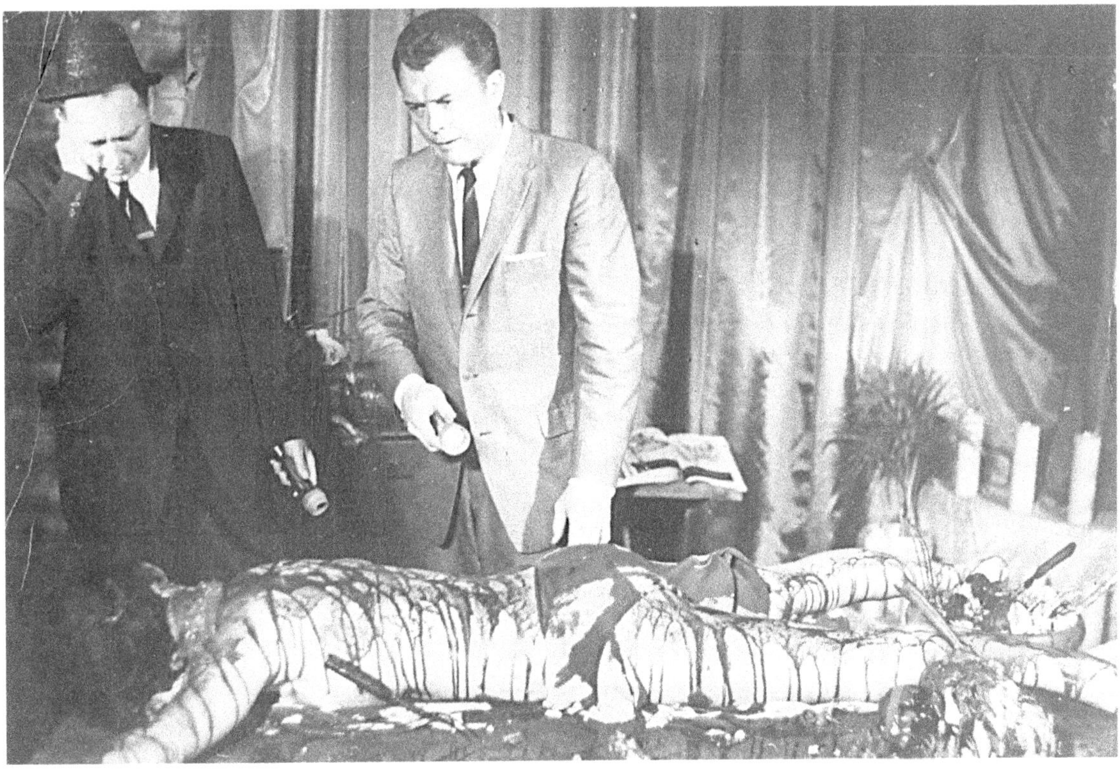

Top: A look behind the "No Admittance" sign in Fuad Ramses' Exotic Catering restaurant. The human detritus scattered around the chopping block includes a hand and a realistic decapitated head with an embedded cleaver. Like many of *Blood Feast*'s promotional photographs, this still shows some gory details that were obscured in the film itself. *Bottom:* The Police Captain (Scott H. Hall, left) and Detective Pete Thornton (Bill Kerwin) discover the latest blood-spattered victim of Fuad Ramses' cross-country cruise for creepy cuisine. While it was all right to dwell on close-ups of hacked-off legs and yanked-out tongues in *Blood Feast*, someone decided it would be improper to show a woman's bare bottom on screen, so a towel was carefully draped across this actress's derrière.

effects. But with the kind of schedule we had, once that first trace of stage blood has got on you, you've got to go the whole route. There was no time for scrubbing down the actress and going back to do it a second time. Once the blood appears you carry it to conclusion and give the actress until the next day to wash up."

Better was the discovering of the victim by the police captain and his sidekick, Pete Thornton. They find the body covered head to toe with streaks of blood. Scott Hall's ludicrous "Ohhhhh!" response never fails to elicit laughs instead of gasps from viewers. Lewis added a long pan down the length of the body so audiences could see just how much red stuff was splattered on the table. For those who looked carefully (or at least got to see the 8 × 10 publicity still) there were also a couple of gory "extras" on the table: a severed hand and a head with a cleaver buried in the back of the skull. (Look closely and you can even see the facial features.)

There is also a very brief shot in which Fuad Ramses, preparing the main course for his Egyptian feast, bakes a leg in a pizza oven. The scene called for Mal Arnold to open the oven door, pull out the cooking tray, and check on the progress of the leg. It was a very minor sequence, but Herschell wanted the audience to see a cooked leg, so to prepare for the shot he took a mannequin leg into the street, doused it with gasoline and set fire to it. The leg went up in flames beautifully — but so did the gasoline, as well as the asphalt. By the time HG, stunned and wide-eyed, was able to put out the fire, it had burned a nice, round hole in the street. "We tried melting some asphalt to fill it in so no one would notice," Herschell recalled, "but the street never looked quite the same after that."

Lewis was never one to let evil reign for very long. None of his horror pictures ends with the villain triumphant, a plot twist that occurred so frequently in the genre during the 1970s that it eventually ceased being a twist. (Only in *Two Thousand Maniacs!* do the townsfolk escape justice as they literally fade into the sunset to begin their long, ghostly sleep — but then, they were dead to begin with.)

Lewis maintained a set of rules he refused to break. He was adamant that the killers in his pictures always got their just desserts. In addition, he felt the villain had to become a victim of the same kind of violence that (s)he had perpetrated against others. It just wouldn't do to have a mad Egyptian caterer who ripped organs out of his victims end up being handcuffed and led away to a paddy wagon. Third, the story line must never endanger a child. Modern terror tales like *Mimic*, which feature monsters that victimize children as well as adults, are just not Herschell Gordon Lewis's cup of tea. "It's generic to my kind of gore picture that the victims are always young women," Lewis explained. "Audiences are not interested in watching geriatric patients [being] disemboweled. They've got to be nubile, fairly voluptuous if possible, girls between the ages of 18 and 30, say. Let's give them some breadth there. Children — never. We *never* touch a child. That's not playing the game. But as you perfectly well know, girls between the ages of 18 and 30 are to be used and thrown away anyway."

Lewis envisioned a particularly gruesome end for the heavy in *Blood Feast* — getting trapped in a garbage truck and squashed to death. In the film's climax Fuad Ramses is at the Fremont house preparing to sacrifice Suzette (Connie Mason) when he is interrupted by Mrs. Fremont's timely arrival. Escaping out the back door, he runs in the general direction of the Miami garbage dump. This is a bad move, folks. The cops are hot on his trail and catching up fast. *Too* fast, as a matter of fact. Recalled Lewis, "When we were filming that scene we kept having trouble because no matter how hard I yelled and screamed, the police who were chasing Mal Arnold kept passing him. They just wouldn't maintain their distance. They refused to stay behind him. Apparently they thought it was some kind of contest where they had to catch him!" To avoid the expense of numerous retakes, Lewis elected to piece the scene together later during editing.

Lewis and Friedman had asked the city of North Miami Beach for the loan of a garbage scow for one day of shooting, and the city officials were more than cooperative. A driver showed up ahead of schedule on the designated day with the cleanest, whitest, shiniest garbage scow Lewis had ever seen. "To be cooperative, the night before we shot the scene they had the whole thing repainted. It was their contribution to show business!" Lewis laughed.

As neat as Fuad's death sounded on paper, the filming proved problematic. It turned out to be the movie's un-goriest gore scene, succeeding by suggestion more than anything else. Herschell conceded, "The last gore shot in *Blood Feast* is lacking in gore, unfortunately, because the construction of that kind of garbage truck included an immense wall that came down with a steel trap that closed over it, and you can see nothing behind it. We had no way of carrying the effect. If we had known more about the way it worked in advance, we probably could have had more gore there — at least an arm getting severed and some gore and gristle coming out of the end of it, or something. But, all we could do was sprinkle some blood around the mashing mechanism. We used what we had." In fact, there is a brief clip of a hand disappearing beneath the mashing mechanism and a bloody bit of torn clothing stuck to the whitewashed metal surface. The scene was lacking compared to the film's earlier gore shots, but it was still a good, gruesome idea, and audiences didn't seem to feel cheated by the quickie climax. (How could they, after seeing everything that went before?) For an amusing capper, Lewis added a line of dialogue to the end of the script: "He died like the garbage he was." Quaint.

After *Blood Feast* was edited, Lewis turned his attention to the music score, which he composed himself. He wanted to use a minimum number of instruments to give the film an off-kilter sort of flavor. "I got hold of Cecil Forsythe's book on orchestration," said HG, "and using it as a guide, I worked and worked on this piece of background theme music." Using a trombone, a cello, a kettledrum, and an organ, with occasional dissonant piano chords in the background, he composed the score in about ten days — longer than it took to shoot the picture! Herschell played the kettledrums himself but noted, "I had the world's worst timing. It took longer to record the score than it did to shoot the film, but it became a challenge that I just didn't want to back down on. It was an ego point, but it was something I never wanted to do again."

Someone who has never watched a Herschell Gordon Lewis picture by now may be beginning to understand how and why his horror films are considered so much more perverse than *Friday the 13th* and its ilk, which customarily impaled their victims, sliced open their throats, or stuck meat cleavers in their heads. All generate feelings of discomfiture, certainly; but compare that to what H. G. Lewis offered audiences who paid to see his homegrown horrors:

Chop off leg (*Blood Feast*)

Slice open thumb, then cut it off leaving gaping hole in hand (*Two Thousand Maniacs!*)

Hack off arm, then barbecue and eat it (*Two Thousand Maniacs!*)

Slice through forehead and yank off victim's scalp (*The Gruesome Twosome*)

Use automated press punch to ram a hole through woman's stomach (*The Wizard of Gore*)

Drive railroad spike into temple until it emerges from other side, pull out dislodged eyeball, and stick finger in the empty socket (*The Wizard of Gore*)

Drive rusty nails into barrel, push victim into barrel, then shove it down an incline (*Two Thousand Maniacs!*)

Prop up disemboweled body and squeeze dangling organs so they ooze blood into waiting bowl — then use blood to paint a picture (*Color Me Blood Red*)

Mutilate woman's face with shards of shattered mirror, then squeeze her dangling eyeball until it pops, squirting black glop all over the place (*The Gore-Gore Girls*).

Need I go on?

While Lewis's gore effects became more and more outlandish with each succeeding picture, even in the beginning he was doing things specifically designed to turn stomachs. No picture had ever sprayed as much blood into the faces of audiences as did *Blood Feast* when it opened in 1963. Although Lewis and Friedman knew exactly what they needed to do to get *Blood Feast* booked into as many theaters as possible, after it was finished they found *themselves* horrified by the film's bloody effects. Compared to today's standards, *Blood Feast* appears pretty archaic, but at the time of its release it was considered shocking and offensive. Lewis recalled, "When we got back to Chicago and began cutting the film, friends would wander into the editing room and look at the footage on the Movieola, and they'd fall down and turn green and throw up and I'm sitting there going, 'What's happening here?' It wasn't that they found it so repulsive pictorially — though of course it was — but because they found it repulsive *psychologically*. Dave and I were working so closely with it that we didn't realize the effect *Blood Feast* would have on other people. Look at this: Here are sophisticated people and they can't stand to look at our picture. It's *that* upsetting."

HG disliked allowing actors to see film rushes because he felt it could become an inhibiting factor for them, but Dave Friedman had promised Connie Mason she could see the rushes she was in. Before long it seemed that everyone involved with the picture in front of as well as behind the camera was coming in to watch. Lewis recalled, "Even knowing Dave and myself, and knowing how much of a joke we thought the whole thing was, and having been there and seeing firsthand how everything was done, they just couldn't sit through it. That told me the effects were going to do fine for us. The real question was, who was going to play this picture? Would it play at a midnight show on Halloween and then disappear? Who would show a film of this type? Who would come to see it? We really began to have second thoughts about the playability of *Blood Feast*. We thought perhaps we had gone too far."

Whether or not the picture went "too far" was a purely subjective matter. There are people who have watched *Blood Feast* in recent years who find it as repulsive as did audiences in 1963, and there are those who have seen the film who dismiss it as an antiquated exercise in silliness. *Blood Feast* has remained a controversial work ever since its debut. "I can't imagine anyone taking this film seriously," remarked Lewis, "although there are those who do." Certainly some members of individual state censor boards took it seriously, because they hounded Lewis to cut back on the film's violence. Before *Blood Feast* could be shown in the state of Kansas, for example, Herschell was forced to cut the tongue scene. He recalled, "The three young ladies of the Kansas censor board — who totaled two hundred years of age — insisted that I cut down that particular scene. So, to get the film played in Kansas, I agreed to cut it. I cut, as a matter of fact, a total of about 10 feet of film. So they could say they did their job, I suppose, and I can say I did mine. I also ran into problems with the MPAA [Motion Picture Association of America], although not on *Blood Feast*, because *Blood Feast* was released before the MPAA instituted their ratings. But it never made sense to me, when you're making a specialty picture like this, to make those kinds of cuts. If you take the gore out of *Blood Feast* all you have left is about 58 or 60 minutes of bad acting, and that's no excuse for a picture."

Primarily because of the reaction the film got from those who saw it being put together, Lewis and Friedman decided it would be best to open *Blood Feast* quietly, to see how it would be received. Stan Kohlberg owned the Bel-Air drive-in theater in Peoria, Illinois, and Lewis zeroed in on it to watch what would happen. "We figured if we died in Peoria, who would know?" remarked Lewis. "And if it made a lot of money or people liked it, we could build our own hoopla around it. So we opened *Blood Feast* on a late summer night in 1963."

And the feast began.

CHAPTER 7

How Did It Play in Peoria?

> I had always been regarded as something of an oddball, so I don't think it surprised anyone that I made *Blood Feast*. Bear in mind that for some years I had been making nudies, so this was a step up. It's like somebody getting out of jail and going to a halfway house. He's regarded as being re-admitted to society.
>
> — *Herschell Gordon Lewis*

When *Blood Feast* opened at that lone drive-in theater in Peoria, cinema history was made. Nobody knew that yet, of course. Although it would take many years, Herschell Gordon Lewis's macabre movie generated the kind of "trickle-down" effect that Ronald Reagan always talked about. But instead of dollars trickling into the economy, which was what Ronny was after, *Blood Feast* trickled rivulets of blood that would swell into a torrent a decade later, when other filmmakers began making their own gory stories.

At the time that *Blood Feast* was scheduled to open in Peoria, neither Lewis nor Friedman had any idea that they might have created, however inadvertently, a new subgenre of the modern horror film. There had been dismembered hands shown on film before: The British mystery/horror picture *The Hand* (1960) depicted a severed hand inside a box, although the film was made in black and white; and Hammer's 1956 production, *The Curse of Frankenstein*, included a color close-up of a severed hand. There had even been a quick shot of a grisly, hacked-off leg in Herman Cohen's 1957 cheapie, *I Was a Teenage Frankenstein*— but again, that was in black and white and the scene went by quickly. Only Herschell Gordon Lewis dared to *dwell* on blood and gore.

Blood Feast opened against some stiff competition. Herschell recalled, "It was the weekend of the heart of the Illinois Fair, and that year the fair was in Peoria. We'd been forewarned not to expect a big gross—and since it was in Kohlberg's theater, you'd have to wonder what the gross reporting figure was anyway!" Lewis and Friedman were holed up in Chicago but Friedman began to get antsy. He telephoned Herschell and talked him into driving to Peoria to see how the picture was performing.

The journey was long and uneventful, but the air was electrified with anticipation. "We had been encouraging each other on the way there," said Lewis. "I would say to Dave, 'Just remember, we didn't mount a big campaign,' and he would say, 'And the fair's in town,' so we were trying to keep our hopes in line with our expectations." The picture had been paired with their earlier sex comedy, *Boin-n-g!*, creating one of the strangest double bills ever to be seen on the silver screen. "That was a real Odd Couple if ever there was one," quipped Lewis. As they got closer to the theater, traffic became snarled and slowed to a crawl. When Herschell saw police along the highway directing traffic he figured they were nearing the state fair. What he didn't know was that they were nowhere near the fairgrounds yet; the traffic backup was coming from all the people crowding onto the exit ramp that led to the theater playing *Blood Feast*! "Cars were packed up and down the highway," recalled Lewis. "From that moment Dave and I knew we had a winner on our hands."

When they finally arrived at the Bel-Air drive-in, they tried to get around the carloads of people coming in at the ticket booth by explaining to the manager that they were the picture's producer and director. The Bel-Air's reaction was basically, "Sure, buddy, and I'm Darryl F. Zanuck." But Lewis and Friedman didn't give up. "We had all sorts of trouble getting in," Lewis said. "We told them that we had made the pictures playing there, and of course these fellows didn't believe that. 'You're not from Hollywood! What are you doing in Peoria?'" They finally just paid the admission fee. Who the heck wanted to waste time butting heads with overzealous ticket booth attendants from Peoria?

Lewis pulled into a parking space close to the front. "We wanted to gauge the audience reaction," he explained, "but it's difficult to get an audience reaction at a drive-in, especially in Peoria, where they bring in five people inside the car and two or three more in the trunk. Nobody had any idea who we were, of course; it wasn't like we were there as part of a publicity stunt. So instead of watching the picture, we watched the audience. Here are all these fellows sitting on their fenders with their girlfriends, yelling and laughing and screaming. 'Hey, wotta lousy movie!' And then comes the tongue scene, and suddenly everything goes dead quiet, and all you can see are these white eyeballs staring up at the screen. That one brought 'em up short."

Lewis and Friedman worked on the *Blood Feast* advertising campaign together. Herschell wanted to use a phrase on the poster that said, "splattered with gouts of blood," but Friedman claimed that the word "gout" couldn't be used in such a context; he insisted it was a word used to describe a medical condition involving inflamed joints. HG countered, "No, you're wrong. When blood spurts out, that's gouts." Friedman didn't believe it and Lewis eventually gave up trying to convince him. Instead, ads and posters screamed, "A weird and unspeakable ancient rite horrendously brought to life! You'll shudder and recoil at the bloody mutilation and defilement of his nubile young girl victims!"

Cheaply printed in a two-color process (black and red on white), the posters were crassly effective. (Incidentally, Lewis was right about the phrase "gouts of blood," and he used it several years after his partnership with Friedman had ended, in the promotional material for his 1967 feature, *A Taste of Blood*.) A *Blood Feast* paperback novelization was prepared by Paul Neimark, an editor at Novel Books, who was a Chicago neighbor of Lewis. Lewis and Friedman gave away copies to everyone who attended the Theater Owners' Convention the year of the film's release.

One of several promotional ad mat designs for *Blood Feast*.

"We handed them out to anybody who passed us," recalled HG. "We gave away at least 5,000 books. It's a rare document now." The remaining copies of the original press run were sold commercially.

There was also a bit of a problem in some territories with the film's title. In the 1960s and '70s — and, in some suburban markets, continuing into the 1980s — newspapers would actually censor movie advertisements containing the word "blood." It wasn't unusual to see some really odd film titles listed as playing some theaters in, say, the New England area. Hammer's *Taste the Blood of Dracula* would be advertised as *Taste the Red of Dracula*. The Hemisphere film company made a series of low-budget chillers featuring John Ashley in the early 1970s with titles like *The Mad Doctor of Blood Island* and *Brides of Blood*, which invariably turned up with corrupted titles that sounded either silly or just awkward. *Blood Feast* was in for trouble in these markets as well, and Lewis realized it long before the film was finished. "I knew some newspapers would reject the title," he acknowledged. "The word 'blood' was somehow controversial in those antediluvian times. I didn't care because it was a whole new world. Blood was more important than the plot, it was more important than the cast. And it would be on theater marquees."

David Friedman came up with the idea of dispensing "vomit bags" to everyone who bought a ticket to *Blood Feast*. Lewis recalled, "We had a simple line of copy on the vomit bags which said, 'You may need this when you see *Blood Feast*.'" Although the vomit bag giveaway wasn't widely distributed, it was the first time such a gimmick had been used to promote a motion picture's utter vileness. (In 1970 Hallmark Distributing promoted Michael Armstrong's notorious *Mark of the Devil* as "the First Film Rated 'V' for Violence" and also gave away vomit bags to ticket buyers. The campaign ran into trouble with the MPAA, which objected to the phony rating, and Hallmark was forced to delete their "V for Violence" blurb on the redesigned advertising material. The vomit bag gimmick was retained, however.)

For years there has been a controversy surrounding the depiction of brutality and bloodshed in films and other media: Does it have an adverse effect on young people? Arguments on both sides were stirred up once more when *Blood Feast* began to be noticed, and on the surface it appeared that the makers of the film were concerned about the potential for psychological damage, because included on the movie posters and newspaper ads for *Blood Feast* was an admonition which read: "This is no 'Publicity-Stunt' warning. If you are the parent or guardian of an impressionable adolescent, DO NOT BRING HIM or PERMIT HIM TO SEE THIS MOTION PICTURE!" It sounded good, but the truth was that Lewis and Friedman were merely trying to generate word of mouth for their film. HG confessed, "That admonition was basic Psychology 101. People like to take a challenge. Suppose we said, instead, 'There are some gore effects in this movie which some of you may find offensive.' That would keep people *out* of the theater. The word 'offensive' gives a person reason to pause. But there's nothing that provokes a

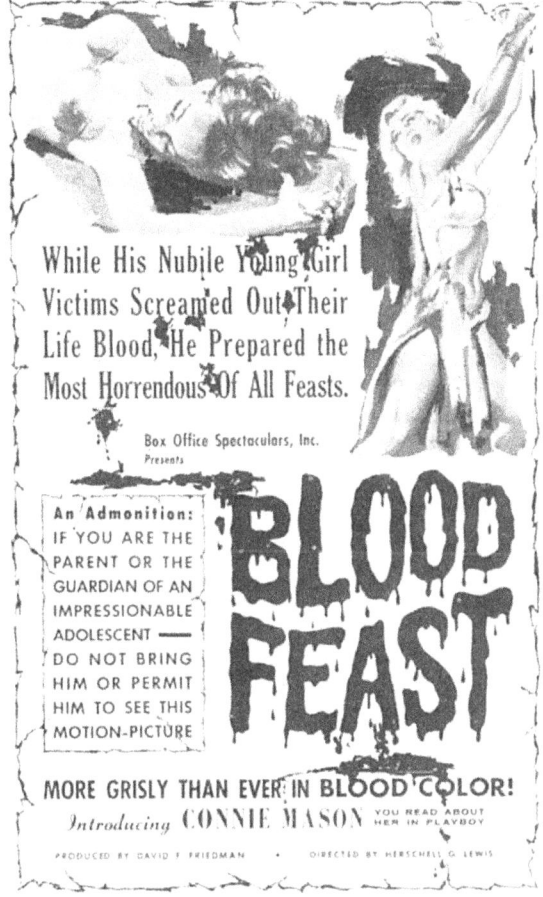

The ad campaigns for *Blood Feast* utilized some of the most compelling artwork ever designed for a Lewis movie. The "admonition" to parents was merely a publicity ploy to stir up interest in the film and it worked like a charm.

response so much as a dare, so we dared them to see *Blood Feast*. And it worked."

Lewis and Friedman designed an unusual "coming attraction" trailer for the picture. Instead of using a conglomeration of film highlights and voice-over hyperbole, actor Bill Kerwin simply delivered a monologue directly to the audience. Reciting a sort of extended variation on the one-sheet's admonition, Kerwin warned, "Ladies and gentlemen, you are about to witness some scenes from the next attraction to play this

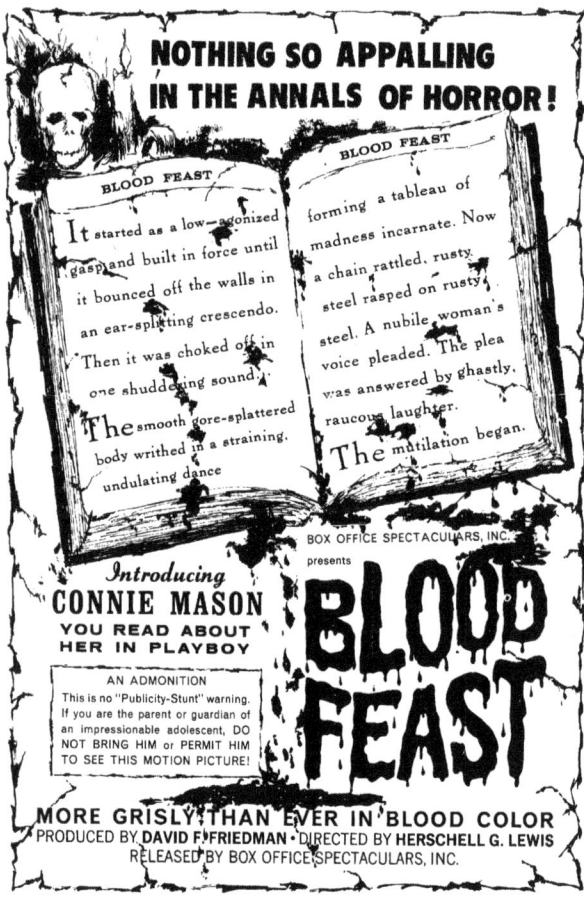

This ad mat from the *Blood Feast* pressbook provided an interesting alternative to the standard promotional campaign which featured a wild-haired assassin with a meat cleaver threatening a partially unclad woman. The "text" version was utilized in communitites that might object to elements of the original design. Note, however, that the author still manages to work in the favored terms "nubile" and "mutilation."

theater. This picture, truly one of the most unusual ever filmed, contains scenes which under no circumstances should be viewed by anyone with a heart condition, or anyone who is easily upset. We urgently recommend that if you are such a person, or are the parent of a young or impressionable child now in attendance, that you leave this auditorium for the next 90 seconds."

Said Lewis, "We figured if that didn't keep them in their seats, *nothing* would."

Obviously, Herschell didn't take the "violence in media" controversy too seriously. He stated, "I don't believe that gore films harm anyone. Great heavens, did Sophocles cause people to marry their mothers when he wrote *Oedipus Rex*?" The point is well taken. If President Clinton honestly believes that a rash of high school shootings can be attributed to the latest round of Hollywood thrillers, who or what can society possibly blame for the reign of terror perpetrated by Jack the Ripper in nineteenth-century London? Where can we point to explain away the back-breaking tortures of Torquemada and the Inquisition? Or the bloody Crusades?

The potential to harm our fellow humans comes from within, not without, but society continues to search for convenient scapegoats on which to blame its ills. "If we can just get Hollywood to make decent pictures"—the thinking goes—"if we can just ban violent comic books, if we can clean up television, if we can just do this or just do that, all our problems will be solved." From this sort of thinking have sprung the crusades against comic books in the 1950s, monster magazines in the 1960s, heavy metal music in the 1980s, video games in the 1990s. Horror films are no exception. They have come under scrutiny more times than just about anything else, suffering periodic backlashes from overzealous senators and congressmen who, as self-described "protectors of humanity," jump on whatever current bandwagon seems to carry public sentiment, promising an end to the rampant immorality and violence generated by films/games/comics/magazines/what-have-you.

Nevertheless, reason generally prevails in the end. "I don't think anyone has ever said, 'This film is doing evil things to our children,'" Lewis said. "I think what people are saying is 'this film should not be shown.' They may have a point for some people. We titillate some, we irritate some. Some people laugh and say how camp it is. Some people scream because they are getting tremendous fright out of it. They're undergoing a catharsis of emotions, which is good. Some people sit dully, which they will do no matter what you present to them! Some people involve themselves, and I suppose it's that group that critics say should not be exposed to this kind of thing.

"But who is exposing them to it? Any gore film is rated 'R' or 'X' or 'NC-17' so the theaters have control and the parents have control. The producer doesn't cause someone to go out and dismember someone else because that person has seen *Blood Feast*. I've heard that accusation made from the day I saw my first movie, and I've heard it said about comic books, I've heard it said about magazines, I've even heard it said about newspapers."

"It's a little bit different with television," Lewis concedes. "The proof of that is that whenever somebody commits a ghastly crime, such as poisoning people with Tylenol, there are imitators who spring up. Now, what causes them to imitate? The person who poisoned the Tylenol, or the person who publicized it? I'm not saying the media are at fault, or the company that made the Tylenol is at fault. It's the low-grade moron who first poisoned somebody, without even knowing who it was he was poisoning, *that* person is at fault. He's the sort who should be strung up by his thumbs, at the very least, although that kind of mindless, animalistic slaughter shows you that person is obviously deranged."

Although the technical aspects of the gore effects in *Blood Feast* have been surpassed many times over by other filmmakers, some moviegoers still find Lewis gore unsettling despite its age. HG offered, "Many films of today use blood, sometimes lots of blood — but to us, blood was just one of four or five components of gore. Blood doesn't make a gore film. That may be where the term 'splatter movie' comes from, but it's a corruption. Gore won't splatter because gore is viscera; gore is messy. People can replace blood with a transfusion. They cannot replace their intestines, their heart, their liver, their lungs. In that respect, *Blood Feast* can still shock because even if a person has seen a so-called 'splatter film' that doesn't mean they've seen a *gore* film."

The success of *Blood Feast* in Peoria became a blood barometer for the picture's popularity on the national level. Everywhere it played it pulled in the bucks. Lewis and Friedman were ecstatic because their little horror was making big money. Keeping in mind that Stan Kohlberg downplayed the success of the film at every opportunity, it's anybody's guess what the real margin of profit was for *Blood Feast* in its horror heyday.

CHAPTER 8

A Little Southern Hospitality Never Hurt Anyone ... Much

> If a big rock falls on you, what happens? It may scrape you where it hits, but what really happens is that it chops up your insides and blood gushes out of your mouth.... We drilled through a girl in *The Wizard of Gore*, but that wasn't as effective as having a rock fall and smash someone and having stuff come out of her mouth. There is something about blood coming out of the mouth that horrifies people.
>
> — *Herschell Gordon Lewis*

Though HG would periodically wander back (*Suburban Roulette* and *Linda and Abilene*) his days of nudie-cuties were mainly behind him. His primary concern was to follow up *Blood Feast* with another horror hit. It should equal *Feast* in terms of cinematic violence, but not repeat what had gone before. "Prior to *Blood Feast* no one had seen blood gush, people die with their eyes wide open, their organs ripped out and squeezed. We really caught the cinematic world unaware. Now that they *had* seen it, what could we do for a follow-up? I had a theory — and this can show you just how naïve somebody can be — that if *Blood Feast* could generate the profits that it did, think how much better we could do with a *decent* picture." Thus the Jacqueline-Kay group embarked on its second gorror project, this time with a little more than $30,000 — 25 percent more than what had been spent on *Blood Feast*.

Like James H. Nicholson of American International Pictures, Herschell Gordon Lewis had a knack for coming up with movie titles that virtually sold themselves. The new film would be called *Two Thousand Maniacs!* and that was no exaggeration — there really were two thousand maniacs in the picture. Not all of them carried axes; not all of them wandered through trails of murderous mayhem; but every last one of them clapped and hollered and raised holy hell whenever anyone earmarked for death bit the big one, and that kind of behavior is nothing if not maniacal.

No one can dismiss the originality of Lewis's horror film plotlines. In *Two Thousand Maniacs!* a group of Northern travelers becomes lost on a back road in Arkansas and wanders into Pleasant Valley (population: 2,000 ... heh, heh), a remote country town whose residents seek revenge for atrocities visited upon them by the Union army during the Civil War. In a surprising twist ending, it is revealed that the residents of Pleasant Valley (and even the town itself) are ghosts from the past who reappear every hundred years to avenge their deaths. With this synopsis in mind, how many other movies could one possibly confuse with *Two Thousand Maniacs!* In contrast, how many horror plots from the 1970s, '80s, and '90s might be mistaken for one another? Not counting sequels (which would increase the total count by at least another 19 titles), there were *Terror Train, The Burning, Scream, I Know What You Did Last Summer, Halloween, Friday the 13th, My Bloody Valentine, Prom Night, Hell Night, Blood Sisters, Mother's Day, Graduation Day, April Fools' Day, Bloody Birthday, Happy Birthday to Me, Don't Open Till Christmas, Black Christmas, Silent Night Deadly Night, New Year's Evil, He Knows You're Alone, Don't Answer the Phone, Don't Go In the House, Night School, Girls' School Screamers, Slaughter High, Zombie High, Alone in the Dark, Afraid of the Dark, Hide and Go Shriek, Chopping Mall, The Prowler, Maniac, The Texas Chainsaw Massacre, Hollywood Chainsaw Hookers, Slumber Party Massacre, Sorority House Massacre, Microwave Massacre, Nightmare* ... so many movies, so few variations.

The story and screenplay for *Two Thousand Maniacs!* were solo efforts by Lewis, who used the film script for a paperback novelization published by Novel Books to coincide with the picture's release. Like the *Blood Feast* novelization, the book was illustrated with scenes from the movie and became an instant collector's item. (In the 1980s Lewis authorized the release of new versions of the *Blood Feast* and *Two Thousand Maniacs!* books, which became sought-after collector's pieces.)

With the larger budget afforded his second gore film, Lewis was able to hire more and better actors, enlarge his crew, and spend additional time and money on pre-production, with the result that the picture acquired much more polish than *Blood Feast*. "We went down to Orlando to cast *Two Thousand Maniacs!*" said Lewis.

"That's where I found Ben Moore [who played Lester, one of the two main hillbilly roles]. Ben subsequently appeared for me in *Suburban Roulette*, which was made several years later. We also got Taalkius Blank [who played Mayor Earl Buckman], a fine actor who did a number of pictures for me. He later appeared in *This Stuff'll Kill Ya, Moonshine Mountain, Year of the Yahoo,* and *Something Weird*. Overall we wound up with a fairly good cast. There are a few weak spots, though. The weakest actors were those who played the nondescript roles — some of the Yankees. They didn't have that much to do, except get killed. The people of the town were universally well cast. We had a good mixture there."

Connie Mason also was featured in *Two Thousand Maniacs!* and just as in *Blood Feast*, hers was the only female character to make it through the picture alive. Herschell commented, "By the time we got into production on *Two Thousand Maniacs!* we had people coming to us from every direction wanting to play parts in our pictures. We were in Chicago, and we were the only crap game in town. You want to be in a feature? Go see Herschell Gordon Lewis. We had no shortage of talented people who wanted to be in a feature who would work for any logical amount of money in exchange for a screen credit, and who were willing, in fact, to pitch in [to work on crew]. That, in fact, was the key in trying to determine who to hire, and that was one of my objections — though certainly not the only one! — to Connie Mason. She didn't pitch in. She was a misfit within the group."

David Friedman was still starry-eyed when it came to the girl with the 78-tooth smile, and he wanted her to be in *Two Thousand Maniacs!* Friedman finally learned his lesson, though. "Dave was not blind," HG allowed. "After *Two Thousand Maniacs!* he

agreed with me that it should be her last picture. When we began shooting I had not yet reached the point where I felt I had to say, 'I can't take it anymore, get her out of here.' Although it didn't take long! I simply began taking lines away from her. Certainly Marilyn Monroe could sulk in her dressing room, Elizabeth Taylor could demand her hairdresser, Sinatra might have asked for his bodyguards to be on hand at company expense, but Connie Mason? She had no right to make any demands at all. She was instantly replaceable. The only problem we had was that we'd already begun the picture with her. In the last days of shooting *Two Thousand Maniacs!* when it was clear that she was doggedly refusing to learn her lines, we just gave them to someone else. In one of the last scenes where she and Bill Kerwin are sitting in a car with the little boy and trying to get away from the townspeople — and there is genuine suspense building there — about half the lines which Bill Kerwin recites were originally Connie Mason's lines. I'd had enough, and I guess she realized it. And finally Dave had enough as well."

HG's favorite among his own cast members was undoubtedly Bill Kerwin, who billed himself as Thomas Wood. "Bill was a consummate actor," said Lewis. "He knew where to stand. If you asked him to do the same thing four times, he would do it exactly the same way each time, so there was never any problem cutting to a close-up on him."

More effective than any tag line or blood-barfing blurb, the title *Two Thousand Maniacs!* virtually compelled attendance by genre aficionados.

Production got underway in the autumn of 1963 in St. Cloud, Florida, a small town near Orlando. At that time St. Cloud was a quiet retirement community that offered the kind of down-home hospitality that Lewis wanted his fictional Pleasant Valley to (falsely) exude. The officials of St. Cloud were delighted to have a band of bona fide filmmakers in their midst, and they gave Lewis permission to shoot wherever he liked. "You'd have thought Burt Reynolds and his crew were there," laughed Lewis. "They treated us like royalty!" Thanks to the town's willingness to help out, Lewis was able to capture a variety of scenic vistas on film that helped imbue the picture with a genuine sense of scale.

When Lewis wanted to shoot major, time-consuming sequences along St. Cloud's main street, the town fathers loaned the production unit a cherry picker so Lewis could get high-angle shots for dramatic crowd scenes. You couldn't ask for better cooperation. "Basically we just went in and took over the town," Lewis joked. "In 1963 St. Cloud was a sleepy little place, but it eventually became part of Disney World, so it's not sleepy anymore! Thanks to the town officials, *Two Thousand Maniacs!* became a much more polished production than *Blood Feast*. Compared to what we thought we could make, *Blood Feast* was a bad gore picture. The effects were primitive because we were just feeling our way. We decided we would try to make a better picture because Stan Kohlberg suggested that the Exchange National Bank in Chicago might very well finance a permanent production company. Our reputations were growing quickly, and by this time our grosses were well known in the film trade. When you add in the relationship between a film's negative cost and its gross, you have what could well be an enticement for a financial backer or financial institution."

In comparison to *Blood Feast*, *Two Thousand Maniacs!* was a quantum leap forward in filmmaking technique. Herschell had no problem shopping around the finished product as a $400,000 production — more than ten times what it actually cost to make! United Artists and American International were two distributors that took a look at the film and made financial overtures, but Lewis and Friedman ultimately decided to maintain control of their product and release it on a regional (state-by-state) basis under the Jacqueline-Kay moniker.

"*Two Thousand Maniacs!* was a very good, strong picture," judged Lewis. "It had a solid story line, it was well-acted all the way through, the effects were good, it had good photography, a traveling camera and lots of motion, and there were big crowd scenes that helped make it appear more extensive than it really was. And believe it or not, it was actually fairly well received critically, which is rare for a picture on my kind of budget."

Instead of repeating the same kinds of effects that put *Blood Feast* over the top, Lewis opted to make *Two Thousand Maniacs!* a "fun-and-games" picture — if that terminology can be applied to a movie that cuts, rips, dismembers, cooks, punctures, and squashes its cast for 80 consecutive minutes. In actual fact, Lewis saw the film as the flip side of *Blood Feast*. Instead of saying to audiences, "Here is a madman who delights in pulling out a girl's tongue and fondling the ganglia, isn't that awful," in *Two Thousand Maniacs!* Lewis said, "Look at these crazy people playing twisted versions of carnival games and using human beings as prizes." The gore was still there, but the silliness of the story's black humor made it significantly more palatable. Much of the film's amusement can be attributed to some over-the-top acting by principal maniacs Ben Moore and Gary Bakeman, who constantly bicker in good ol' boy fashion about who gets to chop off the arm or shove the spiked barrel down the hill. It's so far out it becomes funny, which was precisely HG's intent. As he explained, "There were no ratings back then, and we really caught the censor boards unaware with *Blood Feast*, but we knew we weren't going to be able to do that again. We had no nudity in these films. There was no obscenity. How, therefore, could they rate it 'adults only'? Yet, quite obviously, *Blood Feast* and *Two Thousand Maniacs!* should have been designated as adult features. So we knew, despite the fact that they had no background in which to categorize *Blood Feast*, that when we came back with *Two Thousand Maniacs!* they would be waiting for us." He was right. Once again, in lieu of a national rating, individual states decided whether to show *Two Thousand Maniacs!* uncut, cut, or totally emasculated. Washington, D.C., for instance, permitted showings of the film but only on condition that close-ups of dismembered limbs be eliminated. In neighboring Maryland, however, audiences could watch these sequences intact.

When word got out that the makers of *Blood Feast* were preparing to produce another stomach-churning horror, an entire population of conservative, knee-jerk activists stirred up an "anti-gore" campaign. H. G. Lewis recalled that the San Diego *Union* published an editorial suggesting that concerned readers write to the film's producers to voice their displeasure. "I never found out exactly what kind of editorial they ran," admitted Lewis, "but we knew it was organized, because all the letters came from the San Diego area, and every one of them referred to us as 'wreckless men!'" It made no difference whether the letter-writers were unthinkingly copying a misprint from the newspaper or following an ignorant writer/editor's mistaken terminology; the scary thing was that the paper had seen fit to print such a piece in the first place. But HG took it in stride, laughing each time another diatribe was delivered to his doorstep. "The biggest laugh I got out of all that," said Lewis, "was that somewhere in their story, the writers had said, 'these aren't even Hollywood producers.' As though being a Hollywood producer was some kind of badge of honor!"

In *Two Thousand Maniacs!* the innocent travelers who wander into Pleasant Valley include John and Bea Miller (Jerome Eden and Shelby Livingston) and David and Beverly Wells (Michael Korb and Yvonne Gilbert), Illinois residents all. Not far behind them are a Pennsylvania couple, playgirl Terry Adams (the indefatigable Connie Mason) and schoolteacher Tom White ("Thomas Wood"), who get sidetracked by the same phony detour signs that waylaid the first two couples. Greeted by Pleasant Valley's boisterous mayor, Earl Buckman (played by Taalkius Blank, who acted under the name Jeffrey Allen), all six visitors become guests of honor at the town's centennial celebration. As Tom will eventually determine, the residents of this town are on a vengeance kick, resolved to punish the Yankee outsiders for the widespread slaughter of innocents committed in the name of freedom a century before, when Major General Sherman's army marched on the town in the midst of the Civil War and burned it to the ground.

Bea Miller, a natural-born flirt, catches the eye of local ruffian Harper Alexander (Mark Douglas). While Bea's husband is preoccupied with the charms of bosomy Southern belle Betsy (Linda

Cochran), Harper leads Bea to a secluded spot and "accidentally" slices open her thumb with his hunting knife. The hysterical girl demands that Harper "fix it"—so he slices straight through to the bone, severing Bea's thumb entirely. Harper drags her to Mayor Buckman's office, where celebration co-chairman Lester McDonald (Ben Moore) chops off her entire arm with a fire axe. That night Bea's arm is roasted and devoured at a centennial barbecue.

The utter horror of the sequence is turned topsy-turvy by its twisted presentation, which puts as much emphasis on having a jolly good time and enjoying a hearty laugh as on insanity and brutality. Here, H. G. Lewis took a step forward with his trademark blood and gore. Rather than showing the aftereffect of a lethal wound, as he had, for example, in the "LEGS CUT OFF!" scene in *Blood Feast*, in *Two Thousand Maniacs!* the atrocities seem to happen almost in front of the viewer's eyes. When Harper cuts through Bea's thumb, Lewis includes a scene of the thumb being wriggled away from the hand and dropping to the ground. Harper retrieves it as Bea stares in shocked disbelief at her mutilated hand.

In the scene that follows in the mayor's office, Buckman unwraps a blood-soaked towel from Bea's hand, and Lewis cuts to a close-up. There actually appears to be a hole in the girl's palm. Lewis was rightfully proud of the effect. "That was her hand," he confirmed, "not a prop. We taped her thumb down and covered it with a pool of blood. Then, with the ingenious use of chicken skin, we could make it appear that there was a hole there instead. People laugh when I say we used chicken skin, because it's so available and such an unromantic commodity. But what it does is give you an extra layer of what looks like human skin." (Anyone who believes this sounds too silly to work needs to see the film.) Added stage blood concealed the edges of the chicken skin. The end result was appallingly effective. "It looked for all the world like there was a hole in her hand," Lewis affirmed. "We really caught the audience with that one, because they knew there was evil lurking, but that's all they knew. I've sat in the audience on most of my films, to gauge reactions, and of course they have no idea who I am. But I noticed people were nervous watching *Two Thousand Maniacs!* There is no chance for them to settle back and relax. It may be because of the title or it may be because of the mismatch between the rather pleasant music and the overtones of ominous disaster about to hit. But people definitely became nervous watching that picture."

The audience barely has time to catch its breath before the scene blacks out, a visual cue that usually indicates the end of a story segment or a time transition. But—surprise! When the film fades in again, the now-thumbless Bea is bleeding all over the mayor's office. The gore continues with Bea held down by Harper, Rufus (Gary Bakeman), and Mayor Buckman, while Lester dislodges an axe from a pile of logs and gleefully chops off the girl's arm at the shoulder. (Same arm that lost the thumb, incidentally. At least they were being consistent.) Lewis keeps the camera running as Rufus delicately runs his fingers over the glistening meat hanging from the truncated arm, until the scene ends with another fade-out. This effect was easier to pull off than the thumb (ouch!—pun intended) because there was no camouflaging involved; a mannequin's arm was simply substituted for the real thing. (Shelby Livingston's real arm was placed through a hole in the top of the table.) On camera, unfortunately, the arm appears as

Top and Bottom: A hike into horror in *Two Thousand Maniacs!* Good ol' boy Harper Alexander (Mark Douglas) whoops it up as he slices off the thumb of self-confessed seductress Bea Miller (Shelby Livingston).

stiff as a — well, a mannequin's arm. Still, in 1964 the scene carried quite an impact.

Bea's husband, John (now technically her widower), might wonder where she's been all day, but Betsy the belle has been keeping him so full of moonshine that he can barely think straight. He notices something vaguely familiar about the meat roasting on the spit, but before he can ask any difficult questions, Rufus is at his side, insisting he play the Pleasant Valley version of horse racing. John will be the one racing the horses, and to make sure he doesn't take a dangerous fall, Rufus ties him down securely with rope. No betting is allowed during this event, however, because this horse race involves four horses — all racing in different directions. With just one rider, you can imagine the result. While the Pleasant valley populace looks on, the race begins — and John, stretched in four directions at the same time, begins to come apart at the seams. There's hootin' and hollerin' from the crowd, followed by a strange, eerie silence as the camera cuts from a medium shot of a limb or two being dragged across the ground to an extreme close-up of a torn-off arm on the ground trailing tattered flesh behind it. The onlookers, who were partying only moments before, abruptly fall silent as they drink in the awful carnage. Rufus commands, "Let's hear some music!" to get the festivities flowing once more, but the singing now has a forlorn feel to it. It's an odd capper to a wild scene.

Although this is the only time it happens in the film, Lewis was attempting to make a statement here. (You know how these auteurs are.) The people of the town suddenly realize that they have been cheering on the destruction of an innocent man. It's not a time for a hootenanny, it's a time for introspection and reverence. (In a Herschell Gordon Lewis film?) "When John gets ripped apart by the horses, the townspeople realize what they have done," remarked Lewis, "and at that point, the leaders call for more music because they realize the people are saying, 'Oh my god, what are we doing here? We're acting in an uncivilized way.' The townspeople realize *they* are the killers. It's not like the one guy chopping the finger off or the ringleaders cutting off the arm; now the whole town is involved and they realize what's been done. They had to rebuild their enthusiasm. That was the whole purpose of that scene, and it worked just the way I intended."

Tom and Terry manage to sneak away from the "festivities" and discover a memorial plaque recalling the legend of the Pleasant Valley massacre during the Civil War. Tom, bright boy that he is, figures that the town's residents are using the centennial as a cover for some kind of blood vengeance rite. Terry, who will believe anything (this *is* Connie Mason, remember), agrees to stick with Tom and try to escape when the coast is clear.

Meanwhile, the centennial celebrants lure David Wells to the top of a hill for the barrel-roll contest. When he reluctantly climbs through the barrel, Rufus and Lester grab his feet and hands and hold him while Mayor Buckman drives a fistful of spikes into the barrel — and shoves it downhill. As he bounces around inside the onrushing barrel, David's body is punctured like a Swiss cheese. The crowd follows him downhill, waving their rebel flags amid peals of raucous laughter. Lester checks David's pulse to make sure it isn't there and exclaims, "This is the best dog-goned centennial anybody ever had!" (More fun than a barrel of Yankees!)

Lewis especially enjoyed working on the barrel-roll effect because the idea was suggested by his twelve-year-old son,

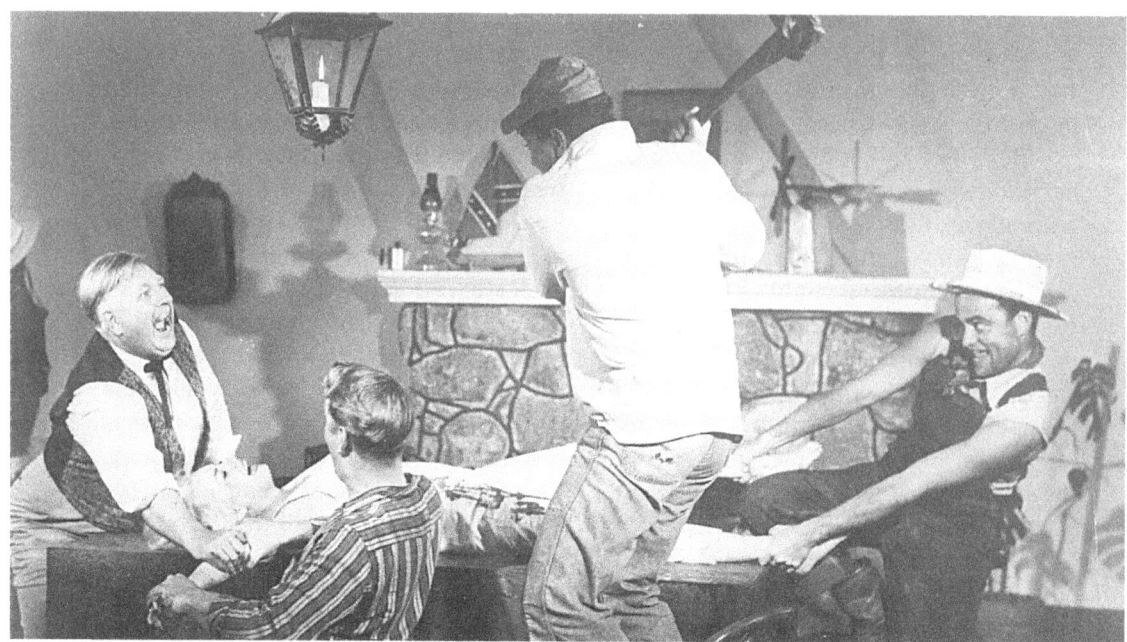

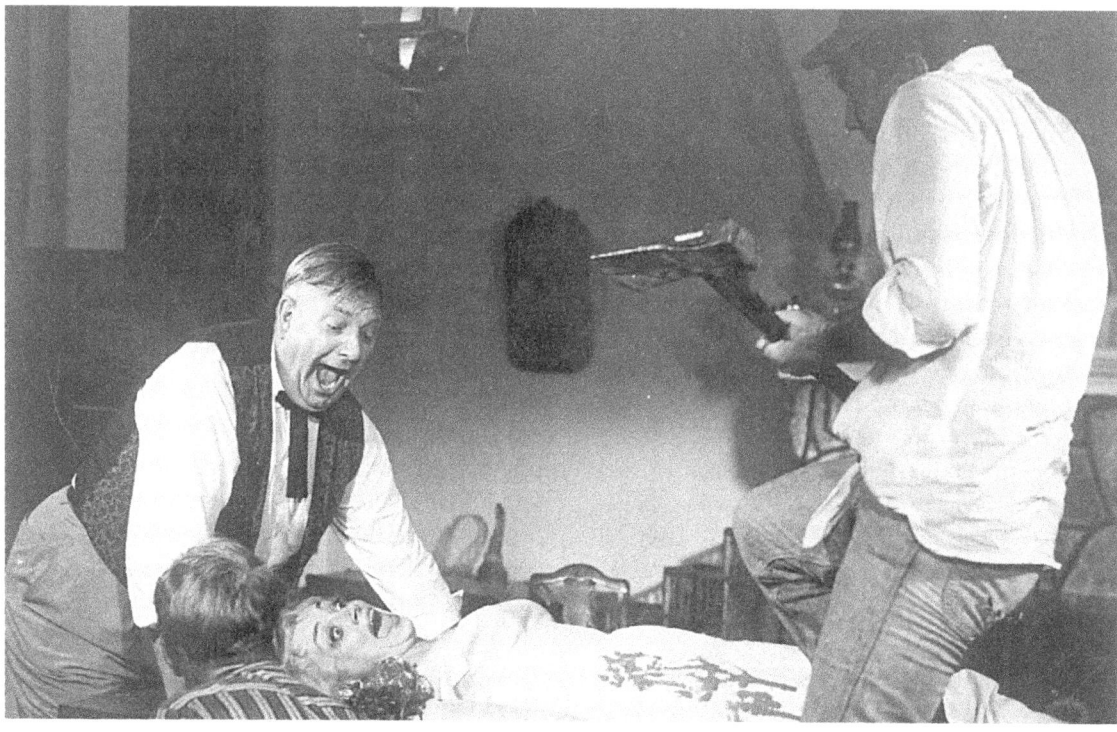

Top: Surrounded by some of the town's most prominent citizens, unlucky Bea Miller is about to make a contribution to Pleasant Valley's Centennial barbecue in *Two Thousand Maniacs!* Left to right: Taalkius Blank (a.k.a. Jeffrey Allen) as Mayor Buckman; Shelby Livingston as Bea Miller; Mark Douglas as Harper Alexander; Ben Moore as Lester; Gary Bakeman as Rufe. *Bottom:* Swipe One! Everyone — well, almost everyone — seems to be having a good time at Pleasant Valley's fear festivities.

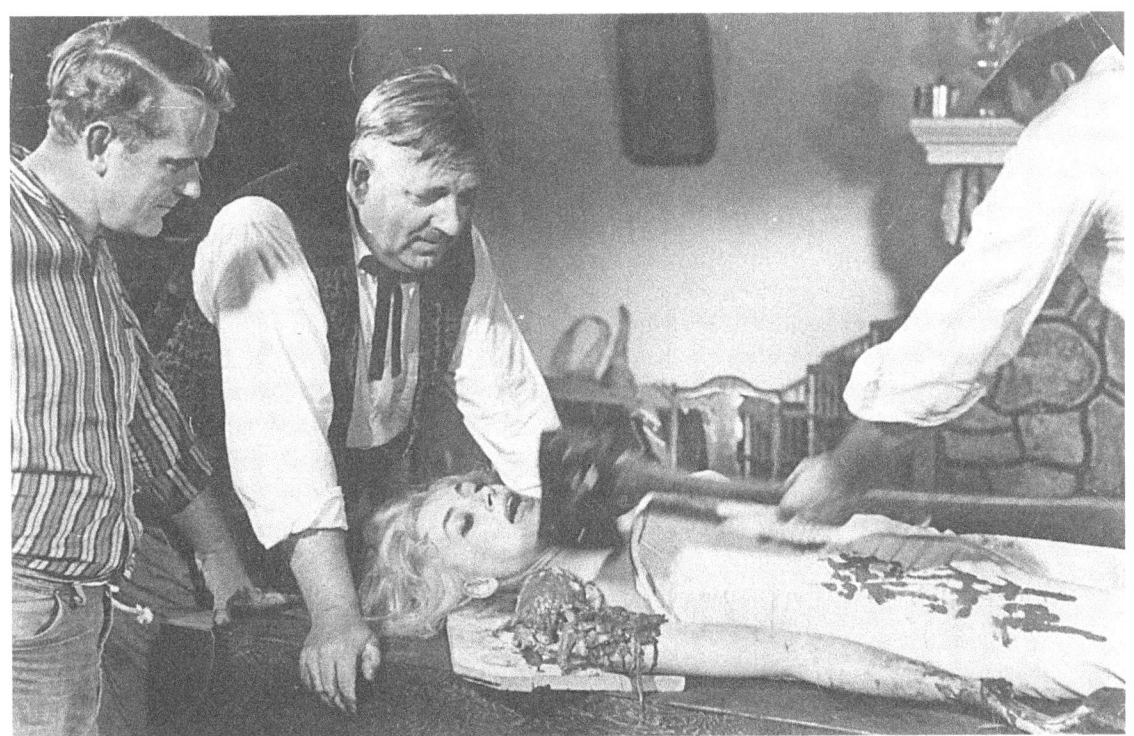

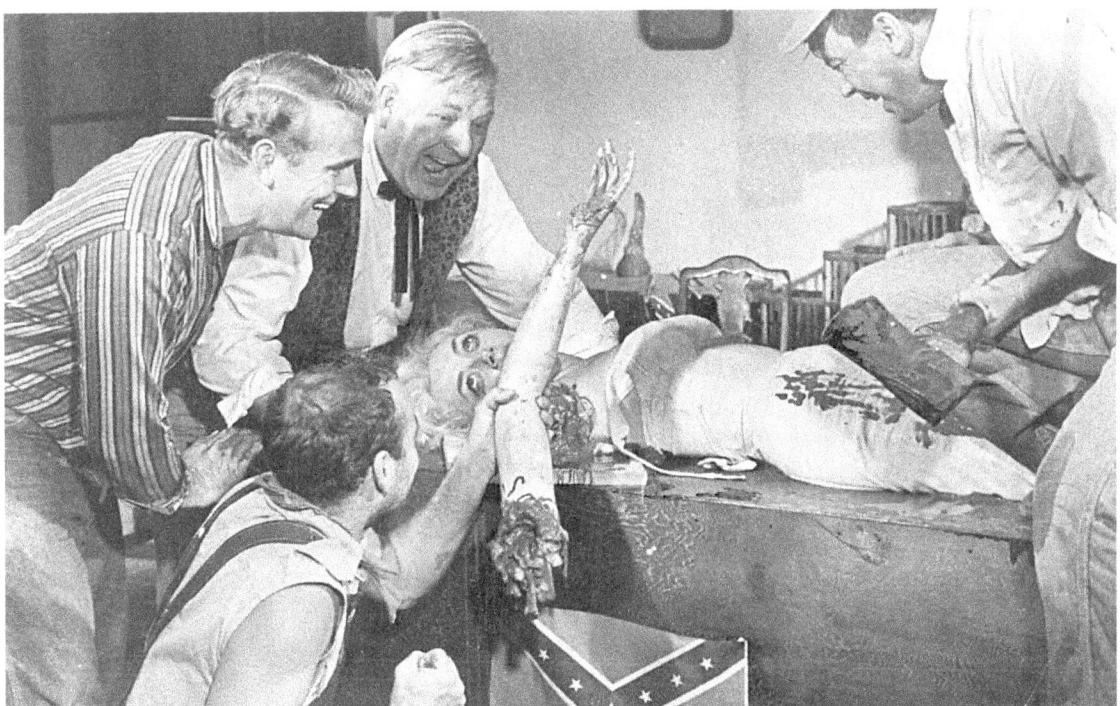

Top: Swipe Two! Although actress Shelby Livingston's real arm is concealed inside the table, axe-slinger Ben Moore had to have an eye for accuracy in order to avoid any truly messy mishaps. *Bottom:* Swipe Three and she's out! Those *Two Thousand Maniacs!* are such cut ups.

Robert. (By the time *The Gore-Gore Girls* went into production almost a decade later, Robert Lewis would be working the crew, occasionally helping his father devise gore effects. He even doubled actors who didn't want to get messy sticking their hands into the gore components.)

The last gore scene of *Two Thousand Maniacs!* involves an elaborately staged setup with a relatively chintzy "payoff." Besides our heroine and hero, Terry Adams and Tom White, only Beverly Wells remains alive. While Tom and Terry sneak around hand-in-hand trying to discover where their car has been hidden, Rufus and Lester introduce Beverly to Teetering Rock — a huge boulder resting atop a precarious wooden structure. Beverly is strapped to a wooden "altar" directly underneath while the townspeople take turns throwing softballs at a bullseye target attached to a dumping mechanism built into the side of the structure. Every time someone misses the target, Mayor Buckman waddles up to Beverly and insists she repeat the words. "It ain't fallen yet." Between sniffles and whimpers of fear, the girl responds, "It hasn't fallen yet."

"Well, pardon my grammar," chuckles Buckman.

The Teetering Rock scene is elaborately staged, especially for a Herschell Gordon Lewis picture. "That was a difficult scene to set up," acknowledged

Rufe (Gary Bakeman, left) and Lester (Ben Moore, right) try to convince centennial guest John Miller (Jerome Eden, caught in the middle) to join in the festivities by taking a part in the Pleasant Valley horse race in *Two Thousand Maniacs!* The blonde-haired youngster to the left is Billy (Vincent Santo), the kid who keeps a pocket noose instead of a pocket knife on hand, to take care of any bothersome stray cats.

What's more fun than a barrel of nails? David Wells (Michael Korb, bottom) is declared the winner of the Pleasant Valley Barrel Roll Contest. Southern belle Betsy (Linda Cochran) and loopy Lester (Ben Moore) take a gander at their horrific handiwork in *Two Thousand Maniacs!*

Lewis. "It took us a long time to get things ready, and by the time we were ready to shoot it was getting late in the afternoon and the shadows were creeping in. The boulder was made out of papier-mâché, but nevertheless it still weighed about 300 pounds! I was lying on the ground beneath it, trying to get a good p.o.v. [point of view] shot, and if something had gone wrong and it had fallen and hit me, that would have been the last scene in the picture that *I* would have shot!"

The tripping device for the Teetering Rock platform was built by local carpenters according to plans that Lewis and Friedman had worked up, and the finished structure towered over fifteen feet. The bullseye board really worked, too. Although the scene plays well, Lewis didn't particularly care for the way it turned out. One reason was that he originally wanted the character of Beverly Wells to be stoned to death. However, "I had a feeling that effect wasn't going to work the way I envisioned it," Lewis recalled. "In fact, I did a trial run with a crew member at short range, and it didn't work. We tried using polystyrene stones saturated with stage blood but it was a waste of time. So Teetering Rock was a substitution."

There were other problems involved in shooting the scene, and in the end HG didn't think the effect was worth all the effort involved in producing it: "There's just not much to it," he complained. "We didn't show the boulder landing on her because we couldn't; like I said, it weighed 300 pounds. If we could have shown it hitting her, now *that* would have been good. We might have been able to fake it somehow by moving the platform [on which she was lying], but the shadows were crawling across the platform and we couldn't do it." Instead, Lewis used a p.o.v. shot of the boulder falling toward the ground followed by a forced perspective setup. The papier-mâché boulder was balanced against the platform and Yvonne Gilbert squeezed as much of her blood-stained body as she could underneath it. Lewis's famous Kaopectate blood was poured in her mouth where it was retained until the director yelled "Action!"—whereupon Yvonne jerked her head to one side and spat it out. It was a satisfactory spit, Lewis felt. Yvonne tried to clean up as best she could after the scene was in the can, but according to HG, "she spent the next 24 hours in *my* bathroom trying to get the blood off because she didn't want to go home that way." (Oh, the vagarious horrors of low-budget filmmaking.)

Lewis thought being crushed by a falling boulder was one of those ideas that sounds better than it plays. The idea of one's body being smashed—ribs broken, organs mashed, lungs crushed, pelvis pulverized—sounds terrible, but what would you actually see in such a circumstance? This was Lewis's Teetering Rock dilemma. "The real reason we didn't have much gore in the rock scene was medical," Lewis explained. "If a big rock falls on you, what happens? It may scrape you where it hits, but what really happens is that it chops up your insides and blood gushes out of your mouth. If she's crushed, the horror doesn't come from having her explode, or having the rock go through her. We drilled through a girl in *The Wizard of Gore*, but in my opinion that wasn't as effective as having a rock fall and smash someone and having stuff come out of her mouth. There is something about blood coming out of the mouth that horrifies people."

Another problem Lewis encountered during the filming of the scene involved his exposure meter, which quit working after they had already begun shooting. Herschell's assistant cameraman was Andy Romanoff. "At that time, Andy was still young and full of energy," remembered Lewis. "We made a great team. But his exposure meter, by pure coincidence, also quit dead. We were filming on a Sunday, and we couldn't find another exposure meter, so we were guessing at the exposure the rest of that day, with the sun in and out of the clouds and the shadows getting deeper and longer as the day wore on. But—here's the funny part—every exposure was absolutely right on the nose." Nevertheless, the experience left him drained, so in retrospect it isn't too surprising that the entire Teetering Rock sequence became one of H. G. Lewis's least favorite gore set pieces.

Herschell also felt that, stylistically, *Two Thousand Maniacs!* was not the kind of motion picture that lent itself to hardcore gore. "The idea with this film was not to have people dripping with gore," he clarified. "Take for example the scene where the fellow is pulled apart by the horses. We could have had significantly more gore in that scene if we wanted. I had a fellow down in Orlando, a multiple amputee, who offered me his services. I didn't use him because I felt that human dignity deserved more than that. I just couldn't see taking an amputee, handling his stump, and dressing it up with gore. I felt that, once again, that was not playing the game. Of course they do it in today's pictures [director John Carpenter used an amputee in his 1982 remake of *The Thing*], and perhaps I would do it today if I were to return to filmmaking. But I had a morality back then that I don't have any more! I may have become corrupted by my own films, I don't know, but I felt more diffident about it than he did! It would not have bothered him to let us make up his stumps for the picture; he volunteered himself. But that really wasn't the purpose of *Two Thousand Maniacs!* We were trying to superimpose evil onto gore, which makes the gore that much more horrifying."

Two Thousand Maniacs! ends with Tom and Terry making good their escape from Pleasant Valley with Harper giving chase on foot and accidentally falling into a pool of quicksand. By the time Tom and Terry relate their experience to a local policeman (Andy Wilson), Mayor Buckman, Rufus, Lester, Betsy and little Billy (Vincent Santo) — a Pleasant Valley young 'un who uses a miniature noose to strangle stray cats — have decided to call it a day. "It's time, Harper," Rufus calls out, "it's time." Unexpectedly, Harper rises from the quicksand pool, covered head to toe in mud and muck, and catches up to the others — walking home, back into the long-lost past. Rufus speculates on whether the next centennial celebration, scheduled for 2065, will have guests riding in rocket ships instead of automobiles. Meanwhile, Tom and Terry locate the general area they think corresponds to Pleasant Valley, but the trail appears overgrown with weeds. The cop tells them there hasn't been a town with that name since the days of the Civil War, when Union troops marched through Pleasant Valley and destroyed every last man, woman, and child. Whatever Tom and Terry think happened must have been an hallucination, he says. Tom is beginning to think he's right — until he discovers little Billy's miniature noose in the backseat of the car.

H. G. Lewis recalled that everyone had a good time making *Two Thousand Maniacs!* despite the problems caused by Connie Mason and a few mechanical failures on the part of malfunctioning photographic equipment. "We had a few complicating setbacks on that picture," said Lewis. "We had rented some equipment from a place called Camera Equipment Company, which was later known as F & B Ceco. We rented an Arriflex camera, and somebody had left a number 85 filter in the lens. We didn't even know it until we got the rushes back. All the indoor shots were off by one stop, and the color was off. All the outdoor stuff was similarly bad because we had double filtration." The filtration complications could be compensated for during the film processing; but there was also a problem with the sound recording of the barrel-roll scene. Their equipment recorded the actors' voices at the wrong speed and hence the wrong pitch. Although David Friedman was able to adjust post-production synchronization, the voices remained off-pitch and were never corrected for the final print.

There were a few unexpected benefits from choosing to make *Two Thousand Maniacs!* in the retirement community of St. Cloud. Most important, the story required big crowd scenes. There was no money in the budget to hire bona fide movie extras, so Lewis and Friedman persuaded the St. Cloud populace to help them out gratis. Lewis had some reservations at first: How would these retired workers react when they found out what kind of picture was being made in their midst? As it turned out, Lewis needn't have concerned himself, because for the most part they were delighted to be a part of it. "That it was a gore film didn't seem to bother them," he said. "If we had had four-letter words in it, that would have bothered them. Each person's morality is individually arrived at. The folks in this community had grown up with a background where four-letter words were bad—but blood? There was no concern there, because there was no yardstick until we invented it. Nudity—bad. Of course, we didn't have nudity, and didn't even come close to it with *Two Thousand Maniacs!* so what was there to moralize over? We did bring a little money to the town of St. Cloud and enlivened their lives somewhat. We certainly put all of them in the movie, and we gave them all a hamburger, because that was all we could afford to do." He was amused by a couple of the town's older citizens, who had no idea they were looking at a prop banner made for the film which had been strung across St. Cloud's main drag. The banner read: "Pleasant Valley Centennial 1865—1965." Lewis recalled, "We shot that in the autumn of 1963. I came out on the porch of the hotel where we were all staying and noticed two fellows looking at my banner. One of them said to the other, 'I wonder why Pleasant Valley is having its centennial here?' And the other guy said, 'What I don't understand is why they put their banner up so far ahead of time.'"

One of the reasons the residents of St. Cloud only got a burger for their part in the picture was that Lewis and Friedman allocated most of their resources to an extended shooting schedule. "We had a 12-day schedule for that picture, which was enormous compared to what we had been used to," explained Lewis. The difference

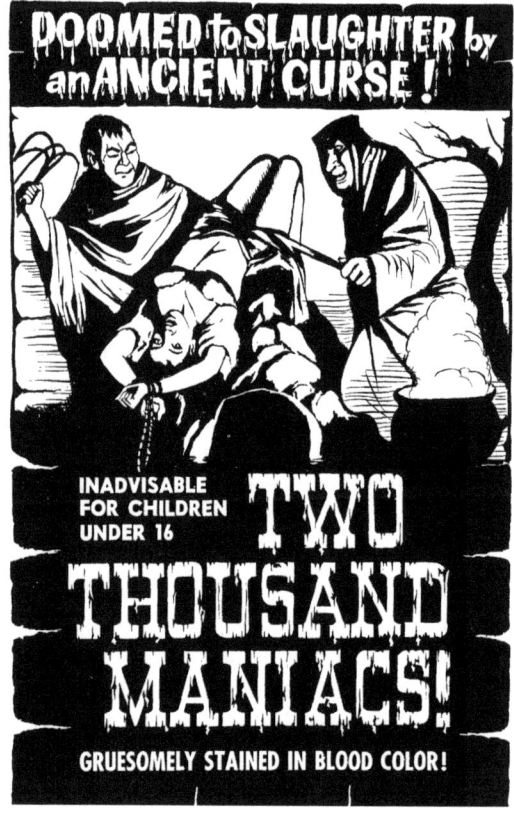

What's witches and warlocks got to do with it? One of several different advertising campaigns devised for the promotion of *Two Thousand Maniacs!*

in budget between *Two Thousand Maniacs!* and *Blood Feast* translated into double the shooting schedule. "Spending more for better actors wasn't going to give us a better picture, and we weren't going to spend more for equipment or locations, we just had more time, which makes all the difference. It's easy to sit here and look back and say, 'Well, why didn't you do this or why didn't you do that?' but at the time we didn't want to spend any more money than we had allotted already. We didn't have a front office to call and say, 'I need another million to finish the picture.' We *were* the front office. We had only ourselves to ask."

Two Thousand Maniacs! was the first picture to feature "hillbilly music" of the sort that played regularly on television's *The Beverly Hillbillies* and *Green Acres* sitcoms. Herschell Lewis penned the lyrics and music for the movie's opening tune, "The South's Gonna Rise Again," performed by a group of musicians from Orlando who went under the name The Pleasant Valley Boys. (They also appeared in the picture behind the opening titles.) Lewis recalled, "We had a good set of musicians on that picture. Chuck Scott, whose real name was Chuck Glore, put together that band. Chuck later played the hero in another of my films called *Moonshine Mountain*."

Historically, critics generally ignored horror films — especially low-budget horror films, and particularly *violent* low-budget horror films — so it isn't too surprising that most of them weren't aware of the finger-pickin' soundtrack music that permeated *Two Thousand Maniacs!* Herschell pointed out, "In 1967 when *Bonnie and Clyde* was released the critics said, 'Gee, what an innovative music track,' but it was just the same thing that we had already done in *Two Thousand Maniacs!*" (A double-soundtrack album containing music from *Two Thousand Maniacs!* and *Blood Feast* was produced many years after the pictures were released.)

When the film was finished, edited, and scored, Lewis and Friedman put their heads together to work up an effective advertising campaign. "We knew we had a good picture on our hands," said Lewis. "Although it was a much better picture than *Blood Feast* and a much more polished production, it never made the money that *Blood Feast* did. *Two Thousand Maniacs!* was written with care. I put my integrity on the line with that film. It's a gore film, but it's a well done gore film. It's well acted and well produced. Yet as good as it was, it grossed only about half what *Blood Feast* had grossed. Actually, it couldn't gross as much, because *Blood Feast* was the first; it was lionized. Within a year it had become a cult film." (It still is — perhaps even more so.)

"*Two Thousand Maniacs!* was a good picture, but there's no relationship between a good picture and making money," declared Lewis. "The picture was well received, which was rather surprising, because you must bear in mind that we competed for playing time not only with other independents, but with Warner Bros., Universal, Columbia, Paramount, and Fox, so the same critics who reviewed our pictures might have seen something earlier that day on a par with *The Exorcist* or *Ben-Hur* or *Jurassic Park* or some other huge-budget picture. Our film would be reviewed in the same frame of mind; there's no special dispensation. That is one reason why the critics are sometimes unkind: not because the audience is displeased, but because they use a different set of yardsticks altogether." And while *Two Thousand Maniacs!* certainly got its share of poison-pen reviews, it didn't do as poorly in that department as had *Blood Feast*. Things were looking up!

"Most of our 'bigger' pictures, like *Two Thousand Maniacs!*, got reviewed fairly regularly in local newspapers," asserted Lewis. "We even had reviews in *Newsweek* and *Time* and *Esquire*, but I generally ignored the reviews on our pictures because you cannot expect the critics to judge such a film within its production context. We couldn't pass out a sheet to people saying, 'We're sorry, folks, but this was a low-budget film and you have to understand that it doesn't have the same production values as this other picture you just saw.'"

"There is a story about *Two Thousand Maniacs!* in a French film criticism magazine called *L'Observateur*," Lewis continued. "And in *Image et Son*, which is a very august French publication, it is listed alongside Roman Polanski's *Repulsion* [1965] and Hitchcock's *Psycho* [1960] as one of the all-time great terror films. So *Two Thousand Maniacs!* is in good company, but that is not the way you keep score. You keep score through film rentals and profits."

While Friedman and Lewis decided to forgo the pseudo-serious "admonition" that appeared so prominently in the *Blood Feast* campaign materials, they did include a statement in the advertising for *Two Thousand Maniacs!* that promised it was "Inadvisable for Children under 16." (Like a lot of other kids whose parents didn't bother researching the content of movies their children wanted to see, I was able to get in to see *Two Thousand Maniacs!* during its first run. The audience was composed mostly of young adults, with some children approximately my own age in attendance as well. Nobody walked out on the picture, but I did hear a few comments from some viewers sitting in the row behind me: "This is sick!" someone complained. A female voice whispered, "I don't know how much more of this I can take." Herschell Lewis would have been delighted.)

CHAPTER 9

Canvassing for Corpuscles

> We had the makings for the intestines, the gore, on ice. The power went out one night and when we came to the set the next day you could smell that stuff from half a mile away. Nobody wanted to get near it!
>
> — *Herschell Gordon Lewis*

It was 1965, and the team of Herschell Lewis and David Friedman seemingly could do no wrong. Ever since they had begun collaborating, it seemed only good things had been happening. Disagreements over "gouts of blood" blurbs and Connie Mason notwithstanding, the two filmmakers never had a bad word to say about one another.

But ... things change.

Two Thousand Maniacs! went into release in 1964 backed by an effective campaign that promised to reward paying audiences with grisly "adult horror." The one-sheet poster ominously warned, "Madness Incarnate! Brutal ... Evil ... Ghastly Beyond Belief!" while newspaper ads exclaimed, "Doomed to Slaughter by an Ancient Curse!" or "Doomed to Slaughter by a Town of Madmen!" Interestingly, the company advertising brochure offered several different ad mat illustrations, only one of which accurately portrayed events in the film. In the first illustration, evocative of an African locale, a trio of savages carry a screaming lass through a field of tall grass. If that doesn't make much sense, the second illustration makes even less: Robed, hooded monks threaten a young woman who seems to be tied upside-down on a pile of rocks. What the heck was going on here?

What was going on was that Lewis and Friedman were trying to sell their movie with the most effective campaign materials at their disposal, accuracy be damned. Of course, that's really nothing new when it comes to promoting and selling motion pictures, especially exploitation pictures. Roger Corman did it all the time. The ad mats were designed with regional audiences in mind. Lewis believed that the average ticket buyer for one of his pictures lived in a rural area south of the Mason-Dixon line, was a male between the ages of 25 and 45, not very highly educated, and was probably fairly prejudiced. (That may have been an accurate assessment in the early 1960s, before Lewis became a cult figure, but it's way off the mark today. Now the average Herschell Gordon Lewis fan is the polar opposite. He's usually a Caucasian male between 17 and 30, solidly educated, and liberal minded to a fault. If you put a 1964 Lewis fan in a room with a 1994 Lewis fan, there could well be more blood shed in five minutes than in 70 minutes of any Lewis gore film.)

With what appeared to be another winning cinema collaboration under their belts, Lewis and Friedman began planning their next move. Since gore seemed to be their hottest commercial commodity at the moment, it only made sense to slaughter onward. Herschell wrote a script entitled *Color Me Blood Red*, which became the picture known incorrectly as "the concluding chapter in the Lewis/Friedman gore trilogy."

First of all, neither Lewis nor Friedman set out to make a trilogy of movies, gore or otherwise. Secondly, the term "chapter" is a misnomer. It suggests that each film is part of some larger whole. And thirdly, *Color Me Blood Red* was not intended to conclude anything, though it was in fact the last picture on which Lewis and Friedman collaborated.

"Our films competed quite successfully with the kind of expensive, commercial product that was being made under studio conditions," Lewis confirmed. "We weren't regarded as oddballs except by some people who asked, 'Why are you doing this? Why aren't you shooting movies in Hollywood?' There's supposed to be some magic in the air there — or at least something other than pollution." Lewis didn't feel the need to go to Hollywood to make features, and neither did David Friedman. They had proven it was possible to make profitable movies almost in their own backyards.

Lewis and Friedman couldn't have been happier when they learned how much money *Blood Feast* and *Two Thousand Maniacs!* were making individually. It even seemed as if *Two Thousand Maniacs!* might overtake *Blood Feast* in terms of film rentals, according to the periodic statements issued by Kohlberg's office. But Lewis couldn't shake the feeling that something was wrong somewhere, somehow.

That feeling had an impact on the production of *Color Me Blood Red*. The enthusiasm he initially felt for the project began to wane. After the gallons of "grue" that had been dumped into viewer laps during the unspooling of his first two horror pictures, what was on the table in *Color Me Blood Red* seemed anemic by comparison. "It definitely was not one of our major pictures," conceded Herschell. "We just didn't have our hearts in that one in quite the same way. The effects are not as good. It eventually did all right from a business standpoint, but it was no *Blood Feast*."

Color Me Blood Red seemed jinxed from the beginning. Obstructive circumstances constantly interfered with the production. One of the first problems the team faced, before the picture even got underway, was locale. Instead of returning to Miami or St. Cloud, the filmmakers settled on the west-coast Florida town of Sarasota — an unfortunate geographical choice for reasons that will soon be apparent. Lewis wanted to shoot in Sarasota because *Blood Feast* had been "banned" there. What had actually happened was that one of David Friedman's publicity ploys backfired. Friedman had sworn out an injunction to keep *Blood Feast* from being played in Sarasota, purely as a gimmick. He was hoping that the story would leak out to the press. But the injunction stunt worked too well, and *Blood Feast* really did get banned in Sarasota. Friedman even had to go to court to get the injunction lifted.

Lewis and his crew rented a house on Longboat Key and began setting up their equipment. The crew consisted of five people: Gordon Oas-heim, Jerome Eden (in fairly good shape despite having been on the losing end of the horse race in *Two Thousand Maniacs!*), Scott Hall, Friedman, and Lewis. It was not a large entourage, but then *Color Me Blood Red* was not a big picture; it was merely a bad picture. "When you make a bad film, you are immortalizing your mistakes," HG warned. "My intention had always been to make the most amount of film for the money I had available. They can put that on my tombstone and I won't object."

The plotline of the new film was totally unlike anything that had gone before. Scripted solely by Lewis, *Color Me Blood Red* concerns an artist, Adam Sorg (Gordon Oas-heim, acting under the name Don Joseph), who forever seems at odds with his paint palette. No matter how he mixes his oils, he just cannot get the right shade of red for his expressionistic paintings. (Uh-oh. That should tell you something right there.) Sorg has a small following at a local art venue called Farnsworth Galleries. Unbelievably, *Blood Feast*'s police captain, Scott Hall, was hired to play the role of the gallery owner, Farnsworth. Had Lewis lost his mind?

Hall had actually improved in the interim. He no longer shouted his lines; he just stumbled over them. Lewis liked him because he knew his way around the crew. "Most of the other roles were given to local actors," Lewis remarked, "although we took along Gordon Oas-heim and the girl who played his girlfriend, Elyn Warner. Elyn also worked on the crew, and that's how we justified taking her down to Sarasota. She did a very credible job, I felt. She was a local [Chicago] actress, a very serious young lady." Indeed, Warner gave one of the best performances in the picture. (Of course, that's not saying much.)

When Sorg's live-in girlfriend, Gigi (Warner), accidentally cuts her finger on a nail sticking out of a wooden frame, *ka-ching!* Adam's eyes light up. Imagine — Gigi's blood is just the shade of red he's been searching for. Adam tries painting with her bleeding finger, but that turns out to be almost more trouble than it's worth — especially when she runs dry. Possessed by the painting that seems to be coming to life with his new technique, Adam grabs a razor blade and slices into one of his own fingers. The oozing, crimson rivulet gives him a reinvigorated sense of purpose, and he paints with his own plasma until he can squeeze no more out. Then he picks up the razor blade and slices another finger ... and another...

When Gigi later finds Adam slumped on a sofa, his fingers stained with dried blood, she gets an inkling of just how "dead"-icated an artist he is. What she doesn't know is that Sorg has come up with a wonderful new idea that will help simplify his work. Using the palette knife still tightly gripped in his hand, he abruptly drives the blade into Gigi's temple, killing her instantly. Now he has four quarts of blood at his disposal — enough for several more paintings, at least. If only he'd thought of this sooner!

The first gore effect in the story occurs so quickly there is hardly any "effect" involved. When Adam Sorg slices open his fingers with the razor blade, the audience sees almost nothing. While "finger painting," the actor held onto a tiny container of stage blood, which he used to streak the canvas. It was a rather awkward effect, and viewers cringed more from the idea than the execution. The palette knife plunge was judiciously put together in the editing room, allowing HG to show the knife imbedded in Gigi's temple only momentarily. Figuring the blood-from-mouth routine was always good for turning a few stomachs, he added a short clip of Elyn Warner drooling some of the famed Kaopectate concoction. This was enough to get the idea across, but it was a far cry from *Blood Feast*'s "LEGS CUT OFF!" or *Two Thousand Maniacs!*'s arm-wrenching horse race.

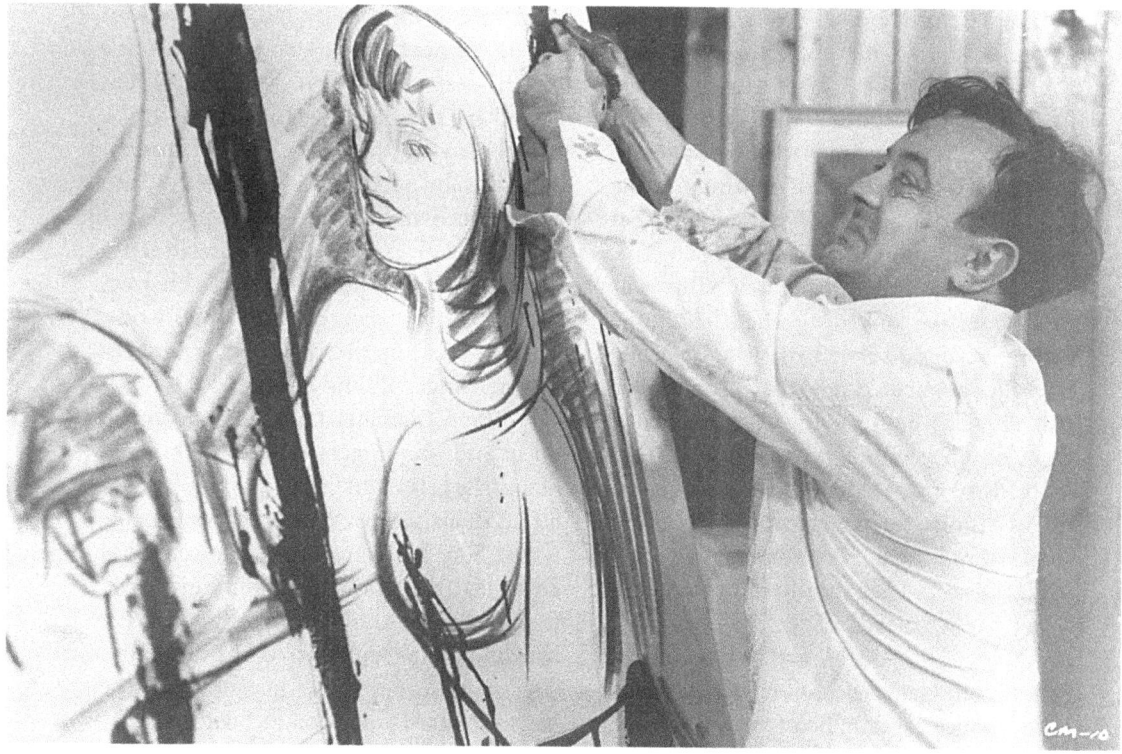

Screwy modern artist Adam Sorg (Gordon Oas-heim) just can't find the right shade of red to give his paintings that realistic edge — until he discovers the hue of human hemoglobin. *Color Me Blood Red* (1965) was the final Lewis-Friedman collaboration.

Sorg buries Gigi outside his beach house. (Dumb move on Adam's part.) Almost immediately a total of six people show up, but luckily for Sorg, they go their separate ways. Rolf (Jerome Eden, appearing for the third time in a Lewis gore film), April (Candi Conder), and the annoying hip-hop duo of Sydney (Patricia Lee) and Jack (James Jaekel) bop on down the coastline, leaving a third pair of young lovers to climb aboard a couple of paddleboats floating innocuously in the water nearby. Their frolicsome fun doesn't last long, though, because Sorg has decided he needs fresh bodies for his work. He climbs into his speedboat and mows them down, spearing the boy in the chest and running him over while the outboard motor turns him into julienne fries. (Well, there went one whole body of blood.) The girl screams hysterically when she sees her boyfriend's torn, bloody clothes floating in the deep red sea, but Lewis neglects to let us in on how Sorg does her in. She merely turns up in the following scene, which features the movie's best gore effect.

The double murder on the paddleboats was supposed to be the film's high point of horror. But something seemed to go wrong with every single effect on *Color Me Blood Red*. It was as if the producers had been cursed from the first frame. The script called for a scene in which the boy on the paddleboat is speared. A harpoon rig was outfitted with a balloon loaded with stage blood, affixed to the blade end (from which the blade had been removed — we hope), and when Lewis called for action the shank was pushed against the boy's chest and the balloon burst, spurting its contents magnificently. Thick streams of crimson stage blood shot out in ribbons at least two feet long. It was one of the best blood squirts ever photographed. But (there is always a "but" qualifier for *Color Me Blood Red* effects), whether it was a slip of the actor or of the camera, or perhaps the impact of the harpoon shank against the actor's chest, the victim's body moved too close to the top of the frame. Only 15 frames of the jet-like sprays of blood were captured on film before the action moved completely outside the frame. Fifteen frames last slightly more than one half-second during projection. Blink and you miss it.

Lewis had a decapitation in mind for the scene immediately following, in which Adam Sorg runs over the boy's body with his motorboat. The crew fashioned a false head using a real cow skull (!) for the base. "We were able to shape it into a human head using mortician's wax," Lewis explained. "We used a cow skull because it had the eye sockets and the teeth and some of the other components. We stuffed the thing with Styrofoam so it wouldn't sink." Nevertheless, it sank. "We threw it in the water and it sank like a stone. It went down so fast we didn't even *see* it go down!

Suffering for his art hurts way too much, so Adam Sorg (Gordon Oas-heim) decides it would be better to hurt others instead. In this early scene from *Color Me Blood Red*, Sorg finds a sweet source of bloody inspiration — his girlfriend, Gigi (Elyn Warner).

You'd have thought it was made of cast iron. We never did find it. So, somewhere on the bottom of the water off Sarasota is a cow's skull filled with Styrofoam. Divers are probably wondering how the heck a cow stumbled into the water and drowned."

Lewis was determined to have gore in the motorboat scene, so he decided to substitute pieces of meat for the decapitated head. Real animal entrails were almost always used for the gore in Lewis's pictures, and for *Color Me Blood Red* the parts had been supplied by a meat-processing plant in Tampa. "As usual, Scott Hall was working crew as well as playing a small part in the picture, and he was in charge of putting ice on the gore every day, which we kept in a refrigerator," said Lewis. "Well, the power had gone off the day before and Scott could barely get near that place because of the smell. We were only able to retrieve a few pieces of meat, but I figured that was better than nothing at all, so we took what we could salvage and doused it with Pine-Sol. Here we are working with this stuff that no matter how much we sprayed it with Pine-Sol, the smell kept oozing through. Finally I decided, let's just throw it in the water and shoot it and be done with it. We start throwing pieces of meat in the water and suddenly we had about 3,000 seagulls swooping down at us, scooping the meat out of the water. A piece of meat wouldn't even hit the water before the gulls had it. So I gave up on *that* shot. In the end, all I could think to use were bloody pieces of clothing, and that's what you saw in the film. These are just some of the unforeseen events which sometimes affect the course of human destiny."

The flip side to this sequence worked out better. As Sorg continues working on a new painting, he dabs his brush into a bowl of blood which he uses like a palette. Deciding he must have more pigment, Sorg walks into the back room and the audience now sees that he has kidnapped the girl who survived the paddleboat attack. She's definitely dead now, though: The artist has tied her to a wall and ripped a hole through her abdomen. He reaches in and grabs what appears to be a kidney (only surgeons in the audience would know for certain), squeezing it until a stream of blood gushes out the bottom, which he catches in his "blood palette." It's a wonderfully disgusting scene, and it was shot without using a single piece of actual viscera. HG explained, "After wasting all that meat in the paddleboat scene we were left basically with nothing. What we had was no longer fresh; it stank so badly we couldn't keep it. So in the scene where the artist is squeezing the blood out of the disemboweled girl, we were forced to use ersatz materials. We used wood shavings, we used pieces of sponge, we used almost anything for the intestines and things that were supposed to be hanging out of her. There was no real gore in that scene." The actor was actually squeezing a balloon partially filled with stage blood. A pinhole in the bottom of the balloon allowed a stream of blood to run out when it was squeezed. The effect was startlingly realistic, and it became the gore highlight of the film.

Meanwhile, the first two couples that arrived outside Sorg's place earlier in the day are still frolicking at the other end of the beach. April, the leading female character, wanders off in the direction of Sorg's shack and finds the artist standing outside, considering a blank canvas. He invites her in to pose for him. She declines because her friends are waiting for her, but Sorg's persistence pays off; he eventually convinces her to come back that evening.

Captivated by Sorg's artistic pomposity, April returns to the shack after the sun sets. Meanwhile, her boyfriend Rolf builds a beachside fire while maintaining a lonely vigil. Jack and Sydney help out by gathering wood for the fire. It's while digging through the sandy brush that they discover a woman's leg buried underground. Within minutes they have uncovered the rotting carcass of Sorg's first victim, his axe-girlfriend, Gigi. (A poor pun indeed, but so hard to resist when one is dissecting Herschell Gordon Lewis movies.)

The discovery of the girl's body on the beach was to be another featured fright in *Color Me Blood Red*, but this time Lewis wanted to shock audiences in a more subtle fashion. Instead of slapping them in the face with viscid viscera, HG wanted to show a corpse in the process of decomposition. His script even specified that worms would be crawling in and out of the rotting tissues — one of the most potentially horrifying images in the entire H. G. Lewis canon. *But—*

Yes, there was another "but." Belatedly, Lewis discovered to his chagrin that *there were no worms* in Sarasota. "We didn't find out until the day before we were supposed to begin shooting there were simply no worms to be had," Lewis laughed. "The soil is too sandy there." Determined not to give up, Herschell queried Sarasota residents to find out where some worms might be unearthed. Acting on an unbelievable-sounding tip, the crew visited a nearby retirement village. "Sure enough, there's a guy who raises worms for a *hobby*," Lewis exclaimed. He asked the fellow how much he wanted for two dozen of the big, fat nightcrawlers. *But—*

"But he wouldn't sell us any worms because they were his *pets!*" Lewis chuckled. "Finally he ended up *loaning* us 24 worms, provided we would return them the next day."

With worms in hand (or jar), the crew returned to Sarasota and began setting up on location. The worm scene was shot night-for-night, the same as the brain rip-off in *Blood Feast*. By this time, thankfully, the troupe wasn't nearly as light-deficient as they had been, so the beach scene in *Color Me Blood Red* was well illuminated. A plastic mannequin head stood in for actress Elyn Warner. The face was smashed to obliterate the features, fortuitously leaving a nice, gaping hole that was filled in with black paint. This actually gave the head a neo-realistic appearance, as if it had rotted from the inside out. Since the character had been murdered by a stab to the temple, this tied in well. The nose, chin, and one cheek remained intact, giving the audience an opportunity to identify the image as a girl's caved-in head.

"We shot that scene the same night we got back from the retirement village, and we didn't get finished until about 1:30 in the morning," Lewis said. "Everyone was exhausted. Finally we started gathering up the worms. We could only find 23 worms. One worm was missing! There we were, scrounging around in this sandy loam in the middle of the night, trying to find one damned worm. Finally someone on the crew shouted, '*I'll* give you 24 worms,' and he grabbed a knife and cut one of the worms in half. I said, 'All right, friend, you now have 24 worms; *you're* the guy who's going to return them tomorrow!'" The funny thing was, no one ever said anything about the discrepancy in worms. "Maybe that fellow didn't look to see that he now had two short worms in the batch," Lewis speculated. Even with 24 — or possibly only 23 — worms on camera, it's difficult to spot the things wriggling their way around the damaged head. They're there, but you have to look hard. (Frame-advancing a video copy of the film helps.)

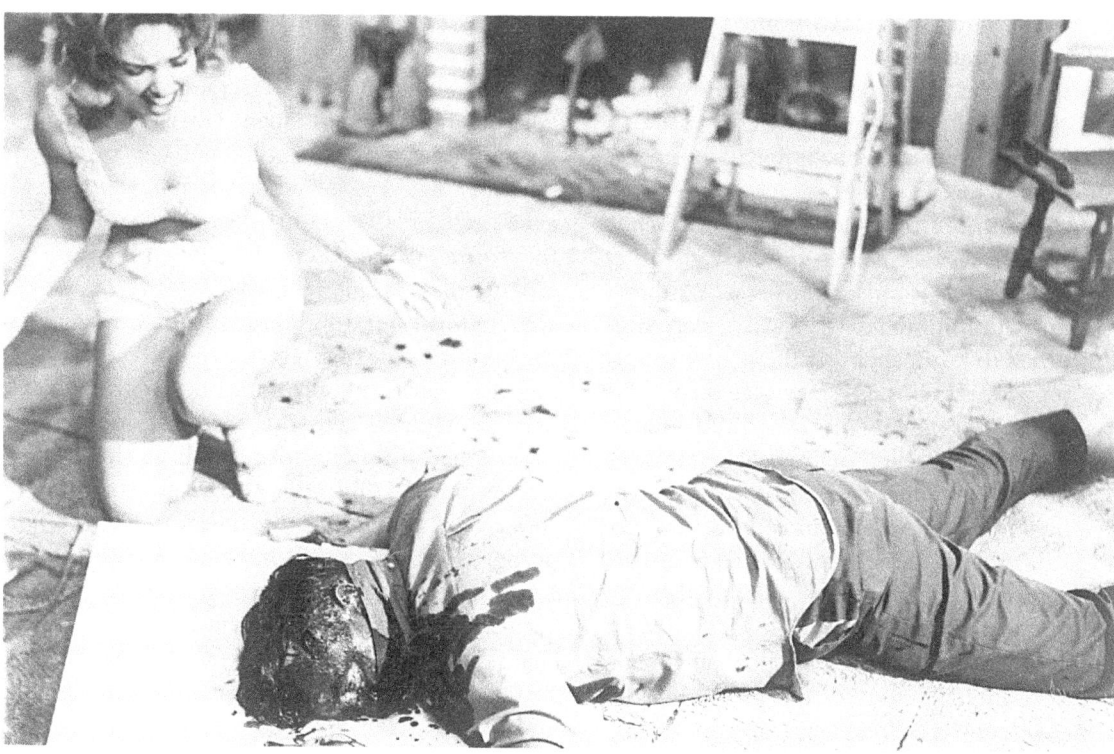

Top: The classic conflict of good versus not-so-good. Rolf (Jerome Eden, left) prepares to take down Adam Sorg (Gordon Oas-heim, right) with a shotgun blast to the head in *Color Me Blood Red*. April (Candi Conder) threatens to show off her pectorals in the background. *Bottom:* Nominal film heroine April (Candi Conder) reacts in horror to a sloppy self-portrait of Adam Sorg (Gordon Oas-heim) in the climax of *Color Me Blood Red*.

The discovery of Gigi's worm-riddled corpse lights a fire under Rolf, who determines to retrieve April from Sorg's clutches. By the time he arrives at the shack the artist is about to make April showers — of blood. Rolf grabs a loaded rifle (conveniently lying on the mantel above a fireplace) and unloads a round directly into the madman's face. Most head shots kill instantaneously, but Herschell Gordon Lewis often exercised "artistic freedom" to make a personal statement. Here, the director apparently is saying, *Avoid getting shot in the face*. Of course, Herschell wasn't making a statement; he was just trying to draw out the movie's final messy moment to compensate for the under-abundance of hard-core gore.

Sorg's death is disappointingly ordinary. No real gore effect was used in the climactic showdown; Gordon Oas-heim's face and head were simply doused with standard Lewis blood and his clothing was appropriately spattered. His blood-encrusted hair *almost* gives the impression that the scalp has been blown away, but this was mostly a matter of luck, as the reflection of the movie lights off the stage blood accentuated the effect.

While the film fails to match the madness of *Two Thousand Maniacs!* and *Blood Feast* overall, it is still a solid, low-budget shocker with at least a couple of scenes that are ghastly enough to elicit screams and groans from some viewers. (I can vouch for this; I saw the film during its first run in a suburban Maryland indoor theater.)

Lewis has often remarked that *Color Me Blood Red* is his least favorite of his own gore pictures, primarily because the gore effects are, on the whole, unremarkable. But Lewis also disliked his own screenplay: "It's an original story, but it's rather dumb because the artist thinks he needs human blood to paint with. If he'd just realized that chicken blood is about the same color, we would have had no film!"

A number of the film's scenes were filmed in the Farnsworth Galleries — an art connoisseur's paradise reconstructed in H. G. Lewis terms and budgets. The gallery appears to consist of a single room with about nine chairs facing one wall, a stage with a display of easels and paintings, and one lone man sitting in a chair. The set almost literally shouts *Low Budget*. On the other hand, it could be chalked up as an interpretation of Germanic expressionism. (Not that anyone would believe it.)

"My biggest triumph in *Color Me Blood Red* was in lighting that art gallery with only six lights," enthused Lewis. "It's a technical problem that doesn't mean anything, unless you're on the other side of the camera, as I was, trying to light the damned thing." More impressive to the casual film fan was Lewis's one Hitchcockian tracking shot, which begins with the camera centered in front of the gallery's closed door (complete with press-on letters that read, in part, *Closed Saturday*s, with the third "s" misplaced). The "door" opens and Lewis's camera glides in, a neat little move that brings to mind the complex camera movements in films as diverse as *Foreign Correspondent*, *Psycho*, and *Frenzy*.

A variety of paintings were needed to be put on display as the work of Adam Sorg, not only for scenes taking place in the gallery, but for those in the artist's workshop. "I wanted those paintings to be big, bold, garish things, but we really didn't have money in the budget to pay an artist to do them," Lewis admitted. "So where were we to go?" Where they went was to the offices of Ringling Brothers and Barnum & Bailey Circus. A staffer put Lewis in touch with the person who painted their circus tents. The artist turned out a nearly a dozen paintings and sketches that were used throughout the picture.

Color Me Blood Red has some funny one-liners and there is plenty of over-the-top black humor that rivals the dialogue Lewis penned for *Two Thousand Maniacs!* For example, after Sorg has gouged Gigi with his palette knife, he carries her body to his easel and begins painting the canvas with her head! It's a brief moment, partially obscured by an overlay of kaleidoscopic images representing everything that's going through the artist's demented mind, but it's darned funny. At the film's conclusion, when gallery owner Farnsworth is creating a bonfire of surviving Sorg paintings, master critic Gregorovich (Bill Harris) dryly observes, "You could have at least saved the frames."

In spite of the good-natured, if black, humor, the production became a nightmare for Lewis and Friedman — in more ways than one. "Dave and I had, in one respect, a perfect partnership," HG pointed out. "He respected my ability to make pictures, and I respected his ability to campaign them. The only argument of substance we ever had was over the casting of Connie Mason." Mason missed this movie (she was living in the Playboy mansion by then), but Friedman was having another problem. The sound-recording equipment was picking up unwanted noise during the filming of the beachside scenes in *Color Me Blood Red*, and there were a lot of beachside scenes in the film. "The noise of the lapping waves was interminable," Lewis complained. "Dave did what he could to filter it out, but it was there through the whole picture." Indeed, some of the dialogue was drowned out because of the problem. Post-production sound synching helped alleviate it, but there was another problem as well, because the production was interrupted by a most unwelcome interloper.

"Stan Kohlberg, who can only be described as something of a maniac, created a rift between the partners that made up the Jacqueline-Kay Corporation," Lewis later charged. "The partners consisted of Dave and myself, Kohlberg, and Sid Reich. Kohlberg came down to the set for a day and stood around gawking: 'Wow! Big cameras, just like in Hollywood!' In my opinion he was a terribly disruptive influence. 'What's this? What's that? How do you do that?' After that day, he mysteriously disappeared." And before long there came the explosion that tore apart the investment group.

With *Color Me Blood Red* finally finished, Lewis began the process of cutting it together. Kohlberg, who had been fudging the income reports on *Blood Feast* and *Two Thousand Maniacs!*, indicated to Lewis and Friedman that it would be a good idea to hold back on pocketing the profits being generated by those pictures. Kohlberg's argument was that if they left that money in the bank and let additional profits accrue, he would be able to get the Exchange National Bank of Chicago to finance a permanent film production company. Until this point Lewis had been forced to cut one deal after another with a variety of investors in order to get his pictures made. A permanent production entity would be a dream come true. If Kohlberg could do what he claimed, it made sense to let the money ride.

But as time passed with no further word from Kohlberg, Lewis began to get suspicious. There were supposed to be four equal partners in the Jacqueline-Kay group, but more and more Kohlberg acted as if he were the one in charge. In fact, he was controlling the purse strings. What had sounded like a great idea began to

Gordon Oas-heim played psychotic artist Adam Sorg in *Color Me Blood Red*. The paintings featured in the film were the work of an unidentified Ringling Brothers and Barnum & Bailey Circus sign painter.

take on the connotations of a duplicitous scam. Finally HG decided to take matters into his own hands. He called the bank to verify what was going on. "I spoke to one of the people I knew at Exchange National, and he told me he knew nothing whatsoever about any production company deal," Lewis stated. That clinched it. Lewis got in touch with Friedman and Sid Reich and suggested they sue Kohlberg for the monies due them from *Blood Feast* and *Two Thousand Maniacs!*

It's unfortunate that things turned out the way they did, because HG was never able to get a fair accounting of how much money those pictures actually made. The legal proceedings that followed in the wake of the suit put a cap on incoming profits from the films, which were temporarily shelved until the situation could be resolved in court. Although Herschell Lewis wrote and directed *Blood Feast*, that didn't mean he owned it, and in fact it was Kohlberg who would end up with the rights to all three pictures — *Color Me Blood Red* included — as part of the eventual resolution of the legal suit. "I'll never know how much *Blood Feast* really made," Herschell lamented, "because I could never get a final accounting on that picture."

Until the legalities were resolved by the courts and the monetary issues settled, Lewis and Friedman would have to find another way to generate income for themselves. Lewis had stopped editing *Color Me*

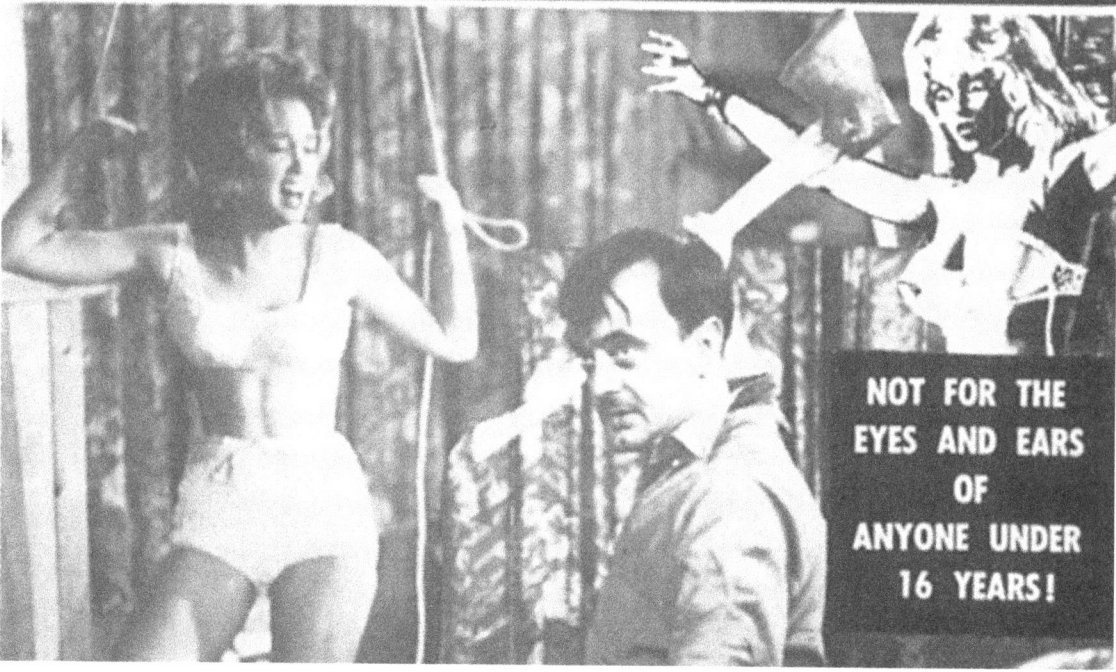

Before the MPAA established its rating system, it was up to film producers and distributors to police their own products. The *Color Me Blood Red* campaign stressed the film's adult approach with an under-16 admonition, which appeared on all of the advertising material.

Blood Red, leaving the film in total disarray. The film negative along with *Blood Feast* and *Two Thousand Maniacs!* was being held by the court while the parties were in litigation. Herschell thought that he and Friedman should begin work on their next feature as quickly as possible. "We already had the title *Moonshine Mountain* registered," Lewis said, "and we were planning to gear it specifically toward our primary audience [Southern blue-collar workers], figuring that something these people could relate to would generate even more money than the gore films." (That didn't happen, but *Moonshine Mountain* at least made a profit.)

While Lewis was working on the *Moonshine Mountain* script, Friedman abruptly cut off all contact. Recalled Lewis, "I had just set up a deal with my distributor in Charlotte, North Carolina, to help us shoot the picture on location there, when Dave just seemed to disappear." *That's odd*, thought Lewis. *Dave should be here getting ready for the shoot.*

What Lewis didn't know was that Friedman had privately settled his lawsuit with Stan Kohlberg and packed his bags for California. When HG found out, he felt betrayed. "I got a call from a man named Al Teton," Lewis recalled. "Teton was Kohlberg's lawyer. He said to me, 'It will interest you to know that there is one less antagonist in the Kohlberg matter.' I asked him what he meant and he replied, 'Dave Friedman settled.' I thought he was joking.

'Dave settled for $10,000 and moved to California.' I was thunderstruck. I tried and tried, but I could not reach Dave on the telephone, which I found inexcusable. I felt that if he was going to settle with Kohlberg he should have told me, especially as close as we were. We had been like brothers!" Some time later Herschell learned that Friedman had made a deal with a film distributor named Daniel Sonney. The deal allowed Friedman to relocate to California and become a partner in Sonney Amusement Enterprises. "Sonney was getting along in years and wanted some younger fellow to come in and run the business," related Herschell. "When I found out about this I just couldn't believe it. I mean, we were only weeks away from shooting *Moonshine Mountain*!"

Lewis then went through a period of soul-searching. He said, "I felt totally lost. I felt like a child abandoned in the wilderness. I was getting absolutely no film rentals out of Kohlberg, it might be three or four years before the suit would be heard in court, and who knows in a Chicago court, anyway? By then the legal fees would probably outweigh any money I might get out of the lawsuit."

And the bad news just wouldn't stop coming. Lewis next discovered that all the footage from *Color Me Blood Red* had been turned over to a fellow named Bob Sinise, a professional film cutter, for consolidation into a feature. Now, there is a big difference between a film cutter and a film editor. An editor makes decisions; a film cutter follows decisions. Sinise was following his own instincts in cutting *Color Me Blood Red*, but he botched much of the picture. "I didn't see the picture until years later," confessed Lewis, "but when I did, I was horrified by it. I felt the editing of it, the scoring of it, the dramatic timing of it, was just not good. The music didn't really go with anything. It was canned music and it was

Lewis and Friedman typically avoided employing Hollywood hyperbole in their campaigns, but a devilish extra "zing" was added to the promo material for *Color Me Blood Red*.

rotten. It sounded like the way you would score an industrial film! There was not much thought to it at all. I watched it again some years later and it was just as bad as I'd remembered. The poor scoring of that film makes it look like somebody's travelogue. It just had no power to it."

Lewis tried to disassociate himself from the film. "*Color Me Blood Red* is not worth watching, in my opinion," he said. "Part of it has to do with the music. I've used canned music before—I used it in *The Gore-Gore Girls*—but this thing was awful. The film is not representative of what I did. My pictures, as cheap and schlocky as they were, were gestalt; they were of one piece. The shooting, the writing, the editing, the campaign, was all one piece; that is, they matched. *Color Me Blood Red* doesn't match; the pieces don't match. I just don't like that picture." Neither did many other people, when they finally got to see it in 1966. From the screwy music soundtrack to the waterlogged dialogue and the low gore quotient, *Color Me Blood Red* was a disappointment for gorehounds everywhere. Unaware of the legal and technical circumstances that so negatively affected the entire film, fans had to wonder, was Herschell Gordon Lewis going soft?

When they found out the director's next picture was something called *Moonshine Mountain*, it seemed their worst fears were confirmed.

CHAPTER 10

Moonshine Monsters

> The picture had been shooting for two years and still wasn't finished. Some of the cast had disappeared and had been replaced by different actors who had nothing to do with the first part of the film. One fellow shot part of his role wearing a hairpiece and the other half not wearing it, so we decided to make him his own brother. That was the only way it would work.
>
> — *Herschell Gordon Lewis*

While the Kohlberg lawsuit dragged on and on, Herschell prepared to shoot *Moonshine Mountain* himself. He reminisced, "Dave was gone, and I wouldn't see him until I went to the next Theater Owners Convention the following November — which became something of a minor event, because everyone was expecting me to show up with a pistol and shoot him — so I went to see Harry Kerr, my Charlotte [North Carolina] distributor. I had planned to shoot *Moonshine Mountain* in Charlotte. [But he didn't.] I told Harry that Dave had backed out of the picture, and that created a real cash-flow problem for me."

Fortunately, Kerr became interested in *Moonshine Mountain* because it was about mountain people, one of his favorite subjects. (Not too surprising, considering that Harry Kerr was a North Carolinian.) Herschell reminded Kerr of another movie that had made enormous amounts of money throughout the South, especially in the Carolinas and Georgia, called *Thunder Road*. Herschell saw *Moonshine Mountain* as another picture in the *Thunder Road* tradition. "It had some comedy in it," Lewis pointed out, "as well as a little bit of gore." (Sometimes it was difficult to get the gore out of Herschell Gordon Lewis.) It didn't take much cajoling and back-slapping to get Kerr to cough up the money needed for the shoot. He wrote HG a check for $8,000, enough to buy the raw film stock, secure the props and locations, and pay the cast and crew. The film processing–lab bills and the cost of prints could be dealt with later.

Herschell traveled to Bullock Creek, South Carolina, to shoot *Moonshine Mountain*, known in some quarters as *White Trash on Moonshine Mountain*. The film was basically a comedy, but with a dramatic overlay. The screenplay was credited to Charles Glore, the real name of actor Chuck Scott, who played the film's main role. Starring alongside Scott was Ben Moore, who had overplayed to perfection the role of Lester McDonald in *Two Thousand Maniacs!* Rather ominously, there also was a cast member with the name Adam Sorg, the name of the bloody painter in *Color Me Blood Red*! (Obviously a pseudonym. We hope.) Pat Patterson, the film's assistant director, helped Herschell on some of the minor gore effects, and also took a small role in the picture.

The *Moonshine Mountain* plotline focused on the life of a popular country singer who jets around the country in his private plane, performing, petting, and partying (though not necessarily in that order). Despite his great fame and wealth, he feels something important is missing from his life. He goes back to his country roots to "rediscover" himself. "That type has almost become a cliché," commented Lewis, "with these private planes and so on. In *Moonshine Mountain*, the country singer comes into a family that owns the biggest 'likker' still for miles around. We built a fake still that was 15 feet high and about 10 feet in diameter, painted red. It was very impressive." (A *red* still? Definitely not a good idea for anyone hiding from the Feds in a backwoods setting.)

The singer becomes involved with the mountain people and falls in love with the daughter of a hillbilly family. After that the plot unwinds fairly rapidly. Tension is generated by the character of the sheriff (Gordon Oas-heim), a typical cinematic bad guy with no redeeming qualities whatsoever. "The sheriff is a plain, evil fellow," confirmed Lewis. "He kills the musician's [former] girlfriend and threatens anyone else who gets in his way." That includes Luther, the town oaf, who is dimwitted but not altogether without sense. He is hoodwinked by the sheriff into killing a couple of federal agents on the trail of the illegal whiskey.

"I had some minor gore in *Moonshine Mountain*," Lewis pointed out. "When the federal agents are searching for the still, we had a scene where Luther comes upon them and lifts them in the air, throws them down, and stomps them to death with his hobnail boots. Obviously, if you stomp somebody with hobnail boots, you're going to do that person damage. Hobnail boots are those boots that have little projections on the soles, almost like golf shoes. I had a close-up of the boot smashing down, and we had a shirt stuffed with these pig ribs inside. The material was pre-cut and rigged so that the least amount of pressure would split the shirt open. So the boot comes down, the shirt rips open, the ribs split and break apart, and all the blood and glop scatters to the four winds — it was quite a good effect." The gore stunts were orchestrated by Pat Patterson whom Herschell met during his visit with Harry Kerr in Charlotte. "Pat's effects were all right, but they were a little bit stagy," Lewis decided. "His work wasn't really designed to be filmed up close."

Another "minor" gore effect HG included in *Moonshine Mountain*—and one which was left intact for the duration of the picture's playoff—came near the conclusion of the film. To neatly tie up the story's loose ends, the sheriff had to die. He had already done away with Luther by this point, so Herschell wrote a scene in which an idiot girl buries an axe in the sheriff's back. He described it this way: "He falls into the still and ultimately the still blows up. We were able to find a local dynamite expert to handle that effect. Then the country singer marries the girl from the hillbilly family and everybody lives happily ever after." A relatively rare circumstance in a Herschell Gordon Lewis picture.

Herschell would eventually realize that by including gore in *Moonshine Mountain* he was alienating the audiences who were paying to see it. With that title, it obviously wasn't going to attract the fans who had liked *Two Thousand Maniacs!* and *Blood Feast*. "We were getting family audiences on *Moonshine Mountain*," said Lewis, "and they began complaining about the scene showing the smashed ribcage. So with great reluctance I removed that episode from the film. I cut the sequence out of every print we had. But I was at a period in my career where I was afraid *not* to have gore in a film. After all, why would someone come to see one of my films if all it had was country music? The *Moonshine Mountain* experience convinced me that I didn't need to include gore in every movie I made. Audiences would pay to see my pictures even if they *didn't* have gore. In fact, audiences will pay to see just about anything, which was something that I had almost forgotten."

No doubt part of the reason for Herschell's "country gore" miscalculation in *Moonshine Mountain* was David Friedman's absence from the scene. "I was still feeling somewhat betrayed," Lewis allowed, "because Dave had left me with a picture to shoot at a time when I had no income from the other pictures. I was forced into being both the producer and the director on *Moonshine Mountain*. On our earlier pictures Dave was the producer and I was the director, although technical titles really meant nothing to us. But I was obviously in a pickle making this picture on my own." It was a real fly-by-the-seat-of-your-pants period in the director's life.

Moonshine Mountain turned out to be a good experience for the director over the long haul. Most of the country music in the film was penned by Herschell himself, who had done an excellent job on the theme to *Two Thousand Maniacs!* "We also had some pretty good chase scenes down country roads in that film," he said proudly, "and the film came in on time and within budget. There was only one dark spot. I had something of a personal problem on the film because one of the actors started drinking. That was not a happy time. But the box-office results of that film I could never complain about. It did very, very well." Lewis's *Moonshine Mountain* screen credit read, "Directed by Herschell Gordon Lewis, who ought to know better, but don't." This single throwaway gag line, tacked onto the film almost as an afterthought, was responsible for kick-starting the production of another motion picture a few years down the road—details of which will be found in a later chapter.

After he completed the film, HG showed the rough cut of *Moonshine Mountain* to Harry Kerr. Kerr liked the picture but thought it would be a mistake to send it out without a backup feature. "There were some areas of the country, such as Dallas, where you always needed a second feature," Lewis stressed. The problem was that there was no money available to make another picture. To see a return on *Moonshine Mountain*'s investment, Lewis needed to get the film out the door and into theaters as quickly as possible. He ended up pairing it with the 1959 version of *Li'l Abner*, a film originally released by Paramount. By 1966 so many people had seen *Li'l Abner* that Paramount offered the picture to Lewis for the princely sum of $15 a day. Herschell said, "We augmented *Moonshine Mountain* with *Li'l Abner* so that I could control the bookings. That way no one could say, 'Well, your film only brought in $100; the other one brought in $1,000.' They can't say that if you control the entire package."

Thematically, the double bill seemed to be a perfect fit: Both films featured plots involving country folk and both contained enough humor to pass muster with undemanding audiences. Still, HG was not happy with the situation. "In my opinion," he said, "*Li'l Abner* was really a mismatch for *Moonshine Mountain*. I thought I could do better with something else as the second feature." Herschell put out feelers to see if there was another independent picture he could acquire for peanuts. If there was ever a god of grade-B greed, he must have smiled upon the filmmaker that day, because Lewis lucked into a situation just begging to be exploited.

"I found out about a film called *Terror at Halfday* which was being made by a fellow I knew named Bill Rebane," Lewis said. "*Terror at Halfday* was an odd title — but the film was even odder. Halfday was actually a little town about forty miles outside Chicago. Well, it turned out that Bill Rebane had been working on this film for almost two years! Some of his cast had disappeared and were replaced by others who had nothing whatsoever to do with the first part of the film that had been shot. There was an army officer whose rank changed because the uniform that they rented changed. Part of the film had been shot in summer, and part of it was shot in bleak, late autumn. It was just a very peculiar looking picture. Rebane had exposed an incredible amount of film on this thing — almost 80,000 feet. That is ten times the amount of raw stock we bought when we made *Lucky Pierre*. Rebane was the original director, writer, producer, and everything else on *Terror at Halfday*. It had a primitive plotline about an astronaut who goes up into space and comes back looking like a nine-foot pizza-faced individual. I felt that, with 80,000 feet of film to work with, there *had* to be a movie there somewhere.

"I was wrong."

Even though, astonishingly, there wasn't a coherent story line that could be extracted from the 80,000 feet of film, Lewis thought he could probably make the picture work if he shot another thousand or so feet of new footage. "I wound up shooting a thousand feet of close-ups," said Lewis. "I shot scenes of feet moving, close-ups of hands, close-ups of telegrams, *anything* to help propel the story forward, to bring this plotline to some sort of a conclusion. One of the things I shot was at night under Wacker Drive in Chicago, in some very odd traffic situations. I also shot some footage at a laboratory way out in the suburbs. Those were my main contributions to *Terror at Halfday*." When he was finished Lewis had 81,000 feet of film instead of just 80,000 — and still no story.

"After I finished shooting that extra film footage, I had it processed and then I took a look at everything again — and I was *still* perplexed," admitted Herschell. "I had only the vaguest notion of what this thing was all about. My film cutter and I put the pieces in the best sequential order we could." Still no dice. It seemed no matter what he did, *Terror at Halfday* remained ... terror-ble. But at last, by juggling the new footage and adding a bit of narration, Lewis was able to eke out something that more or less resembled a story line.

Frank Douglas, the latest NASA team astronaut, journeys into space and returns to Earth a changed man. Radiation has scarred his face and made him tall. (Well, why not?) He wreaks general havoc until the film's finale, when he is at last cornered inside a tunnel — and promptly disappears. (Huh?! Well, what the hey — he's an astronaut, he went into space, any damned thing could happen.) A narrator solemnly intones, "Suddenly there was no giant, no monster, no thing called Douglas to be followed. There was nothing in the tunnel but the puzzled men of courage who suddenly found themselves alone with shadows and darkness. Frank Douglas was rescued alive, well, and of normal size some 800 miles away." That doesn't make much sense, but at least there seemed to be a beginning, a *long* middle, and an end. Sort of.

Terror at Halfday could at least boast an interesting star. "The film had in it Henry Hite, who was billed as The World's Tallest Man," noted Herschell. "Bill Rebane had shot some footage of Hite as his monster from space. Hite used to do an old vaudeville routine. He's dead now, but he used to live in a hotel in Chicago. He was a very likable fellow. I felt immensely sorry for him, because he had such fragile ankles. He weighed so much, he was so big, that it hurt him to walk."

Lewis used Henry Hite's ponderous image in the advertising for the film, which he decided to retitle *Monster A' Go-Go*. "That title made about as much sense as the film itself, so it was a good match," Lewis opined. "In fact, when I looked at all the pieces of film we had assembled, including the new material, it became obvious that this could be nothing but a joke, because it was still impossible to make any sense of it. So I turned the campaign into a joke. The catch phrase was simply, 'An Astronaut Went Up; A Guess-What Came Down.'" The one-sheet poster even warned potential theatergoers, "You've never seen a picture like this—thank goodness!"

"*Monster A' Go-Go*, stupid as it was, was still better than *Li'l Abner* on a ninth run," Lewis insisted. "It's just too bad it had cost Bill Rebane twice as much to make an unfinished black-and-white film than I'd spent on any two of my pictures!"

In order not to tarnish his hard-core gore image, Lewis used one of his stock assortment of pseudonyms on *Monster A'Go-Go*. The advertising materials as well as the film itself credited the direction to "Sheldon Seymour." Lewis had a theory about film credits. "I came to the conclusion that everybody in the film business was named either Sheldon or Seymour," Lewis declared. "I figured that if I put those names together, everyone would be able to identify with it." Actually, Lewis directed, wrote, photographed, and produced under a variety of guises over the years. At various times he credited himself as Herschell Gordon Lewis, Lewis H. Gordon, Sheldon Seymour, Seymour Sheldon, R. L. Smith, Armand Pays, Mark Hansen, and George Parades. "The use of made-up names went all the way back to *Lucky Pierre*," Herschell disclosed. "Our crew was so small we would make up credits so we didn't have to repeat the same names over and over. We even made up nonsense credits, like 'Lenses by Coca-Cola Bottling Company,' just to have a longer list of titles."

The long list of actors who appeared in *Monster A' Go-Go* included Phil Morton, June Travis, George Perry, Lois Brooks, Rork Stevens, Peter Thompson, Robert Simons, Barry Hopkins, Stu Taylor, Del Clark ... it just went on and on. Even Bill Rebane had played a role. Lewis's participation in the film can only be described as less than minimal, and the film could be considered a part of the director's canon only by a long stretch of the imagination. In addition to Lewis and Rebane, Jeff Smith and Don Stanford also received writing credit on the film. (Not that they wanted the credit.) Cinematography was blamed on Frank Pfeiffer.

Unbelievably, Rebane later began work on another picture. Herschell recalled, "Rebane phoned me one day and said, 'I want you to shoot this new film for me, and the only thing I can tell you is, get a snowsuit, because we're going to shoot it in the middle of winter in Minnesota.' I replied, 'If you want me to get a snowsuit because you want to shoot in the middle of winter in Minnesota, I want a $500 advance against my participation.' And he sent me the $500! I thereupon bought a snowsuit, complete with heavy boots, a mask—the works. But I never heard from Bill after that. He may have made the film, I don't know. I kept the snowsuit for about two years and then gave it to the Salvation Army. But it wouldn't surprise me if I was to learn that Bill is *still* making the picture—not after all the time it took him to shoot *Terror at Halfday!*"

While HG was awaiting an influx of rental fees from the playoff of *Moonshine Mountain* and *Monster A' Go-Go*, his income from film production hit an all-time low. Receipts from sporadic showings of *Scum of the Earth, Living Venus, The Adventures of Lucky Pierre,* and even *The Prime Time* kicked in a few dollars now and again, but otherwise very little was happening in the film business for him between 1964 and 1966. This was primarily due to the legal proceedings against Stan Kohlberg, which were still held up by an overloaded court system. The completion of *Moonshine Mountain* and the acquisition and metamorphosis of *Terror at Halfday* into *Monster A' Go-Go* at least helped put groceries on the table; but just as important, the new releases allowed Lewis to begin again the long process of climbing up the ladder of independent feature film production.

Around this time, Sidney Reich, the fourth investor in the original Jacqueline-Kay Corporation, got in touch with Herschell to suggest that they consolidate their lawsuits against Kohlberg. "Up until that time I thought that Sid Reich was an antagonist," said Lewis, "but it turned out he wasn't. He wanted information about Kohlberg, which I gave him, and he then filed our suits in federal court, as opposed to circuit court, where nothing so far had seemed to happen." Before long Kohlberg offered to settle with both men out of

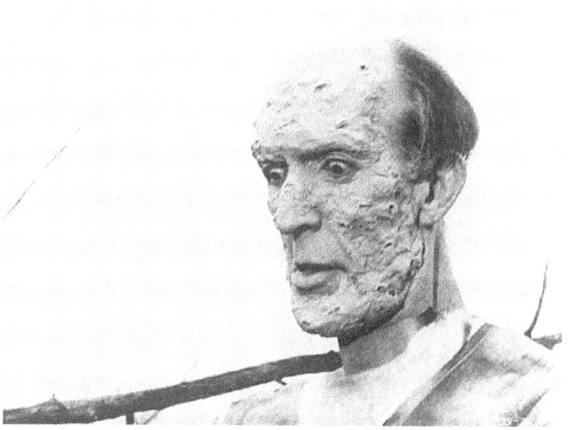

The "tall, pizza-faced individual" (Henry Hite) from *Monster A' Go-Go* (1965), a science-fiction failure partially rescued by Herschell Gordon Lewis. For those who never saw it and want to know just how bad the film is: It's better than ***The Incredibly Strange Creatures Who Stopped Living and Became Mixed-Up Zombies*** but not as good as *Cat-Women of the Moon.*

court, but for Herschell it meant giving up the rights to *Blood Feast, Two Thousand Maniacs!* and *Color Me Blood Red.* It must have seemed as if all the big profits had already been bled from *Blood Feast* and *Two Thousand Maniacs!* Certainly Kohlberg wouldn't make much money on a re-release of either picture. So, figuring that those two films had pretty much played themselves out, Lewis allowed Kohlberg to take control of the films. "I came out of that whole situation with some money," Lewis confirmed, "although it certainly was not as much as I thought I was entitled to. But at least it was a pleasure to be rid of that albatross around my neck."

With the Kohlberg case finally out of the way, Herschell began to feel more like his old self. Coincidentally, new film production offers began to appear, almost as if by magic. "Interesting things began to happen," agreed Lewis. He was approached by several individuals, all of whom happened to be looking for film production partners. One of those individuals was Sid Reich. "I was literally waited upon by Reich, who wanted to make movies. So we decided to make some pictures together."

Lewis's partnership with Reich would lead to a handful of minor productions, as well as another horror-and-gore project, *A Taste of Blood*. Lewis also made pictures with Harry Kerr, James Hurley, and Fred Sandy. In fact, Herschell found himself busier than he had been since the early years when the nudie-cuties were in full bloom. The late 1960s would be the most prolific period of Lewis's film career. It was a time of great social unrest. It was the time of Vietnam, Richard Nixon, Haight-Ashbury, Timothy Leary, LSD, Robert Kennedy, and Jimi Hendrix.

It was also the time of *The Wizard of Gore*. Who could ask for anything more?

CHAPTER 11

100 Percent Weird

> There was no rating system in place at the time I began making motion pictures. There were individual censor bureaus, and that was it. If I made *The Adventures of Lucky Pierre* today, I'm certain it would get a PG rating, but when it was first released it was considered adult fare. That's why there has been an ongoing argument about whether movies are creators of public morality, or reflectors of public morality, or just followers of public morality.
>
> — Herschell Gordon Lewis

With the *Moonshine Mountain/Monster A' Go-Go* combination in release, Herschell could relax a little. Money was beginning to come in again. He hadn't any idea if he could ever make another picture that would match the success of *Blood Feast* in terms of notoriety and box-office profit, but he had to put that behind him and move forward. Kohlberg controlled *Blood Feast* now. Kohlberg controlled *Two Thousand Maniacs!* And though Lewis didn't much care, Kohlberg controlled *Color Me Blood Red*, as well. Those pictures were out of his hands forevermore.

Coincidentally, *Blood Feast* and *Two Thousand Maniacs!* had just been re-released while Kohlberg was preparing to distribute *Color Me Blood Red*. The year was 1966. Word climbed over, under, around, and through the grapevine and eventually reached the ear of Herschell Lewis: *Blood Feast* was back in theaters, but there was something odd about it. The credit crawl at the beginning of the picture no longer listed the names of Lewis and Friedman.

Herschell knew instinctively that Stan Kohlberg was trying to pull another fast one. "It was unbelievable," Lewis said, "but apparently what happened was that Kohlberg took the picture and tried to cut the titles off and put his name on it! Apparently he thought he could do this and thereby become a celebrity. Unfortunately for him, he did it four or five years after the films had been made, and in the industry it was well known who actually made those movies. But that just goes to show you the mentality of Stan Kohlberg. The funny thing is, Kohlberg is the type of person to whom you might say, 'That's the worst picture I ever saw,' and he would thank you. He'd think he was being complimented!"

Lewis was still interested in talking to David Friedman to hear his side of the story concerning his litigation settlement. But no matter where he turned or whom he spoke to, no one was able to provide him with a current address or telephone number for his old film partner. "I still felt betrayed," acknowledged Lewis, "and I needed to talk with him. I felt frustrated. Fortunately, I finally caught up with Dave at the Theater Owners Convention in Los Angeles the following November [1966]. It was quite an event. We made up, and we've been good friends ever since. In fact, we became better friends after the reunion than we had been before." There was no chance that the two men would get back together to continue producing features, though. "Dave was living in California then, and I was still in Chicago," said Lewis, "so the logistics were all wrong for setting up another partnership. I was determined to continue on my own, and Dave had already had a couple of successes by then on his own."

Lewis and Friedman surprised a lot of the industry insiders who had expected them to go for each other's throats at the Theater Owners Convention. They parted on good terms at the close of the show, and each went back to producing the kind of low-budget exploitation items they knew best. Friedman made a horror film called *She-Freak* in 1967, but concentrated on sexploitation pictures after that. Titles like *Thar She Blows!* (1968), *Love Camp #7* (1969), and *The Erotic Adventures of Zorro* (1971) more or less cemented Friedman's new reputation as a soft porn peddler, but he was really only making newer versions of the kind of nudie-cuties he and Lewis had been doing in the early '60s.

Meanwhile, back at HG's Chicago film headquarters, Herschell began working up a list of subjects to tackle in the aftermath of *Moonshine Mountain* and *Monster A' Go-Go*. Exploitation continued to be the name of the game, but Lewis's idea of what constituted exploitation differed from other independent filmmakers — sometimes by a wide margin. Many years after he got out of the film business, Lewis remarked, "I would regard *Jurassic Park* as the ultimate exploitation film. An exploitation film is a motion picture in which the elements of plot and acting become subordinate to elements that can be promoted. If you look at *Jurassic Park* with a cold-blooded eye, the acting level is junior high school. People read their lines as though they're seeing them on a TelePrompTer for the first time. A film like *Cyrano de Bergerac* [1950] with José Ferrer—now, that's a motion picture. There are no exploitation values at all. There are no dinosaurs eating people or chomping off arms. *That's* exploitation — elements the promoter can grab on to and shake in the face of theater owners to get them to play the picture and in the face of the public to get them to see it." [Quoted in *The Sleaze Merchants* by John McCarty, pp. 38–39; St. Martin's Press, 1995.]

Never let it be said that Herschell Gordon Lewis didn't try making a motion picture without at least some redeeming value. Strange as it may seem, the man who pulverized patrons with shock-hops like *The Wizard of Gore* and *Two Thousand Maniacs!* also made ... a sweet, warm, gentle, nurturing children's film. Lewis recalled, "The next film I did [after *Monster A' Go-Go*] was a children's picture called *Jimmy, the Boy Wonder*. A fellow named Hal Berg came to me with the idea to do this, because his wife had a children's show on a local television channel in Philadelphia. For some reason, Hal had acquired the rights to a 12-minute cartoon which had been made in Italy. It was a nice cartoon. It was actually kind of charming. Hal's idea was to weave a feature around the cartoon, and he wanted his wife to star in it." (Shades of *Bell, Bare and Beautiful*, only without bosoms.)

Jimmy, the Boy Wonder, a 1966 release, was not a project that Lewis had penciled in on his production slate. Like several other minor pictures that bore his name in the credits, it was the kind of film that he made at the behest of someone else — a project that fell into his lap unsought. HG was hired as the director and cinematographer. "Hal Berg had put the deal together," Lewis noted, "and he gave me a percentage for shooting it. It turned out to be a good feature, but nothing ever happened with it." (In other words, it didn't make any money.) "There really was no plotline to the film," he admitted. "What little bit of story there was involved a boy who makes a wish and stops the flow of time. Everyone in the world is frozen in time, and he has to go into the 'netherworld' to start up all the clocks again. He is chased by 'Mr. Fig,' a heavily made-up, evil entity who postures and gestures away the whole time. A wizard's daughter, Aurora, tries to help him get the world started up again." The mystical figure of Aurora was played by Berg's wife, Nancy. She, along with an ancient, absentminded wizard, helps Jimmy defeat Mr. Fig. It's the kind of so-cute-it's-sickening plotline that only very young children would appreciate.

That didn't matter to Herschell. "We shot the picture in Miami, and I had a good time making it," he remarked. "A lot of it was filmed in a building called the Coral Castle, which was a strange construction with furniture made completely of stone." If nothing else, *Jimmy, the Boy Wonder* provided another opportunity for HG to hone his filmmaking skills. That kind of hands-on involvement always proved invaluable to someone working in low-budget productions, because whatever expertise they gained from one picture could be applied to the next one. Lewis was never one to claim he knew everything there was to know about the filmmaking process. He saw each project as one more opportunity to pick up new techniques and refine old ones. In HG's view, you never stopped learning. "That's why I quit hiring cameramen," Herschell said. "Going back to *The Prime Time*, I didn't want to pay money to people who couldn't do something as well as I could do it, even if that was what they did for a living. I already knew how to operate a camera. I'd learned that years before, when I was making industrial films. After that first day of shooting I just grabbed the camera and took over, because I knew I could move faster than the cameraman we hired."

Jimmy, the Boy Wonder was occasionally shown under the title *Jimmy, the Wonder Boy*, although at this late date no one seems to know why. Those who have seen the film do not hold it in very high regard. "The only reason to ever show this film is if you have children you want to punish," said Brian Marshall in a posting on the Internet Movie Database. Marshall described the fairy godmother as looking like actress "Kathy Bates with a bad hangover."

Lewis was later asked to photograph and direct a film entitled *An Eye for an Eye*, but as sometimes happened in the low-budget independent film business, the project fell apart before it could ever be completed. "The person for whom I was making that picture took it and disappeared, and I don't know what ever happened to it," Herschell stated. "In production it wasn't bad. It was about a man who wills his eyes to whoever can get them. It then turns out that his eyes have special powers. He was actually part of a group that planned to take over the world, and his only way of getting out was to kill himself in an automobile crash and have his eyes go to somebody else who might then be able to break up this unholy ring. But as far as I know, the film never saw the light of day."

Between 1966 and 1969, Lewis was involved in no less than a dozen film productions, from major gore extravaganzas like *A Taste of Blood* to minor "director-for-hire" situations like *Alley Tramp* (1966). *Alley Tramp* was co-written by Herschell's old acting and writing associate, Allison Louise Downe — the same A. Louise Downe that came up with the idea for *Blood Feast*. Her writing partner for *Alley Tramp* was Paul Gordone. "I shot that in black and white for Tom Dowd," said Lewis. It was actually made in 1962 but not released until 1966. The story concerned a girl and her mother who were socially and financially challenged (in other words they were street bums). They both fall in love with the same truck driver. (Not much of a surprise there, considering what has gone before.) The film's advertising tag line, "She Went for Anything in Pants," was used in a total of three different campaigns, as the film saw release under several titles. Besides *Alley Tramp*, it was also known as *I Am a Woman* and *Pleasure Me, Master*. Herschell took credit as cinematographer and director on the film.

Although Lewis's output would begin to wind down as the 1960s segued into the '70s, in general his pictures were becoming bigger and better. Lewis knew an instructor named James Hurley who was on the faculty of Triton College. Like Sid Reich, Tom Dowd, Al Sack, and others who had crossed Herschell's path, Hurley wanted to get into the motion picture business. He had a script, which he had written himself, ready to go before the cameras, but he needed guidance; he needed expertise; he needed Herschell's help. Together, the pair filmed Hurley's story, which was titled *The Sensitive*. Before the film was released, Lewis prevailed upon Hurley to come up with a more exploitable title. They eventually decided to call the film *Something Weird* (1967). It wasn't so much a better title than an oddball title — just odd enough, thought HG, to lure the curious into theaters to see it. (By the 1980s a title like *The Sensitive* might have generated as much money at the box office as any similarly titled horror film — *The Sender*, *The Omen*, or *The Legacy*. But in 1967, when the picture went into production, horror films had titles like *The Conqueror Worm* and *The Vengeance of She*. *The Sensitive* was too "soft" sounding, in Herschell's opinion.)

Something Weird is not a gore film. There are scenes of violence in it, but in no way does the film resemble *Blood Feast* or even *Color Me Blood Red*. "It really isn't like the other [gorror] pictures," agreed Lewis. "*Something Weird* is about ESP and witchcraft. It's a strange picture."

The film featured a large cast, especially compared to some of Herschell's earlier efforts. Taalkius Blank, the mayor in *Two Thousand Maniacs!*, returned in a main role, working alongside top-lined Lawrence J. Aberwood, Lee Ahsmann, Mudite Arums, and William Brooker. Kathleen Koenig was credited as the "Ghostly Apparition" who seals the curse. Larry Wellington, who had composed music scores for several of HG's pictures, also showed up in a minor part. The finished film ran 80 minutes.

Lewis was proud of the special effects he was able to add to *Something Weird* using simple trick camera work. (The costs involved in using laboratory opticals were prohibitive to a filmmaker on the kind of budget Lewis generally had at his disposal.) Nevertheless, he thought he managed reasonably well to add some visual zing to the picture.

"This film had some nice visuals in it," Lewis said. "We had a woman who turned into a witch, we had a ghost running through a chapel, all of it done in the camera. I exposed the film twice at stopped-down shutter speeds to get those effects. Using the same procedure I had a fellow disappear through a wall, and it looked impressive, but it was not the least bit difficult to do."

Although *Something Weird* is not the most evocative film title Lewis came up with, it at least alerted potential ticket-buyers that this was a motion picture which offered something out of the ordinary. "It's the story of a man who is horribly burned in an electrical explosion and left with a scar on his face," offered Lewis. "Along with the scar, he is also given extraordinary mental powers. A witch appears and offers to give him back his good looks in exchange for his [sexual] favors. To him, she looks like the ugly witch she really is, but the rest of the world sees her as this beautiful girl. Eventually a doctor who specializes in telepathy comes to investigate this fellow, and the witch then falls for the doctor. She causes the doctor to fall against one of the warning lights that are used in road construction, and he burns his face, thus becoming her next victim. In between, there are a lot of very odd effects."

Perhaps because of the unusual subject matter, *Something Weird* was not a hit. Audiences couldn't seem to figure out whether it was a fantasy film, a horror story, or a drama with supernatural overtones, and the picture lost money from the first day it played theaters. Lewis hadn't lost money on a film since *The Prime Time*. Brainstorming for a quick fix, in a moment of inspiration he decided to return to the gold mine he had first excavated four years earlier.

He decided to pour on the gore galore.

CHAPTER 12

Whatever Flips Your Wig

> The heroine was supposed to poke out the eye of the homicidal son who had been killing these girls for their scalps. Louise Downe, who was handling props on *The Gruesome Twosome*, came up with a sheep's eye. We used sheep almost exclusively. But this sheep's eye looked enormous. It was at least 30 times larger than a human eye. Now, that may be what's behind our eyeballs, but nobody would ever accept it. We just couldn't have that much stuff hanging inside our heads! We were scrambling around trying to find something else to use, and all I could find was a fish. So we ended up using a fish eye.
>
> — *Herschell Gordon Lewis*

When the box-office results for *Something Weird* were first tabulated, H. G. Lewis and James Hurley were devastated. The film was performing nowhere near the level either man had hoped. "*Something Weird* was just not strong enough to stand on its own," Lewis reasoned. "It's what they call in the industry 'a nice, little picture.'" He decided to make a quickie that could be used in double-bill situations to support the Hurley picture. (There is an argument to be made here that *all* of Herschell Gordon Lewis's movies are quickies, but if one confines oneself to the Lewis universe, rather than considering motion pictures in general, then films like *Blood Feast*, *Two Thousand Maniacs!* and *The Wizard of Gore* are "major" productions, and *The Gruesome Twosome* and *Monster A' Go-Go* are "quickies." Heaven help us.)

In 1966, H. G. Lewis met Fred and Jerry Sandy, a father-and-son team who were long-time insiders in the film business. Jerry Sandy was in charge of American International's Washington, D.C., exchange. He and his father, Fred Sandy, joined forces with Herschell to create a partnership similar to the Lewis-Friedman production entity of the early 1960s. Under the umbrella of Mayflower Pictures, Inc., the two produced a handful of mostly profitable ventures, including two of Lewis's later gore features. The first gorror movie that came over on the Mayflower was *The Gruesome Twosome*.

Lewis was under pressure to turn *Something Weird* into a moneymaker. The picture couldn't be changed, but it could be augmented by adding a co-feature. Lewis was able to come up with a script for his new horror quickie that outdid most other shockers when it came to originality. (Originality, gore, and attention-grabbing film titles were this filmmaker's forte.) *The Gruesome Twosome* is, in a nutshell, about two nuts who operate an establishment called The Little Wig Shop. Their wigs are so lifelike, you'd almost swear they are the real thing. (Heh, heh.) "When I made *The Gruesome Twosome* and

After joining forces with Fred and Jerry Sandy, Lewis embarked on the most prolific portion of his film career, making in rapid succession such films as *Suburban Roulette, She-Devils on Wheels, A Taste of Blood, Something Weird, How to Make a Doll, Blast Off Girls, Just for the Hell of It*, and others, as well as his first "goremedy"—a comedy with gore—*The Gruesome Twosome* (1967).

coupled it with *Something Weird*, the combination started making some real money," HG said. "It wasn't one of my major pictures; it was made with a specific purpose, which was to save *Something Weird* from becoming a flop. But there are some [fans] who think it is a classic! I like it, personally, because it has such good humor."

Historically, humor and horror don't mix. The number of successful horror comedies produced between 1930 and 2000 can be counted on two claws. Only when the humor is as twisted as it is here does the mixture of goosepimples and guffaws seem to work. *The Gruesome Twosome* works. "Basically it's about a little old lady who runs a wig shop," Lewis said. "Her idiot son, who lives in the basement, gives her the makings for the wigs which he takes from the girls he kills. The old lady lures the young girls in through the other door on the pretext of renting them a room, and then the son cuts their scalps out." High good humor, indeed.

Lewis got the project in front of his cameras and completed in a mere six days. Even though *The Gruesome Twosome* was the most rushed of any H. G. Lewis gore film, it turned out respectably well. "I thought it was a charming little picture," HG opined defiantly. Not everyone can say that about a movie in which people are scalped, gutted, gouged, and carved up with an electric knife. "It's really whimsical," the director added with a wry smile. "It's gore served up with a sense of humor. We were starting a new pattern, either out of boredom with what we were doing, or just because we thought we'd burned everything else up, I'm not sure which."

Although Lewis sometimes employed a cameraman, as often as not he was behind the camera himself. "If I know what I want in a shot, I'll say to my cameraman, 'Let me make this shot,'" HG explained. "And sometimes I'll just stay on the camera, and he'll move over to being the assistant cameraman, or second cameraman, and whoever was the second cameraman will then do something else on crew. Lewis's musical chairs! But by doing that, things get moving much faster. That's especially important when you're trying to stay within your budget. And that's what you have to do to finish a film — stay within budget. That's how I was able to get *The Gruesome Twosome* finished so quickly."

The film opens with a static shot of talking heads — literally. Not the kind of heads you might expect to see in a Herschell Gordon Lewis film, like decapitated ones; these are wig holders, painted and decorated with scraps of colored construction paper to resemble cartoon faces. And they talk to each other. And talk. And talk. They talk so much, some movie patrons must have begun wondering if this was all there was to *The Gruesome Twosome*. "The reason for that sequence at the beginning," Lewis interjected, "was that our timer [the crew member responsible for keeping a tally of the film's accumulated running time] was off by about ten minutes. I discovered, when I was cutting the picture, that it was too short. So in order to get it up to the 70 minute mark, I added that scene of the talking heads at the beginning." (Mistakes will be made, after all, but this was ridiculous.)

One head proposes to tell the story of Mrs. Pringle, the Little Wig Shop, Napoleon, and Rodney. "That Rodney sure knew how to handle a knife," the head sighs. A hand holding a switchblade enters the frame, "scalps" the other head, and stabs it through the crown. Lewis added some bonus gore here as the knife pops a hidden blood balloon, sending the red stuff squirting skyward. Fortunately, the rest of the picture isn't as dumb as this intro suggests. (Well, not quite.)

In a pitch-black night-for-night scene, Lewis focuses a long shot on the film's first victim-to-be, a raven-haired lass who is interested in renting a room from the proper Mrs. Pringle. Mrs. Pringle runs two businesses out of her home: renting rooms to whatever pretty young things happen across her advertisement in the newspaper for "Rooms to Let"; and selling 100 percent natural human-hair wigs through her "Little Wig Shop." Coeds from the nearby college campus contribute the raw material for the wigs — unknowingly, of course, and most unwillingly. It's all rather a convenient setup ... until the tables are turned on the Pringles. (Did someone name a potato chip after these characters?)

One half of *The Gruesome Twosome* is about to coax a victim into the hair lair. Dianne Raymond (left) and Gretchen Wells in a subdued scene from Lewis's fourth "gorror" film.

In grand H. G. Lewis fashion, there is a murder before the credits even begin to roll, and it's one of the director's best. Mrs. Pringle leads her visitor to Rodney's room and shoves her inside. (It's a gargantuan room, but then he needs all that space to kill in.) Moments later, rattlebrained Rodney has her pinned to his worktable, mouth agape and tongue hanging out. (And that's just the girl. Imagine what Rodney looks like.) Rodney whips out a butcher knife and proceeds to go to work, pressing the blade into the girl's scalp. With the aid of some pliable mortician's wax (a standard makeup item in Hollywood until the advent of rubber prosthetics), a wig, stage blood, and that old standby — animal tripe — Lewis presents the genre's first on-screen scalping.

The scalping scene is truly revolting: It goes on and on, with the knife blade slicing through the girl's "skin" as Rodney pulls the scalp away from her head inch by inch. Look closely and you'll even see some strands of gristle still attached to the crown of her head. Lewis keeps the camera centered on a medium close-up of the action until the scalp has been pulled almost all the way off, then cuts to a reverse angle showing part of the bloody skull. All this is gruesome enough, but as we well know by now, H. G. Lewis doesn't give up the gore easily. His camera returns for another front shot, followed by a medium shot of Rodney as he picks up the bloody scalp by its gore-streaked hair. As he holds it aloft, streams of blood run down his arms, along with chunks of flesh and musculature that drop out behind it. (Yes, it's overkill, but don't forget that in a Herschell Gordon Lewis picture, it's the splatter that matters.)

"As technology catches up with you, some of these effects get easier to do," noted Lewis. "Whereas before we used regular wax and chicken skin, in *The Gruesome Twosome* we used mortician's wax, which slices well. If we had been able to make *The Gruesome Twosome* later on, with the motorized, rubberized arms and legs they now have — ah, yes! I would have a marvelous time with those. That's why I think it's funny that they have such dumb effects in these films today. They don't understand what gore really is. Those films may make the term 'splatter movie' apt for what they are doing, but it is not apt for what we did. The only film we had where blood splattered was *The Gruesome Twosome*, but we also had plenty of viscera as well."

It's too bad that the quickie nature of the production turned what could have been a minor Lewis gore "classic" into a sloppy, only occasionally effective comedy-horror. Kathy Baker and her boyfriend, Dave, are one of the most annoying, do-gooder couples ever seen in a genre picture. Kathy is an angelic snoop, who thinks there is a conspiracy taking place around every corner. As might be expected in a production of this type, she is the one who uncovers the dastardly deeds being perpetrated by Mrs. Pringle and her son at The Little Wig Shop. During a good-natured pajama party with her friends (it's so good-natured, it's sickening), Kathy talks incessantly about the recent disappearances of three college coeds. She's certain they've come to some kind of harm. Ominously, at that very moment, the radio show the girls have been listening to is interrupted by a voice which advises, "Please stand by for an important announcement regarding the murders in this area." (It's HG saving money once again, folks! A newspaper refers to "disappearances." Later, the cops refer to "disappearances." Only HG's radio persona says anything about "murders." Must be because he's read the script.)

Kathy begins a snooping investigation on her own, and the film wastes a good seven or eight minutes as she trails the college custodian, who was seen sneaking bones out of the campus eatery. It turns out he gives the bones to his dog every year on the mutt's birthday. Naturally, today's his birthday.

Meanwhile, back at The Little Wig Shop, Mrs. Pringle recites Rodney's favorite fairy tale, *Rapunzel*. (It figures.) As a reward for being such a good boy, she gives him an electric carving knife. And wouldn't you know it — he puts it to good use on his very next victim. One of Kathy's pajama-party friends, Dawn, turns up at the Pringles' to rent a room, but before she can get the money out of her purse, Rodney takes it out for her — in blood. "We had Rodney slobbering around, dribbling saliva all over the place, to make it more grotesque," said Herschell. It is here, in the film's second gore sequence, that blood finally splattered in a Lewis picture.

The script called for Rodney to use his new electric knife to slice through Dawn's throat. The crew concealed a plastic hose under a false neck appliance worn by the actress to allow stage blood to be pumped out during the filming of the scene. "He was supposed to slice her right across the windpipe," Lewis detailed, "and for that effect I had the tube going all the way up the girl's leg, under her clothing, to her neck. Rodney was supposed to cut *through* the tube which would then splatter blood. Well, once we had it set up it looked like it was going to be too dangerous to do it that way. We had the girl standing upright, with a false neck that could be cut through, but it just wasn't working. What we ended up doing was positioning her horizontally [to allow gravity to do some of the work on the bloodflow] and using a stagehand to blow through the tube to get the blood to come out."

But when they began filming, nothing gory happened at all. Lewis described the frenzied activity going on behind the camera: "Our crew man couldn't get the blood to come out. The film was rolling. I was yelling, 'Blow harder, blow harder!' Somehow the stage blood had coagulated during the period in which we were trying to put this shot together. So I said 'Gimme that tube' and I blew on it, and I blew on it, and I blew on it. Finally the tube burst and it blew blood all over the place. It got on the plants in the room, it got on the camera, everybody had stage blood all over them, and that stuff was *hard* to get off." At least Lewis got the shot he was after.

Later in *The Gruesome Twosome* there is a beach scene featuring one of the worst bands ever to appear in a professional motion picture. (And that's saying something, because there have been some bad bands in some bad movies. Remember the Del-Tones in *The Horror of Party Beach*?) This band literally sounds as if they have just figured out the chords to "Louie, Louie." The lead guitarist plays as if he *might*, with hard work and determination, one day be awful. "That scene is not one of the film's highlights, admittedly," Lewis acknowledged.

Kathy and Dave have an argument and that night Dave goes to the funny car races with his buddies while his girlfriend spends more time trying to figure out what's going on. (Much like the audience.) Meanwhile, victim number three turns up at The Little Wig Shop and Rodney promptly disembowels her with what must be the largest machete in existence. Unfortunately, once more *The Gruesome Twosome*'s rushed nature spoiled what might have been a gore effect to rival the kidney squeeze in *Color Me Blood Red*. As Rodney reaches down to rip out her guts with his bare hands, it becomes pretty obvious that the animal innards substituting for the real thing are simply lying on the actress's belly in a pool of blood. No wound or gaping hole was built up from wax as had done for the heart-ripping flashback in the middle of *Blood Feast*; this was gore on the cheap. There is even an embarrassingly laughable shot of the idiot son reaching *into the girl's pants* to extricate a slice of liver hidden there. (At least this is what we *think* he was reaching for.)

Dave departs the funny car races to check on Kathy's whereabouts and discovers that she has followed a clue to The Little Wig Shop — the last known address visited by Kathy's friend, Dawn. Sure enough, that's where Kathy is, questioning Mrs. Pringle about Dawn. Since Mrs. Pringle is not as idiotic as her son, she merely feeds Kathy enough information to get her to leave. But on the way back to her car, Kathy decides the old bag's answers didn't seem entirely on the up-and-up. She decides to "hide" her car — by backing it up four feet! (No kidding.) Then she sneaks back to the house to do some undercover investigating of her own. Sure enough, she runs into Rodney, waving around the same giant machete he had earlier (although it is slightly stained now).

The resourceful girl grabs a hatpin sticking out of a wig and jams it into his eye.

The police arrive with Dave in tow and find mother and son in the basement. There is a quick close-up of Rodney's eyeball hanging down his cheek — complete with the hatpin sticking out of the pupil! (This is the famous fish-eye scene.) Mrs. Pringle bellows, "Oh, my lovely wig business — all ruined! Rodney, you should just be ashamed!" Poor Rodney. Poor Kathy. Poor viewer.

Lewis shot *The Gruesome Twosome* in his favorite filmmaking city, Miami. "We didn't have any particular problems on that picture," he noted. "It was made to fill a hole in what we laughingly called our release schedule, and to support *Something Weird* in double-bill situations. Overall, *The Gruesome Twosome* did *extremely* well. It was made quickly, but it was the least troublesome gore film I ever made. Everyone had a good time making it. The cast showed up [that's always a plus], we had nobody pulling locations on us, it was simply a production-line kind of film. We had a policy of using every foot of film we could find. That did enter into the decision-making process of including some of the scenes which looked like they might not have belonged."

There were several familiar names in the cast of *The Gruesome Twosome*. Ray Sager was in the film, but he would make a bigger impression in the title role of Lewis's later gore extravaganza, *The Wizard of Gore*. Barbara Kerwin and Kim Kerwin also appeared in the film, along with Herschell's two sons, Michael and Robert. The campaign for the film played heavily on the story's black humor. Only one gore scene was featured in the promotional materials — the opening scalping, which is in fact the picture's best horror highlight. Screenplay credit went to Louise Downe, who also doubled as the crew's production manager. (She was the one who found the sheep's eyeball that HG rejected in favor of a fish eye.) Allison Louise Downe had been with Herschell since the beginning, and continued to work with him until the '70s. She was a versatile crew member, a good writer, and a functional actress. (She had appeared in several of HG's early nudie titles, but refrained from acting in his gorror efforts.)

Herschell took credit as *The Gruesome Twosome*'s producer and director, awarding his partner, Fred M. Sandy, credit as executive producer. As the premiere Mayflower Pictures release, the film's box-office business boded well for future Mayflower bouquets.

Chapter 13

Sex-O-Rama

> It was impossible for us to fall behind our shooting schedule. We always scheduled outdoor scenes first so that if it rained we could switch to indoor. A number of film people go out to a location, shoot the indoor scenes because they are more controllable, then it starts to rain or it clouds over, and they're trapped. They can't do the outdoor scenes, so they sit around and play gin rummy for three days. You can bet that never happened to us.
>
> — *Herschell Gordon Lewis*

Next up for Herschell was something that aimed in a different direction entirely: *Blast-Off Girls*. "I didn't take a writer credit on *Blast-Off Girls*, even though I wrote that one," Lewis said. "I usually don't take a writer credit unless it's a solo job. That picture was made as part of a package. The co-feature was *The Pill*. The actual title is *The Girl, the Boy, and the Pill*. Originally I wanted to call it *The Girl, the Body, and the Pill*, but it made more sense to call it *The Girl, the Boy, and the Pill*. We were able to change the whole campaign just by dropping one letter!"

Blast-Off Girls follows the sleazy career of rock promoter Boojie Baker, who convinces a young up-and-coming band to work for him. Boojie makes all sorts of promises to the band members, and visions of dollar signs and groupies are soon dancing in their heads. They agree to join forces with Boojie, and before long their name—"The Big Blast"—is up in lights. Unscrupulous Boojie arranges publicity and playdates for the band and secures for them a recording contract with a major label, all by coercion and corruption. Utilizing the T&A talents of a bevy of bosomy beauties to keep everyone happy (or at least silent), Boojie has it made—he keeps the money while The Big Blast blows their collective wad. When the band members threaten to walk, Boojie sets them up for trouble with the cops. In the end, it's beauty versus brains versus brawn, with Boojie on the losing end of the schtick.

Blast-Off Girls was filmed primarily in the Chicago area. The story included exchanges that occurred in a nightclub setting, and rather than build expensive sets or rent a club in the Chicago area, it was more cost-effective for Lewis to pack the cast and crew on a bus bound for Cleveland in order to shoot at a club owned by a friend of his. "*Blast-Off Girls* was one of the first pictures to have psychedelic lighting in it," HG pointed out. "We had all sorts of lights flashing around. Since it was a rock group picture, that was appropriate, especially for the year it was made. Basically the story was about a rock group and their manager who uses girls to keep the musicians 'tame.' But they finally rebel and the manager loses it all. It was a comedy-drama with rock music, but it was made before rock-and-roll got so loud, before the sameness crept into rock. In my opinion, it had some pretty good music in it."

Although the two pictures are miles apart in terms of production values, set design, cinematography, acting, directing, and just about anything else you can think of, some writers have drawn comparisons between *Blast-Off Girls* and the Beatles blockbuster, *A Hard Day's Night*. "The story is basically about the girls who follow rock-and-roll bands," noted Lewis, "so the only real similarity I see between it and *A Hard Day's Night* is that they're both about the rock music scene." HG takes more interest in the film from a production standpoint, as any director usually will when discussing one of his own works. "*Blast-Off Girls* is really about the rise and fall of an unscrupulous rock music producer, and it was full of very good, uptight [*sic*] music. It's not a bad picture at all, and it's fairly well produced."

Lewis did have some interesting production problems on the picture, though. "We had sound trouble on *Blast-Off Girls*," he disclosed — the sort of problem that could have removed the picture's entire raison d'être. After all, who would want to pay money to watch a movie boasting a soundtrack brimming with rock-and-roll when there is a fault with the sound? As Herschell explained, however, the problem didn't really affect the movie's music. "I didn't find out about the sound problem until long after the 'Captains and Kings' [the source of the music] had departed, and we could not then go back and re-record," he sighed. "What I had to do was try and filter the sound as best I could. There was still a problem, but fortunately, it didn't really affect the music. Other than that, *Blast-Off Girls* is a fairly well-made picture."

The co-feature that played with *Blast-Off Girls* was *The Girl, the Boy, and the Pill*, a melodrama with a dash of sexy elements to appeal to the viewer's prurient interests. The film's credits plainly stated that the picture was produced and directed by Herschell Gordon Lewis — something of a surprise since Herschell usually preferred to use one of his numerous pseudonyms on projects that relied on sex as a gimmick to get people into the theater. HG's willingness to attach his real name to the production of *The Girl, the Boy, and the Pill* suggests that the picture is a relatively tame, PG-minded affair on the subject of birth control — or lack of control. "*The Girl, the Boy, and the Pill* was not a comedy," Lewis stressed. With that title, though, it's doubtful many people thought they were coming through the door to watch a drama.

The story centers around a high school teacher who begins a series of sex education classes without the endorsement of the school faculty. The classes rapidly grow in popularity as more and more students become interested in the sex lectures. (And what teenager wouldn't? Just think of the homework assignments.) Eventually the teacher locks horns with the school board and is fired for being too forward-thinking. Undaunted, she invites the students into her home where she continues providing sex education in a less formal setting.

Lewis dismissed the film as a minor piece of fluff. "That picture is really about the relationship between a girl and her mother, who are at odds with one another," he said. "The daughter substitutes saccharin for her mother's birth control pills so she can take them, and the mother then gets pregnant and has to have an abortion. The girl and her mother finally have a reconciliation and all works out well." (Whew — we were wondering for a moment there.)

The Girl, the Boy, and the Pill is a prime example of bedrock exploitation filmmaking. Birth control, teenage pregnancies, and the moral and legal ramifications of abortion were hot topics in magazines and newspapers at the time. Opportunities, actions, and the consequences of one's actions invariably make for interesting melodrama, all the more so when they are related to sexual issues. Herschell couldn't have wished for a better combination of subject matter on which to base a film. "*The Pill* was a very timely movie," he affirmed. "During that period — 1966, 1967, 1968 — the birth-control pill was big news. Now it's old hat, but if you think back, abortion was a topic many people shied away from." And it was prime exploitation movie material.

Several cast members who loaned their talents to the production of *The Girl, the Boy, and the Pill* turned up in more important pictures for Lewis. Roy Collodi, who also was credited with the cinematography for *The Pill*, played the role of Pike Grover. George Brown, Valedia Hill, Kay Ross, Nancy Lee Noble, and Otto Schlessinger were all unknowns; but Bill Rogers and Ray Sager both did well enough to score leading roles in Herschell's next two gorror pictures, *A Taste of Blood* and *The Wizard of Gore*. "Bill Rogers was impressive, and I decided to use him again as the Dracula character in *A Taste of Blood*," Herschell commented. "In fact, I brought him up from Miami to be in the picture, which was a very unusual thing for us to do." Mulling over his statement, HG added, "I think the reason we did that was that it didn't cost us any more. In fact it had to be that, otherwise we wouldn't have done it." (The lesson to be learned here is that, no matter how good an actor you are, if you aren't cost-effective, you can forget about being in a Herschell Gordon Lewis movie.)

The *Blast-Off Girls/The Girl, the Boy, and the Pill* combination followed Lewis's primary commandment: Thou shalt make a profit. "We opened that double-bill in New Orleans at a 15-theater break [15 theaters all at the same time] and did quite well with it," Lewis enthused. The films continued to make a tidy profit wherever they played.

Probably the best known of Herschell's non-gore pictures made at this time is *Suburban Roulette* (1967). This was another sleazeball potboiler for the sex-n-skin market. As with all of the sexploitation films Herschell made after leaving the nudie-cutie field behind following *Boin-n-g!*, *Suburban Roulette* substituted suggestion for more obvious titillation. The MPAA awarded the picture an M rating, the late 1960's equivalent of a PG.

The MPAA's tweaking of its rating codes over the years has caused confusion in some quarters. The original set of codes — G, M, R, and X — was revised soon after it was created, with the M code, which denoted "Mature" material, dropped in favor of GP, standing for "General Audiences–Parental Guidance Suggested." The GP code was later transposed to read PG, which stood for "Parental Guidance." Years later the PG was augmented with PG-13, which functioned as a kind "hard PG" or "light R" rating. The 13 enforced an age restriction of "13 and older," as did the MPAA's R, which originally prevented persons under the age of 16 from viewing an R-rated film unless they were accompanied by a parent or adult guardian. (Did the MPAA feel that the proximity of an adult guardian or bona fide parent would prevent corruption of the adolescent's moral values?) The R code's age restriction was subsequently revised upward to 18, and later back downward, where it finally settled (to date) at 17. The X rating restricted admission to those 16 and older (later revised to 18, and finally 17). Eventually the X was dropped in favor of a new code, NC-17, which stood for "No Code" (a film that was unrated) with a 17- and-above age restriction. There have been no further changes to the MPAA rating system, although producers of pornography continued to use the "X" code, as well as "XXX" (never legitimized by the MPAA), to denote hard-core adult motion pictures.

In retrospect, *Suburban Roulette*'s M rating seems pretty much on the mark. "That was a very mild film," Lewis remarked. "There was no nudity, no profanity, but the concept was rather far-out for its time. It's about a bunch of suburbanites who swap spouses." In the film, the Fisher family moves to the suburbs to get away from dirty, congested, stressful city life — or so they tell their friends. Actually Bert Fisher (Ben Moore of *Two Thousand Maniacs!*) wants to put some distance between his lubricious wife, Ilene (Elizabeth Wilkinson), and her latest lover. All seems well and good until Ilene begins taking too much of an interest in the family's new neighbors, the Conleys and the Elstons. Innocent backyard cookouts and friendly get-togethers eventually lead to familiar indiscretions. Marty Conley (our old friend Bill Kerwin) and his wife, Fran (Ione Rolnick), are swapping one another with Ron Elston (Tony McCabe) and his wife, Margo (*Blood Feast* co-scripter Allison Louise Downe). Before long, Ilene and Bert join the party, but by the final reel everyone is feeling the guilty repercussions of mate-trading, and begins to make amends to untangle their emotion-torn lives.

The script for *Suburban Roulette* was not an H. G. Lewis original. "I just chanced upon the script and bought it outright," Lewis stated. "It was written by Jim McGinn, who had also written *Living Venus*." In both instances, Lewis rewrote much of the script, filling in holes the writer had left in the original story line. Lewis bought McGinn's *Suburban Roulette* script because the price was right, he was involved in more film projects than ever before, and he knew that eventually the script would come in handy. Lewis hadn't intended to make the picture so soon, however. "The only reason *Suburban Roulette* got made," he observed, "was that I had met a man named David Chudnow who decided he wanted to make pictures with me."

Chudnow had seen *Moonshine Mountain* and was impressed by the film's cross-breeding of good ol' boy humor and modern violence. Chudnow especially liked Herschell's mischievous *Moonshine Mountain* credits, which included a nod to the liquor industry: *Special thanks to Jack Daniels and Jim Beam*. "That film was full of little comments along with each title," noted Lewis. "Chudnow had seen this picture in Milwaukee and he asked the local distributor whose picture it was, and he drove down to see me." Chudnow had begun producing a series of television shows with narration by Akim Tamiroff, an actor from Hollywood's "golden era." Tamiroff had appeared in the title role of *The Great Gambini* in 1937, but by the mid–1960s he was working in low-budget horror productions like *The Vulture* (1967). Chudnow wanted to bring Lewis on board the series, but the director was not interested. "I advised Chudnow not to pursue [the series]," said Lewis. "Instead, if he wanted to make features, he should call me."

In fact, that's just what David Chudnow wanted to do. He asked Herschell what kind of feature they would make, and

HG responded by showing him the *Suburban Roulette* script. That was good enough for Chudnow. Once he helped set up the production budget, they were in business. Jim McGinn, who billed himself as James Thomas III, shared a screenwriting credit on *Suburban Roulette* with Lewis, who pulled his Sheldon Seymour persona out of the hat, dusted it off, and slapped it on the screen. Lewis did use his real name for the producer-director credit, however.

"We shot *Suburban Roulette* somewhere near O'Hare Field," recalled Lewis. There was some concern about the quality of the live sound recording because of the constant takeoff and approach of jet planes overhead. Filming would be problematic. Only Herschell Gordon Lewis would attempt such a feat. Roger Corman probably would have scheduled a substitute location at the cost of a day's shooting. Ed Wood — well, Ed Wood might have attempted it, but he would have rewritten his script to include the noise pollution whether doing so made any sense or not. HG proclaimed that working around the noise wasn't all that difficult. "We had no trouble shooting it," he asserted. "It just meant we had to time our takes carefully." *Very* carefully.

Herschell was more concerned with his *Suburban Roulette* cast — specifically Ben Moore, who had a knack for upsetting the status quo. "Ben was a very good actor, but difficult to work with," HG said. "He had a terrible case of foot-in-mouth disease. Some girl had agreed to let us use her car for something or other, and I thought that was extremely nice of her. Well, Ben Moore went over and told her, 'These fellows will really take care of you for that. You can count on some good money.' There had been no money discussed whatsoever!" Naturally, it fell on Herschell's shoulders to explain that Ben Moore was not speaking for the film's producers when he opened his big, fat mouth. "That was the kind of thing Ben would do," HG allowed. "At the end of the day we gave away the Ben Moore Award to whatever person had been 'Moored' that day, which was anyone who had run afoul of Ben's tactlessness. He was a good actor, a very intense actor, which I liked, because it tends to pull up the actors around you when you take a serious view of what you're doing. Most of these people that we were using were laughing and scratching and didn't really give a damn. Ben Moore gave a damn. He knew his lines, he was there on time, and that appealed to me. In comparison, Bill Kerwin was a natural actor. Ben Moore was a fabricated actor. That is, he didn't have the natural talent that Kerwin had. But he made up for it by the intensity of his approach."

With a clutch of recent moneymakers under his belt, HG decided it was time to try a more upscale production. And what better arena in which to spend extra money than the one he knew best — the gore arena? H. G. Lewis had begun thinking about making a horror movie "epic." The tasteful title would be *A Taste of Blood*.

CHAPTER 14

Gouts of Blood

[The actress] refused to topple into the pool. She said something like "it's cold down there!" I said, "It's hot in hell, which is where you will be if you screw up another take."

— *Herschell Gordon Lewis*

When *The Gruesome Twosome* turned out to be such a success for Mayflower Pictures, H. G. Lewis's other current production partner, Sid Reich, urged Lewis to move ahead with another horror-oriented piece. Herschell was interested in doing another picture with Reich, but he didn't want it to turn into the kind of rush job that *The Gruesome Twosome* had become. He envisioned a film that had a lot of on-screen production value to it: big sets, imaginative costuming, moody lighting — perhaps even decent acting for a change. It might have been that, after a string of recent low-budget features, but HG had forgotten about his own formula for filmmaking success: There is no correlation between a well-made movie and its profit percentage. By the time he made his "upscale" horror movie and got it into theaters, he would be reminded of that equation, because *A Taste of Blood* was not a huge success. In fact, it wasn't even a minor success. Actually, it hardly earned anything. Oh, let's be perfectly frank: "It never made a nickel," confessed Lewis.

Nevertheless, HG felt that *A Taste of Blood* was his best picture. Not his best gorror picture, but his best picture of *any* type. "*A Taste of Blood* was my 'big' picture," asserted Lewis. "About a year before we got underway with [it], a fellow named [Donald] 'Dok' Stanford had come into my office with a script under his arm. Dok was a decent guy, but he was something of a joke. He was a joke because *he himself* was a cliché — an unsuccessful Hollywood type who was about to sell a script. At that time, whenever you met someone who was about to sell a script, it was always to either Sammy Davis, Jr., or Frank Sinatra. Why they picked those two, I don't know. So when he told me this I replied simply, 'Forget it. You're not in my ballpark.'"

Herschell figured that anyone who had a script they thought was worthy of Sinatra's attention was going to want way too much money. The discussion might have ended there except that Herschell noticed the odd way the script was put together. "It just did not look like a professional script," he noted. "Stanford had written it on about 14 different kinds of paper. Some of it was typed, and some of it was even handwritten. I had no idea what he had done before [in the film business] because I dismiss what everybody tells me as bullshit when they come to me with a script. After all, why would anybody come to me with what I pay?" Stanford tried to be reasonable. He said he was willing to sacrifice his multi-colored screenplay for a mere $7,500 — slightly more than the entire budget of *The Adventures of Lucky Pierre*. "I just laughed," said Lewis.

Eventually, however, Stanford sold the script to Lewis, although not for anywhere near his original asking price. (Apparently neither Sinatra nor Davis was interested.) The story was entitled *The Secret of Dr. Alucard*, which is the name "Dracula" spelled backward, as most horror fans are well aware. Stanford's title was a tip of the hat to the 1939 Universal film, *Son of Dracula*, which featured Lon Chaney, Jr., as Count Alucard.

"I became very friendly with Dok Stanford after a year or so of screwing around with his script," Lewis recalled. "Finally, Sid Reich and I made the picture. And it made well, which is the sign of a professional writer. Some films are hard to make. *Something Weird* was hard to make, for example. But *A Taste of Blood* fit together well. The sequence of it made sense. So I had to hand it to Dok Stanford; he had written a professional script, no matter how many different kinds of paper he had used. And whatever hard times Dok had fallen upon that he was forced to sell that script to me instead of Frank Sinatra or Sammy Davis, Jr., or even Christopher Lee [who was still making Dracula movies for Hammer at the time], at least it all worked out well. As a matter of fact, Bill Rogers even looked a little like Christopher Lee." (Just don't tell that to Christopher Lee.)

Although most fans seem to prefer *Two Thousand Maniacs!* Herschell felt that *A Taste of Blood* had greater production values, better acting, moodier photography, and a more interesting story line than his tale of southern inhospitality. "I regard *A Taste of Blood* as undoubtedly my best picture," Lewis stressed, "but if you see it with all the gore cut out, as has happened at some showings I've heard about, then you don't see much of a film. I had cooperation on that film that no one has had before or since. It's two hours long and it's heavily produced. You could almost think of it as *Gore with the Wind*."

It's also the picture on which HG finally employed his favorite unused tag line: "Gouts of Blood." As far back as *Blood Feast*, Lewis had wanted to use this phrase in his film's promotional materials, but at the time, David Friedman objected. (Friedman just didn't seem to understand that one word can sometimes have two different meanings.) With *A Taste of Blood* Lewis used the phrase in newspaper ad mats as well as the one-sheet poster and the campaign pressbook: "A Ghastly Tale Drenched with GOUTS OF BLOOD Spurting from the Writhing Victims of a Madman's Lust!" In addition, other nightmarish claims adorned the ads. "Will Dracula's Avenger Turn Loose His Wrath into the 1970's? ... The Most BLOODCURDLING Motion Picture of All Time! ... A Spectacular Experience in Terror You'll Remember All Your Life, in Shocking Color! ... Only a Stake Through Her Heart Could Appease His Appalling Passion! ... The Most Terrifying Picture of All Time!" (Lewis was obviously a subscriber to the theory of hyperbole.)

A Taste of Blood was filmed in the Coral Gables area of Florida. Lewis recalled, "A man named Bent Kaaber let us use his house and drag our filthy cables across his beautiful white shag carpet. We could not have been more grateful." (Beware if someone named H. G. Lewis shows up at your house with a bunch of camera equipment.)

"Gouts of Blood" at last! And at more than 100 minutes, *A Taste of Blood* is the longest-running film Lewis ever made, as well as the most costly. "There was a lot of production value in that picture," recalled Lewis, "and it never made a dime"—even when paired with a little-seen travesty entitled *Teen-Age Strangler*, which Lewis acquired to beef up the bill.

The film is basically a modernized spin-off of Bram Stoker's *Dracula*. Early in the story, John Stone (Bill Rogers), a successful and wealthy businessman, receives a mysterious parcel from England. The outside of the package is marked "Of gravest urgency." (Sort of a play on words there, y'see.) Inside the package Stone finds a cask containing two ancient bottles of slivovitz, a Yugoslavian brandy. There is also a note enclosed which asks that he drink the brandy in honor of an ancestor on his mother's side of the family. This ancestor has also bequeathed some property in England to Stone.

Although Stone's wife, Helene (Elizabeth Wilkinson), warns John against imbibing the unknown brand of brandy, he ignores her protestations and pours out his first glassful. Since he doesn't keel over, turn green, sneeze, cough, belch, or otherwise do anything distasteful, John figures the slivovitz is just what it purports to be. He makes room for the cask in his liquor cabinet and routinely pours himself a snifter each day. Eventually, Stone begins to experience weird side effects from the brandy. He grows moody and distant. By the time he has finished off both bottles, he has become a night prowler, sleeping when the sun rises, waking at the approach of dusk.

Worried about her husband's health and sanity, Helene reaches out for help from a close family friend, Hank Tyson (Thomas Wood/Bill Kerwin, back in bloody action after sitting out the last two Lewis gore films). She invites Hank to dinner one night so he can see for himself just how much John has changed; but to Hank it appears nothing is wrong. John seems more reserved than usual, but that's all.

"What we were doing with that was letting the audience in on what was happening bit by bit," recalled Lewis. "It's a classic Dracula story in modern-day dress. We focused on a descendant of the House of Crone, which is the basic Dracula family." (Where does HG dig up this info?) "He is sent some bottles of ancient brandy and instructed by the solicitors of his great-great-great-grandfather's estate to take one sip each day for a certain amount of time."

Stone travels to England to claim the land he has inherited, and while there he learns he has become a vampire by assimilating the blood of Dracula — a secret component of the brandy that was delivered to him in America months earlier. A descendant of one of Dracula's original executioners, Lord Gold (Ted Schell), informs Stone that he is in fact a descendant of the king of all vampires, Count Dracula. Stone responds by ramming a pool cue through Gold's body. There follows a series of grisly murders of prominent businessmen, all killed by impalement with wooden implements. Because Dracula was killed with a wooden stake, Stone, as his modern-day avenger, is killing in the same way.

"*A Taste of Blood* was the first film in which we used blood bags," Herschell noted. The low-tech answer to Hollywood's blood squib, these self-contained plastic bags held a quantity of stage blood, all set and ready to pop, leak, dribble, squirt, or gush, depending on the amount of liquid inside and the pressure with which the bag was struck. With one swat of a knife — or pool cue, as the case might be — the blood bag would be punctured and its contents emptied. Previously, balloons had been used to achieve similar results, such as the puncture/gush effect in the paddleboat scene in *Color Me Blood Red* and the dripping "kidney" from the same film; but the balloons had to be hit with a real wallop to get them to pop. (Prophylactics would have worked better, but they could not hold the quantity of stage blood Lewis desired.)

Actor Ted Schell was outfitted with a medium-size blood bag for his death scene in *A Taste of Blood*. The bag was fixed in place with long strips of waterproof first-aid tape to make sure the plastic material would not slip or slide, or work its way loose beneath his clothing under the movie lights. Once everything was set up, Bill Rogers slipped into his vampiric persona and Herschell gave the signal to roll film. At the call of "Action!" Rogers grabbed the pool cue and advanced on his cringing victim. At the appropriate moment, Rogers lifted his wooden weapon and thrust it straight at Ted Schell. With an agonized look on his face, Schell stumbled backward — and stopped. Herschell remembered, "We were standing around wondering what the heck was going on. Those little plastic bags, when punctured, would let the blood flow nicely. But on this take Bill missed the blood pocket, so — it didn't hurt him — Ted just stood there with no blood coming out." When he realized what had happened, Lewis called for a break. The camera was stopped, the latch popped open, and the film removed. Herschell wasn't going to pay a laboratory to process an unsalvageable film error. So he had another 100 or so feet of film leader to put to use later on.

Except for the upcoming swimming pool scene that would go so wrong that Lewis felt like tearing out hair (the actress's, not his own), the other effects in *A Taste of Blood* came off effortlessly. In the story, Stone returns to America and uses Dracula's ring to hypnotize his wife, maintaining her in a trance-like state. "That ring was made with concentric circles so that when the light hit it, it gave off odd colors to the camera," Lewis said. "It really looked as if it could hypnotize someone."

Sleeping in a coffin concealed in a remote area by day, Stone prowls the night for victims to satiate his bloodlust. Stone visits a burlesque theater where he meets "Vivacious Vivian" (Gail Janis), an exotic dancer. Under the spell of the ring, Vivian invites Stone to her apartment. When she accidentally cuts her finger, Stone succumbs to his blood thirst and kills her. "The Dracula character killed some of his victims in different ways," Lewis pointed out. "The girl who is found on the floor of her apartment, he disemboweled." This sequence, though shock-full of the usual Lewis brand of blood and guts, wouldn't hold a cooked leg to the disemboweling scene that was to turn up in Herschell's later "pièces" de résistance, *The Wizard of Gore.*

"There was a reason that we didn't elaborate on the gore in *A Taste of Blood*," Lewis revealed. It wasn't at all like the situation HG found himself in during the making of *Color Me Blood Red*, when a succession of unexpected mishaps ended up stealing the film's thunder and gory. (Oops — there went another bad one.) "Gore simply wasn't the *purpose* of *A Taste of Blood*," Lewis asserted. "Dracula would not have elaborate gore. The story doesn't lend itself easily to the idea of gore."

To advance his murderous mission of avenging Dracula's killers, Stone flies to Houston to destroy another linear descendant, Sherri Morris (Dolores Carlos). During the filming of Morris's death scene Herschell found himself at odds with the owner of the estate where the scene was shot. Lewis wanted the Morris character killed in a swimming pool, because he thought the effect of blood seeping through the water would be gruesome. The property owner was adamant that the pool area not be damaged or stained by the makeup props — including Lewis's stage blood, which (as Herschell always admitted) stained everything it came into contact with. "I was trying my best not to stain the stones outside the pool with our stage blood," HG said. "We had to be very careful. In the scene we were filming, Sherri Morris is talking to her lawyer — heaven help us, that was Sid Reich's part — and when he leaves, the Dracula character comes in and kills her."

Dolores Carlos's one-piece bathing suit had been outfitted with hidden packets of stage blood, rigged to split open at the slightest pressure. The effect was ready to go, but Lewis had a problem with his actress. In fact he would have several problems. By the time they wrapped the scene he had so many problems he was probably wishing he had traded in Dolores Carlos for Connie Mason.

Carlos was supposed to fall into the swimming pool and bleed to death, but she thought the water was too cold and refused to do the scene as it had been scripted. Lewis recalled, "I had her walk to the edge of the pool, and she hears a dog whine or howl, and suddenly the vampire is upon her and dispatches her, and at that point she was to fall into the water. But she stopped cold and ruined the take. She's standing there looking into the water and she said something like, 'It's cold down there,' and I said, 'It's hot in hell, which is where you will be if you screw up another take!'"

To convince the actress that she would survive her death scene with only minimal damage, HG proposed to demonstrate that the water in the pool was not really cold. "The place where we shot this thing did not have a heated pool," Lewis admitted. "We were shooting at night, another night-for-night sequence, and everybody was antsy to get out of there. Dolores didn't want to fall into water that was cold, so I turned to the crew and told them we were going to have to show her the water was not cold so we could get the scene done and get out of there. So in order to prove to Dolores that the water was not cold, the whole crew got in the water, myself included — and we literally froze!" That didn't stop Herschell, though. He was determined to get the scene completed that night.

"We're all standing in the pool, and I'm trying to talk to Dolores without letting my teeth chatter," Lewis continued. "I said to her, 'Now Dolores, when I call action, what you must do is clutch yourself. By doing that you'll release the stage blood which will seep through the bathing suit. You'll then fall into the pool, but remember — you're dead. Even though you may think with the first shock of the water that the water's cold, it isn't. We're all in here, see?' Of course, I'm standing there with my knees knocking together, lying through my teeth! 'So you must fall like a dead body and not move until you have to breathe. You should hold your breath about 15 or 20 seconds.' Somehow, I just didn't think this was going to come off."

Lewis was right on the money with that judgment. Dolores didn't care how many people got into the water, she simply didn't intend to follow them in. Lewis decided to start shooting anyway; the longer they stood around arguing, the later it got and the more frazzled everyone's nerves became. "Well, the first thing that happened on the second take was that she clutched herself, rupturing all the blood bags and releasing the blood — but then she refused to topple into the pool," Lewis said. "I didn't know *what* to do. We're standing around in this damnably cold water, and here's this bathing suit that is now destroyed. I had to send somebody out to find another bathing suit. We finally got the other bathing suit and we re-rigged it, and set up the scene again."

And again there was more trouble. "This time she fell in the water, but as soon as she hit the water she began a dog-paddle that drenched everybody within three city blocks," said Lewis. "She climbed to the side of the pool and pulled herself out, saying, 'This is *terribly* cold,' and as she climbed out she got *all* that stage blood all over the outside area of that pool." By now Herschell was ready to kill for real. "I thought it would have been nice if we had left the blood in the water. And the girl, for that matter," he growled. He ended up redoing the crucial part of the scene over again, this time with a girl that was working on the crew. "The girl on the crew was about the same size as Dolores Carlos," said Lewis, "so she was able to wear the bathing suit, and she fell into the water with no problems. But I had to avoid a jump cut, so we used a different angle. Then we had to sit around with muriatic acid, scrubbing down the outside area of the pool for about two hours." Ah, the joys of independent filmmaking.

While the vampiric Stone is in Texas killing Sherri Morris, his influence over his wife dissipates, and she calls Hank Tyson to discuss her husband's odd behavior. Coincidentally, Dr. Howard Helsing (Otto Schlessinger) arrives from Europe with evidence that links Stone to the English murders. Hank defends his friend, but is secretly disturbed by Helsing's newspaper clippings and other circumstantial evidence that suggests Stone had something to do with the murders.

Stone returns home and learns that Helsing has been there. He plots the doctor's demise, but Detective Crane (Lawrence Tobin) arrives to arrest Stone for the murder of "Vivacious Vivian." Stone escapes and returns to his secret lair, hypnotically willing Helene to join him there. "We had a girl named Elizabeth Wilkinson who played that role," reported Lewis. "She had also been in *Suburban Roulette*. She and my cameraman, Andy Romanoff, became interested in each other, and as their relationship progressed, Andy began moving slower and slower [setting up camera shots]. He became so slow that finally, in desperation, I grabbed the camera myself, which I didn't really want to do on that picture." Wilkinson and Romanoff were married about six months after filming was finished.

Ad mats for *A Taste of Blood* and *Teenage Strangler* used the same photo, making it impossible to tell which film actually contained the shot. (The correct answer? The screaming lass is a victim of the *Teen-Age Strangler*— much like the paying audience.)

In the picture's climax, Hank, Dr. Helsing, and the police trail Helene to Stone's hideaway. "We had policemen running around shooting blanks for this scene," Herschell related. "Everything seemed to be going fine until some back-up police cars pulled in [to the film location] and saw their own police cars working for us. Suddenly we had sirens, we had flashing lights, we had the entire neighborhood down our necks. The police were concerned about us shooting guns off at night. And they were right — we should not have had the guns go off, but at night they have a nice muzzle flash that you just can't get in daylight. In daylight you hear the *bang*, but you don't see anything. We wanted to have the muzzle flash."

In the climactic showdown, Stone uses the unholy strength of the vampire to overcome his human adversaries, but the morning sun's rays force him back into his coffin and Helsing grabs the opportunity to drive a stake into his heart. As Dracula's descendant perishes at last, Helene recovers from her trance. Her husband is dead, but Hank's presence reassures her that life is still worth living. (Break out some more corn, folks.)

"We did have a nice gore effect, or what you might call a splatter effect, in *A Taste of Blood* when the Dracula character is staked in the end," opined Lewis. "The blood really *gushed* out. We used the same setup as in *The Gruesome Twosome*, where the idiot son slices open the girl's neck [employing a blood pump and plastic tubing], and it spurted nobly."

Helping behind the camera on *A Taste of Blood* once again was Bill Kerwin, acting as the unit's production manager. Working alongside him, in a larger capacity this time around, was ever-dependable Allison Louise Downe, who nabbed an Assistant Director credit.

Way down in the casting credits were two interesting names: Sidney Jaye and Sheldon Seymour. Seymour, of course, was one of Lewis's favorite pseudonyms. Although normally Herschell did not appear in his pictures (except by proxy when he overdubbed narration, radio announcer voices, and the like), he took on the role of the British Seaman in *A Taste of Blood* because the actor he had hired for the part never showed up on the set. "The fellow that I wanted to play that scene was a Britisher," said Lewis. "He had a marvelous accent, but come shooting time, he didn't show. Anyway, somebody on the crew — I can't remember who — had a motorcycle, and rushed over to the guy's apartment. There was nobody there. Now we were in real trouble, because we had made arrangements to shoot on board an actual steamship at the Miami docks. I had made arrangements with Emerald Lines' public relations people, who were willing to help out, but they were only going to be able to give us one hour to get on board the boat and shoot the scene while the longshoremen were on their dinner hour. Get on and get off! The longshoremen threatened to throw our equipment in the water if we didn't get off in time!"

Naturally, Lewis was not going to pace back and forth waiting for his tardy actor to show. In such a trying circumstance as this, there was only one thing to do. (No, not call for Scott Hall — he wasn't working the crew on *A Taste of Blood*.) "Bob Vercruse, one of our crew, donated some of his hair to make a mustache, and I played the part of the limey sailor myself," related Lewis. The crew quickly glued the mustache to Herschell's face, helping conceal his features — although why anyone thought it was necessary to disguise him in the first place remains a mystery.

Lewis continued, "I had a stocking cap pulled down over my head, I had this bristling mustache which rolled all the way out to my ears, and I spoke in a thick cockney kind of British accent. I figured nobody would know who it was." No doubt Herschell was surprised at the end of the film shoot, when a fellow watching the rushes turned to him and said, "What are *you* doing in this picture?"

"You can imagine my chagrin," laughed Lewis. "So much for my disguise!"

Even with Lewis's last-minute sailor substitution, the unit managed to abide by Emerald's instructions and get the filming completed on time. "I had explained to them that we were making a horror picture," said Lewis, "and they let us use their hoist to lift up our vampire casket and deposit it in the ship's hold. It was an unearthly scene because that's the only thing in the ship's hold. The vampire goes down to check to make sure the casket is there. The Emerald staff even stopped the [passengers] from getting off, just so we could get shots of them as they disembarked. They were very cooperative." And so were the cast and crew of *A Taste of Blood*, what with the longshoremen standing behind them with their stopwatch ticking.

Sidney Jaye, whose name appeared near the bottom of the film's cast credits, was actually the film's executive producer and HG's investment partner on this endeavor, Sid Reich. He was playing the part of a lawyer. The role was so insignificant that the character wasn't even dignified with a name. "Sid Reich was so bad in that picture, I had to get rid of most of the stuff with him in it," Lewis said. "He was just unbelievable. He was the world's worst actor. He could not say 'Dinner is served.' He could not say 'Tennis, anyone?' He could not say, 'Captain, the enemy approaches.' He couldn't read a *line*. He was that terrible. He had one line, which was something like, 'Well, Joan, your affairs are in good order and I'll see you tomorrow.' I screwed around half the night trying to get him to say that, knowing I was going to have to cut it, too. I only kept two lines of his dialogue, which I had to retain for the plotline."

A Taste of Blood was not only a comparatively "big" production for Herschell Gordon Lewis; it was the longest-running film he ever made. A large chunk of the budget was eaten up by the purchase of raw film stock and laboratory processing costs. Because Lewis considered the film a major project, he focused as much as possible on directing chores, leaving other tasks in the hands of the crew. While he operated the camera on early films like *Blood Feast*, *Boin-n-g!*, and *The Adventures of Lucky Pierre*, that duty was assigned to Andy Romanoff on *A Taste of Blood*. The crew supervisor, or crew chief, was Roy Collodi. Sound recording (David Friedman's specialty in the "old" days) was handled by Alan Tadie. The picture even boasted an "assistant to the producer," L. G. "Pat" Patterson, Jr.—the man who worked on the gore effects for *Moonshine Mountain* (most of which ended up on the cutting room floor). This was in marked contrast to the early H. G. Lewis films, which employed crews so tiny that there was no one available to work the actors' clapper sticks.

Lewis turned over the editing duties on *A Taste of Blood* to Richard Brinkman, who scored a screen credit as Editorial Supervisor. "I knew this was going to be a tremendously long picture," HG said, "and I did not relish the thought of editing it by myself." Herschell brought back his old music composer, Larry Wellington, to score the film.

Besides the usual difficulties that manifest themselves during any exploitation picture's shooting schedule, Lewis encountered problems that were endemic to this particular production. "We had effects in *A Taste of Blood* that just weren't very easy to do," Lewis noted. "More money might have solved them; more time might have solved them — although we had one of the longest shooting schedules of any of our pictures — but given our resources they just proved very difficult to overcome. I'll give you an example. We had a scene involving a mirror that was supposed to reflect everyone in the room except one man. I did not want to get into optics to do that, so we couldn't do anything except position [the cast] to do it. Optics involved laboratory costs, and it was not within our budget."

The shooting schedule was a little longer than average by H. G. Lewis's latter day standards: 14 days. But, as usual, everyone was rushed. "I was personally exhausted at the end of that picture because we had a couple of 24-hour shooting days," Lewis recalled. "And this was dramatic shooting; it wasn't just shooting nondescript footage. It was a peak point, dramatically."

As filming wound down, HG began to enjoy a feeling of personal accomplishment that he hadn't experienced since the pre–Kohlberg days. "As the picture developed, I had a realization that what we were creating was a film that was technically excellent," said Lewis. "That may be why we continued to pour more effort into it than we would have normally. We finished on time and on budget, and it just happened to run two hours. It wasn't as though we set out to spend more money. But the picture did not do well at the box office. That was a terrible disappointment to me, because I knew it was a good picture. Everyone who saw it thought it was a good picture. It was a picture I felt I would not be ashamed to show to anybody. It had a different mood [than other H. G. Lewis films]. But not enough people saw it. And, as you know, there is no relationship between quality, or intended quality, and box office."

Although the picture failed to make an impression at the box office or in critics' notebooks, it floated around the industry for quite some time. In the late 1970s, *A Taste of Blood* was booked into — of all places — the Jerry Lewis Cinemas, to play — of all things — a kiddy matinee. Although the Jerry Lewis Cinemas went out of business many years ago, during their heyday they served two primary purposes. First, they played many of Jerry Lewis's later pictures, which hadn't made much money during their first runs. These were such titles as *Don't Raise the Bridge, Lower the River* (1968) and *Which Way to the Front?* (1970). Secondly, they were earmarked as family theaters: movie houses that parents could count on to show *only* nice, G-rated little pictures. The trouble was, not many G-rated pictures made much money, unless they were released under the Disney banner. (I mean, when a Jerry Lewis Cinema played a Jerry Lewis movie, and nobody turned up to buy tickets, you knew something was wrong.) The chain hung on for as long as it could before going out of business.

But before the Jerry Lewis Cinemas closed, they actually booked HG's *A Taste of Blood* for Saturday afternoon kiddy shows! (I was there; I can vouch for it.) Maybe some JLC bureaucrat misread the film label, and thought he was booking a Jerry Lewis movie rather than a Herschell Lewis movie — who knows? Whatever the cause, *A Taste of Blood* was one of the very few pictures that played to a packed house at a Jerry Lewis Cinema, and that happened only because the kids knew they were coming to see a horror movie! Unfortunately for those of us who went out of our way to catch the film, the version that played at the JLC theaters was totally emasculated. They cut every single *drop* of blood from *A Taste of Blood*. Jump-cuts were rampant throughout the action. The story made no sense. JLC also removed the vampire's entire demise from the end of the film, so that the story just seemed to end arbitrarily.

Well, at least the kids in the audience seemed to enjoy themselves — but then, they weren't watching the movie, anyway. They were too busy throwing Jujubes at the screen and aiming spitballs at the backs of adults' heads. (I discovered one still stuck to my scalp two days later. I thought I had been developing a boil.)

It definitely was not the best environment in which to watch a Herschell Gordon Lewis movie — especially one that had been mutilated as badly as some of his on-screen victims.

CHAPTER 15

Hellraiser

> We were filming the scene where the head goes flying through the air, and the blood flew out and got all over a brand-new pair of white Levis I was wearing. I was furious. I tried everything to get [the stain] out — bleach, everything. One day, in desperation, I dipped it in Axion, which had just come out on the market, and the stain vanished instantaneously. I was so impressed I would have written the Axion Company a testimonial, but I was never sure they'd welcome one of that kind.
>
> — Herschell Gordon Lewis

Neither Sid Reich nor H. G. Lewis was very pleased by the poor ticket sales of their big bogeyman extravaganza, *A Taste of Blood*. Herschell was especially disappointed, not only in the film's performance, but in himself for ignoring his own primary commandment: Thou shalt not spend money unnecessarily.

In a final effort to generate some profits for the picture, he repackaged *A Taste of Blood* as the top half of a double bill with a film called *Teen-Age Strangler*. Originally released to zero fanfare in 1964, *Teen-Age Strangler* was directed by Bill Posner and featured a young, "hip" cast occupied by juvenile-delinquent activities of the day, such as gang rumbles and drag races, while a teenage killer on the prowl victimizes his schoolmates one by one. Although the screenplay was obviously built around teen interests that were popular in the late 1950s and early '60s, Lewis ignored these chronological concerns when he fine-tuned the advertising: "A Caress... an Embrace... Then Defilement and Death!" screamed the tag line. "Budding Young Teenie-Boppers were this Bluebeard's Prey!" (Teenie-Boppers? Well, you have to remember this picture was being re-released at the end of the '60s. Even American International was thinking of making a movie called *The Day of the Teenie-Boppers*, so HG's advertising copy was reflective of that era. Not that that makes it any less embarrassing.)

Despite the revised double-bill campaign, the combination failed to generate any excitement whatsoever. HG thought it best to put the picture behind him and move on to something else. Unfortunately, Sid Reich had a problem going along with the program. With far fewer films under his belt, he found it much more difficult to gamble on a new film production — and lose. Lewis vividly remembered one of the worst mistakes they had made as a team. "We had formed a subchapter S corporation, a legal maneuver which allows you to have a corporate shell, but you are taxed as individuals. The IRS came after us, claiming that we couldn't have a subchapter S corporation because the bulk of our personal income was derived from film rentals. The government wanted all kinds of back taxes from the company. My argument was that this was not a 'passive' rental. In other words, it's not as though you have a building with 18 apartments and the people living there pay you a fixed rental every month. We called it 'film rental,' but everything was a hard-boiled negotiation. It isn't really rental, it's a commission structure, which is individually arrived at [with each picture's release]. So I'm in the middle of this particular argument with the government — and Sid Reich suddenly died."

Whether or not the Feds understood what Lewis was getting at, the bottom line was that they wanted what they perceived as "their" money. The IRS interpreted a "film rental" as a fixed amount of money that should be taxed. That amount would apply to a movie like *The Gruesome Twosome*, which made money, and it would equally apply to something like *A Taste of Blood*, which lost money. "When Sid died, his sons did not want to pursue this argument with the IRS," Lewis disclosed. "They just wanted to get out of the business, so we gave up the ghost to the government. A man named Abbott Schwartz took over the Sid Reich group of pictures, and I don't know what happened thereafter. It bothered me less than it should have, because I was making pictures right and left then. But I don't even know who owns those pictures today."

Herschell would enjoy much more lucrative partnerships with Fred Sandy and David Chudnow. In fact, his work with Sandy produced some of his best film material since the early years with David Friedman. Lewis's work with Chudnow also led to the making of profitable film ventures, but none of them had the impact of the Sandy-Lewis collaborations. "Rosamond Chudnow, who was David Chudnow's wife, had the idea to shoot a picture called *How to Make a Doll*," reflected Lewis. "She just loved that title." The title was not really innovative; there had been numerous "how to" pictures made in Hollywood over the years, such as *How to Marry a Millionaire* (1953), *How to Make a Monster* (1958), *How to Murder Your Wife* (1964), *How to Stuff A Wild Bikini* (1965), and *How to Succeed in Business Without Really Trying* (1967), to name a handful. Nevertheless, probably the best thing about *How to Make a Doll* was its title.

The film featured Jim Vance and Patricia Rhea in starring roles, with Bobbi West and Robert Wood in supporting parts. Herschell recalled, "*How to Make a Doll* was about a young fellow who invents a computer that can make girls — that is, the computer actually creates them." As opposed to being an absentminded professor type, the inventor is merely a nerdy professor type who's too shy to ask for a date. But with the automated girl dispenser at his fingertips, he can finally satisfy his every sexual whim. "It was a perfectly awful picture," Lewis charged. "It was supposed to be a comedy, although it wasn't particularly funny. It was just too harmless. David Chudnow's wife, besides coming up with the title, also wrote the script, I *think* — although it was never admitted." And that's understandable. Who, after all, would want to admit to perfecting awfulness?

In retrospect, Lewis felt that the premise of *How to Make a Doll* was too simplistic. "We shot that in Miami, but it's not the kind of picture we should have ever made," he reflected. "We just didn't have the budget to do it right. It needed effects that we could not manage. We used a lot of flash powder and smoke bombs to make the girls appear in a puff of smoke, but it was really the type of picture that Blake Edwards should have made."

How to Make a Doll was scheduled as a support feature for one of Herschell's personal favorites from his own production catalogue, *Just for the Hell of It* (1968). "That was the kind of movie that should have become a cult hit," HG declared. Patterned in some ways after AIP's biker pictures (*The Wild Angels*, *The Glory Stompers*, etc.) — but without the bikes — *Just for the Hell of It* recalled the youth gang phenomenon of the '50s. In many ways it anticipated the senseless urban violence that arose out of the real-world thug gangs, like the Crips and the Bloods, which dominated inner-city ghettoes in the 1990s. "Get Off the Street," exclaimed the advertising materials. "Here Comes Destruction, Inc. They'll Smash, Wreck, Violate, Demolish ... Blasting the Screen in Color! Mothers: Hide Your Daughters! Police: Don't Turn Your Backs! Innocents: Watch if You Dare! Violence and Vandalism — the New Look in Madness that Laughs and Destroys Anything in its Way — Including Your Life!" Herschell certainly wasn't far off the mark; he was just 20 years too soon.

Just for the Hell of It was no more or no less polished than any other Herschell Gordon Lewis feature, but it received scant distribution. "You've Never Seen Anything Like This!" screamed the one-sheet poster. And Lewis was right: People hadn't seen anything like it. Neither did they know what to make of it, especially in markets where the picture played opposite *How to Make a Doll*—a combination as screwy as the early showings of *Blood Feast*, when it was paired with *Boin-n-g!*

"I had always toyed with the idea of bringing back *Just for the Hell of It*," Herschell confided. "It's the kind of picture that seems to go in and out of vogue. The problem with the idea of bringing it back was that the cars would have been out of date." (Nothing that an opening title card reading "Chicago—1968" couldn't fix, though.)

HG thought *Just for the Hell of It* was one of his most entertaining productions, but he was in the minority. "It's a picture that I like and nobody else does, apparently," he said. "It was about a bunch of kids who smash things. The picture opens with a whole group of people at a psychedelic kind of party. Their faces are painted, they're standing around on one leg, and in the corner is this one huge, hulking oaf. He's sitting alone on the couch and someone decides to empty a goldfish bowl over his head. He picks up the goldfish bowl and looks at it, then he throws it into a plate-glass mirror, and that one event sets off a general carnage of destruction which doesn't end until the entire room is demolished—furniture, walls, *everything*. There wasn't one stick of furniture left in that room when we were finished. We just emptied out the entire studio in that shot." And that was just the film's opening.

The actors, which included Rodney Bedell from *The Gruesome Twosome* and Ray Sager, destined to portray *The Wizard of Gore*, got so into the spirit of the action that Lewis filmed the opening scene without a single cut. "On the covering shot for that particular sequence, we ran over 600 feet of film without a cut," Herschell enthused. "I had two other cameras going for closer shots and particular moments of action. It turned into a fairly hard-boiled little picture, and we ended up getting an R rating."

Not unexpectedly, there were the usual missteps and mishaps in front of and behind the camera. An actress named Agi Gynes had been hired for a prominent part as one of the gang members, and she wanted to impress HG with her acting prowess and devotion to the project — primarily because she also wanted to be in Lewis's next picture, *She-Devils on Wheels*, which was going into production on the heels of *Just for the Hell of It*. What didn't impress the director, though, was Agi's inability to recite portions of her dialogue. She was almost a female counterpart to Al Golden, the man who couldn't say "identify" in *Blood Feast*. "This was one of those times when I spent the whole afternoon trying to get one scene committed to film," growled Lewis. "Agi knew her lines, but for some reason she kept putting the emphasis on the wrong syllable. Her line was, 'They shouldn't listen to that senile old woman.' Instead of saying that line the way one would normally say it, Agi said, 'they shouldn't listen to that senile old wo-MAN.' No matter how many times we repeated that scene, she kept saying 'wo-MAN.' It turned into another deadly day of shooting."

Later in the day, after Herschell had given up the idea of getting the scene finished the way he wanted, a light bulb belatedly popped on inside his head. "I suddenly said to myself, 'You jerk, why didn't you just change her line?' It was too late then, because we had already moved on to something else," he said regretfully.

Dialogue difficulties weren't the only headache that Agi Gynes created for Lewis during the making of *Just for the Hell of It*. "That girl put a pox on my picture," Herschell insisted. "She was a jinx, plain and simple!" The film's original title was *The Smash-In*. At the time the picture was made, more and more people were using the latest "hip" phrases — love-in, freak-out, be-in, sit-in, turn-on — and CBS also had the hit television series, *Rowan and Martin's Laugh-In*. *The Smash-In* seemed to fit his film perfectly, but Herschell eventually decided against using that title. "I figured it would be outdated within a couple of years, anyway," he reasoned. Darned if he wasn't right.

Just for the Hell of It wasn't a gore film, but it was definitely steeped in violence, and that appealed to the younger element of the movie-going crowd. "*Just for the Hell of It* could only be considered gory in the most minor sense," Lewis reported. "There is a scene where the gang cuts up one guy's girlfriend, and carve their initials on her. Other than that, there was no gore. Kids seemed to like the film because it was a slap at the establishment. But I think it was a mistake to release *Just for the Hell of It* and *How to Make a Doll* as a combination, because *How to Make a Doll* was such a terribly weak picture."

As filming on *Just for the Hell of It* began to wind down, the crew quickly prepared to move forward on Lewis's next production, which was filmed in the same locations and with many of the same actors. "It's always cheaper to make two pictures back-to-back if you're going to use the same locations," HG pointed out.

Lewis had already hired most of the girls he needed for the cast of *She-Devils on Wheels*, but Agi Gynes was determined to prove her potential value to the film. She borrowed a bike from one of the other actresses, climbed aboard, and gunned the engine. "Look at me, Mr. Lewis," she cried, as the cycle belched out a roar loud enough to be heard for three city blocks. HG said, "She had borrowed that bike from a girl we called 'Fang,' because she only had one tooth. She was sitting on the bike, waving her arms and shouting, 'Look, look, I can do wheelies!' Now, Agi Gynes could not do a wheelie even if somebody else held the bike up for her. She drove that motorcycle straight into the swimming pool of the motel where we were staying. 'Fang' was quite upset. She wasn't concerned about Agi Gynes, she was concerned about her bike. Meanwhile, Agi is flopping around in the pool, trying to pull off this dying swan routine. I wasn't buying it. We just ignored her. Nobody gave a hoot about her, anyway. We were more concerned with the bike and the pool." Priorities must prevail.

She-Devils on Wheels was made in response to American International's hit motorcycle melodrama, *The Wild Angels* (1966). The AIP film was the first in a long line of "biker" films that persisted in popularity for the next four to five years. Stars like Peter Fonda, Bruce Dern, Nancy Sinatra, John Cassavettes, Tom Laughlin, Dennis Hopper, and Jack Nicholson all played in pictures with such interchangeable titles as *Devil's Angels, Angels from Hell, Hell's Angels on Wheels, The Cycle Savages*, and *The Savage Seven*. The genre enjoyed its peak popularity during 1967-68. Although AIP would eventually make its own "biker bitches" movie — the embarrassingly titled *The Mini-Skirt Mob* (1968) — H. G. Lewis beat them to the punch with *She-Devils on Wheels*, a 1967 release. Lewis admitted, "Our film was inspired by AIP's biker films, but the difference, Jerry Sandy and I felt, was that it was time for a motorcycle picture where the girls didn't just jump on the back of the bike and grab the guy. We wanted to give them what nobody had before. We wanted girls who could actually ride motorcycles. AIP had women in their pictures, but the woman always sat on the *back* of the bike; it was the guy who was doing the driving. We wanted to turn it the other way around. And we had nothing but women who could handle a big Harley or a Norton or a BMW. These were rough, tough women. We gave them violence instead of sex, although the overtone of sex was always there because sex and violence work together in exploitation pictures."

When Lewis started filming *She-Devils on Wheels* in the Southeast, an actor-director named Tom Laughlin was making his own independent biker adventure called *The Born Losers* on the West Coast. (And American International was filming *The Glory Stompers*, Fanfare was doing *Hell's Angels on Wheels*, actor Tom Stern was preparing *Angels from Hell*, eternal teenager Dick Clark was readying *The Savage Seven*, Crown International was spending a little money — as little as possible — on *The Hellcats*; but none of these pictures would cross swords with Herschell's film the way Laughlin's project would. More about this in a moment.)

Lewis's stalwart sidekick, Allison Louise Downe, composed the screenplay for *She-Devils on Wheels*, but took screen credit under the name Vickie Miles. Her script provided the picture with a unique perspective — the female vantage point. She didn't ignore typical biker movie staples like wild parties, fisticuffs, wild parties, cycle racing, and wild parties; but the traditional male and female roles were reversed. Here, the gals were in control; the guys were the gang mamas (or papas), "owned" by the Maneaters. Lewis thought Downe's script was right on the money. Not only did it have the requisite rogue elements indigenous to the modern motorcycle melodrama as defined by Roger Corman's super-successful *The Wild Angels* — which every bike film scriptwriter was then using as a blueprint for their own take on the formula — but Downe had also tossed in a little Lewis gore for the hardcore fans. "There is some gore in *She-Devils on Wheels*," HG confirmed. "When one girl finds out her boyfriend has been betraying her, she hooks him to the back of the motorcycle and drags him around the [drag] strip until there's nothing left of him but a bunch of raw meat." (Still wearing clothes, incidentally.) "We also had a very fine gore effect in there involving a decapitation."

But gore wasn't the focus of *She-Devils on Wheels*. What Lewis wanted was a story that was a reversal of the biker formula, with the female as the dominant figure and the male as the subservient one. Downe's screenplay fulfilled HG's expectations admirably. But as was the case in 99 percent of the motorcycle movies made between 1966 and 1970, the plotline became subordinated to the film's action. These films simply did not have intricate story lines. In Downe's script the Maneaters terrorize a small town (it's *always* a small town) as they race their hogs up and down the streets, over hillsides, and anywhere else they choose. Betting on the outcome of the races, the chicks gamble away their men, who are swapped back and forth between the girls as chance dictates. But their 24-hour-a-day party gets interrupted when they run up against another bike gang — this one a more traditional, male-dominated consortium of thugs — and all hell breaks loose.

When it came to hiring actresses to play the Maneaters, Herschell was adamant that they get as many actual bike-wielding babes as possible. Any woman joining the production payroll had to possess three qualities: first, she had to own a motorcycle — preferably a vroom-vroom Harley or BMW, not a putt-putt Honda. Second, she had to know how to ride the bike, and ride it well. And third, she had to be at least somewhat attractive. (Notice how HG didn't list "ability to act" as one of the job's requirements?)

"We ran an ad in the Miami *Herald* saying we wanted pretty girls who could drive motorcycles," Herschell recalled. His temporary production office (in other words, his motel room) was swamped with women the next day. "They showed up by the hundreds!" he chuckled. "I'd never dreamed there were that many girls who could ride Harleys and BMWs." Still, Herschell didn't get quite what he was after. "We ended up putting together a rather motley crew," he confided. "We had one big, heavy, tough-looking girl, and we had one girl who had a baby on her back in a papoose. I was actually rather delighted with that. Some of them looked like the dregs of humanity, but there were one or two who were really beautiful." As might be expected, it was the lookers who scored the primary parts. "But of course," Herschell confirmed.

The leader of the pack, played by Betty Connell, not only had the look that HG was after; she had the big, badass bike, as well. Lewis said, "We cast in the lead role a girl who was truly beautiful, and whose motorcycle was beautiful. She had a Harley Electroguide, which was a magnificent piece of machinery." The bikes were put through their paces in several racing sequences interspersed throughout the film. The crew set up shop at an abandoned air field outside Miami, where they photographed the cyclists gunning their choppers across stretches of grassy land, churning up patches of dirt and weeds. There was a minor problem in that the airfield personnel had not yet given their permission for Lewis to film there. Nevertheless, Herschell pressed onward. "We had some great scenes of long, flat areas where one person — and it was usually me — would lean out the back of an automobile and show the motorcycles coming straight at the camera," he recalled.

Although he had been relying on such cinematographers as Roy Collodi and Andy Romanoff since the split-up with

David Friedman, Lewis went back on the camera to shoot some specific sequences for *She-Devils on Wheels*. "There were certain photographic effects I was determined to have in this picture," he commented, "so I took the camera away from Roy Collodi and did it myself. There were a couple of scenes where I was on a motorcycle, grabbing hold of the girl driving it so I could get the effect I wanted. It was not an easy picture to shoot!"

Character names used in the biker dramas of the 1960s were outrageously amusing. "Loser," "Heavenly Blues," "Mike" (a woman), "Funky," "Terry the Tramp," "Mouth," "Crabs" ("we call him that 'cause he's got 'em"), and "Frankenstein" are some examples. In *She-Devils on Wheels* Louise Downe gave the Maneaters and their male counterparts names like "Russian," "Supergirl," "Honey-Pot," "Poodle," "Outlaw," and "Doodie." But even some of the actresses' names would raise an eyebrow or two. Playing the part of "Terry" was none other than "Ruby Tuesday" (the title of a Rolling Stones song, in case you've forgotten). At this late date it's impossible to know whether Ms. Tuesday was a real-life biker or a pseudonymous cover for someone on Lewis's crew. And as Herschell would say, "Who the heck would care anyway?"

Several of the actors and actresses who had parts in *Just for the Hell of It* turned up in *She-Devils on Wheels*, including Rodney Bedell in the role of Ted, and Nancy Lee Noble as Honey-Pot. Roy Collodi had a small part as the bartender, but his primary role was behind the camera, as cinematographer. Collodi did passable work as far as Lewis was concerned — except for the picture's single all-out gore scene, which he declined to photograph because he was afraid he would get hurt. (What a wuss.)

As Lewis noted, *She-Devils on Wheels* was not designed as a gore extravaganza. Except for the body-dragging event already described and a few close-ups of knives slicing into outstretched fingers as part of the gang's initiation rite, the film only featured one particularly gruesome scene. Herschell described it this way: "The girls swipe one fellow's motorcycle and he takes off after them on another cycle. They lead him into a trap, where there is a wire strung across the road, neck-high. When he hits that wire at high speed, it slices his head off, and the head goes circling through the air and falls to earth." HG had storyboarded this sequence so the head would follow a very precise trajectory as it described a beautiful arc through the air, raining blood and gore all the while.

Lewis knew exactly what he wanted for the scene, but cinematographer Roy Collodi seemed unable to give it to him. "I wanted to use a CineFlex camera for this shot," said Lewis. "The CineFlex is old — it was made during World War II — but it could do things the handheld Arriflex couldn't do. It loaded like a Mitchell, and it could run at speeds up to 240 fps. That's *extreme* slow motion. But, the CineFlex bucks the way a machine gun will buck. My cameraman literally couldn't handle it. It kept getting away from him. He was afraid. We'd toss the head in the air and as it came down near him he'd turn aside, ignoring the fact that he had just turned the whole scene to the side. He tried it several times, failed several more times, and finally in exasperation, I said, 'Give *me* the camera!' I knew what I wanted and I knew how to shoot it." Lewis got a bit more than he bargained for, though.

To get the best shot of the decapitated head breezing through the air, Lewis decided to lie on the ground and aim his camera skyward. The head, like the precarious Teetering Rock in *Two Thousand Maniacs!* was made of papier-mâché. "That head was made by an art student from the University of Miami," Lewis interjected, "and I thought it was a good-looking head." It even looked reasonably like the actor portraying the infuriated motorcyclist, which was quite an achievement for someone making a film prop without access to body molds, plaster casts, and professional facilities.

With Lewis in position on the ground and the camera nestled against his shoulder, everything was readied for the take. "The head was getting pretty ratty by this time because we had been throwing it around for a while when Roy was attempting to film it," Herschell pointed out. Nevertheless, the team persevered. The head was doused with stage blood and tossed into the air. Lewis followed its trajectory as the head arced across the sky, finally dropping like a stone — straight down into HG's crotch. He wasn't as upset by the pain as he was by the fact that he had just bought a new pair of pants that were now ruined. "I had a brand-new pair of white Levi's on," he said, "and that's when I learned how tough it really was to get that stage blood out of your clothes. I had to go back to the motel wearing a towel around my middle, because no one would believe how the blood got there." Lewis tried everything he could think of to get the stain out of his Levi's, but the only thing that worked was a heavy-duty enzyme product known as Axion. "I tried that stuff and the stain immediately dissipated," said Lewis. "I yelled, 'Eureka! Look what I've found!' Our whole lives changed because of that. We were no longer afraid to tell people to get [stage blood] in their hair or on their clothes because we knew that Axion would get it out immediately." Wonders never cease.

When *She-Devils on Wheels* was finished, Lewis had it scored by Larry Wellington, who had scored most of Herschell's pictures throughout the 1960s. The completed feature looked good, sounded great, and played as well as anything he had made previously. Lewis knew he had a potential winner on his hands, but rather than distribute it through Mayflower Pictures with his partner, Fred Sandy, he wanted to sell it outright for a profit. "I was making so many pictures at that time, it seemed like a good idea," HG explained. "I showed the picture to a fellow I knew in New York named Jerry Gross who had a company called Cinemation Pictures. Jerry offered us $70,000 for the North American distribution rights, excluding Washington, D.C., where Fred Sandy had already set up a 30-theater release. So we would get the money, and Jerry Gross would buy the prints. I felt it was a good deal; we'd double our money, at least. Dave Friedman used to have a saying: Nobody ever went bust taking a profit. But Fred Sandy did not want to sell *She-Devils on Wheels*, because he wanted AIP to distribute it."

Sandy, whose son Jerry worked for the Washington, D.C., American International exchange, was very close to AIP co-boss Samuel Z. Arkoff. The Sandys thought that if AIP distributed *She-Devils on Wheels* the picture would be in the best possible hands, because American International was doing so well with their other biker pictures. In fact AIP was already working on their fifth motorcycle melodrama; the cycle was still very hot. (That there's a pun, as Mayor Buckman of Pleasant Valley might say.)

"Arkoff was a cigar-chomping lout," Herschell charged. "I knew going in that he was not going to give us a good deal. I wanted a negative guarantee, and AIP was not going to go for that. My feeling was that they thought *She-Devils on Wheels* was competitive with their own product, which it was: They were making one bike picture after another in those days. I told Fred Sandy this. Macy's would not go to Gimbel's to have a sale for them! I felt taking *She-Devils* to AIP was an illogical thing to do, but Fred was emotionally involved with this picture, because he knew he had something that would interest American International. He wanted to show off by making a deal to have them distribute."

In fact, although AIP would not agree to the kind of deal that H. G. Lewis was looking for, the company did play *She-Devils on Wheels* in combination with another independent biker film called *Born Losers* that had been brought to them by actor-director Tom Laughlin, the originator of the character "Billy Jack." Laughlin introduced Billy Jack in *Born Losers*, which Laughlin wrote, directed, and performed in. "I decided to let AIP distribute our picture in some territories, and in others we played it regionally," said Lewis. "AIP paired *She-Devils on Wheels* with *Born Losers* on a fifty-fifty deal. But as it turned out, we made far more money in areas where AIP was not the distributor. That's when I told Fred we were not going to see money from this picture if AIP handled it. It's also when I told Arkoff we would accept a negative guarantee, and it's also when he said forget it."

Ironically, Lewis and Sandy later played *She-Devils on Wheels* with *Born Losers* in their own regions, and the Lewis film was the one that got a percentage of the box office. "There was no question of what the exhibitors felt, because *Born Losers* was coming in at $100 flat and *we* were getting the percentage," Herschell laughed. Revenge can be sweet—and profitable.

The association with American International and Sam Arkoff, no matter how antagonistic, eventually led to discussions with one of AIP's top exploitation directors, Roger Corman. Although Lewis would soon travel to California to make a handful of sexploitation features for other producers, at the time he spoke with Corman his filmmaking activities had been confined to the Chicago area and the state of Florida. Corman knew Lewis's background as a writer-producer-director of sexploitation and gore pictures, and seemed interested in bringing him into his own company, Filmgroup. (It is sometimes erroneously reported that Filmgroup was an extension of AIP. Filmgroup was not an extension of AIP, but was Corman's own production company. The only AIP extension was Trans-American Films, a subsidiary that AIP used to release films even they were too embarrassed to claim as their own, such as *Teenage Rebellion* (1968) and *Bora Bora* (1970).)

Of his discussions with Roger Corman, Lewis recalled, "I was talking to Corman about coming out to California. I came very close to relocating to Hollywood. *Very* close. But Corman and I just couldn't get together on anything at all [in terms of film projects that interested both sides]. Eventually I became exasperated. I could not understand why, in fact, he had initiated the dialogue. So it came to nothing."

It's interesting to speculate about the turns Herschell's film career might have taken had the talks with Corman been more productive. Lewis could be in Hollywood today, still making movies. But it's a pretty safe bet that he would never have made another picture like *Blood Feast* or *Two Thousand Maniacs!*

CHAPTER 16

California Cowpoke

> Everybody at the Spahn Movie Ranch was either broken or crippled. The owner, George Spahn, was blind. What made it so difficult to shoot *Linda and Abilene* there was the fact that George had all these telephone lines running into the place. Everywhere you looked you saw telephone wires hanging down. It was very difficult to pretend that [our story was taking place] in the nineteenth century.
>
> — *Herschell Gordon Lewis*

As the 1960s drew to a close, so did Herschell Lewis's partnerships with other film production partners. Jim Hurley, the Triton College instructor who in 1967 had convinced HG it would be a great idea to make a movie about a witch's curse called *Something Weird*, now talked him into working on one final project that was something even weirder.

"Hurley had come up with an idea to make a pure G-rated picture," Herschell related. "In one sense it was almost a bleached-out version of the same story that he had come up with for *Something Weird*." Hurley had removed everything from the plotline of *Something Weird* that might push the film beyond a G into PG or R territory. Instead of a picture about a man who has an electrical accident and acquires psychic powers, he now had a story involving a man who falls off a ladder and acquires psychic powers. In fact, *The Psychic* was the name of the film. However, the film did differ from *Something Weird* in other ways. Instead of meeting up with an ugly witch who desires his sexual favors, the psychic takes advantage of his newfound powers to get into show business and rip off just about everyone he can. When his powers finally begin to fade, the people he snaked seek a little retribution.

Herschell produced, photographed and co-directed *The Psychic*, but it was not a Lewis original. In fact, it was the only motion picture Lewis was involved in where he shared a directorial credit with another individual. In retrospect, Herschell may have wished he had let Hurley take all the credit on this one. "When we finished *The Psychic*, the film just sat on the shelf collecting dust," recalled Lewis. "Nobody wanted to play it. Basically, it was an ego piece of Hurley's. Consequently, the only person who thought the picture had any value whatsoever was Jim Hurley."

Hurley was determined not to give up. He decided that since *The Psychic* could not get any playdates as a G-rated feature, he would splice in some sex scenes and slap a self-imposed X-rating on it; maybe then the adult theaters would play it. "When Hurley suddenly decided to add sex scenes to *The Psychic*," said Lewis, "that picture went from a G to an X. It was a soft X film, but it was a definite X. The problem was, the adult theaters didn't want it, either."

Now Hurley began to panic. There were nameless outside investors who were itchy to see a return on their investment. These investors were people that even Herschell didn't know — and didn't want to know. In a moment of perverse inspiration, Lewis advised Hurley to sell the picture to Stan Kohlberg. "He'll buy anything," promised Lewis.

By 1968, Kohlberg had given up trying to convince industry insiders that he was the man responsible for *Blood Feast*. Nobody ever believed him, anyway. He was now involved in other film pursuits. "I gave Hurley the background about Stan Kohlberg, so Hurley would at least know to exercise some caution in dealing with him," remembered Lewis. Sure enough, Kohlberg took the picture off Hurley's hands. The next thing HG knew, Kohlberg had slapped a new title on *The Psychic*. It was now known as *Copenhagen Psychic Love*. "Kohlberg had a Copenhagen fixation," HG explained. "He'd put the name Copenhagen on almost any picture. I'm sure that when he played the films in his theaters, he called them *The Copenhagen Sting* and *The Copenhagen Exorcist* and *Snow White in Copenhagen*. Maybe even *Debbie Does Copenhagen*. That was simply the mentality of that particular man." (Obviously, time had not healed Herschell's legal wounds.)

Lewis was still occasionally filming nudies for other producers in the late '60s. He made a handful of minor sexploitation pictures in California. *The Ecstasies of Women* (1969) was made to order for Tom Dowd; it followed the adventures of one man as he jumped from bed to bed night after night, leaving a trail of broken relationships and broken hearts behind him. A real tearjerker.

Another picture Lewis made in California was *Linda and Abilene* (1969), which combined elements of two genre staples, the sexploitation film and, of all possibilities, the western. It was the first — and probably only — western to feature lesbian cowgirls. The film had an unusual production history. "We shot that picture in California, at the infamous Spahn Movie Ranch," Herschell revealed. Numerous films had been shot at that location over the years, but it was something else that made the Spahn Movie Ranch more infamous than famous: For a while it was the home of one of the most notorious mass murderers of the modern era — Charles Manson and the Manson "family."

At the time that Herschell made *Linda and Abilene*, the Manson family hadn't yet embarked on its bloody killing spree — but Manson and the girls were indeed living there. HG saw them several times while filming his sex-western. "We all knew that there was a bunch of goofy kids living there," said Lewis, "but we had no idea how goofy they really were. We saw them wandering all around the place, looking like they were stoned out of their heads. They also had an old-time cowboy stuntman living there — I can't recall his name — who had performed one stunt too many; he could hardly walk. His horse was in the same predicament. It had to be at least thirty years old. In fact, everybody at the Spahn Movie Ranch was either broken or crippled. The owner, George Spahn, was blind. What made it so difficult to shoot *Linda and Abilene* there was the fact that George had all these telephone lines running into the place. Everywhere you looked you saw telephone wires hanging down. So it was very difficult to pretend that this was a ranch in the nineteenth century." But Lewis persevered, shooting around the telephone lines as much as possible. "It was definitely a strange place to shoot a picture," he said, "but the price was right." And that was the bottom line, as always.

Fred and Jerry Sandy, whom Herschell had last worked with on *She-Devils on Wheels*, were interested in doing a sex-oriented take-off on CBS television's hit comedy series, *Rowan and Martin's Laugh-In*. Once again, Lewis journeyed to the West Coast to make the picture (although he avoided the Spahn Movie Ranch on this trip). "We called the film *Miss Nymphet's Zap-In*," said Lewis. "It occasionally played under the abbreviated title, *Zap-In*. It was basically just a sexy version of *Rowan and Martin's Laugh-In*." Made in an impossible-sounding four days, the picture was a one-man wonder. Lewis wrote the screenplay, produced, and directed the film. In some ways, *Miss Nymphet's Zap-In* recalled his early smash hit, *The Adventures of Lucky Pierre*. Both films were built around a series of comedy blackouts with only the thinnest connecting story line. "Both of those pictures were very quick-paced," agreed Herschell. "*Miss Nymphet's Zap-In* was more visual, I believe. It was just a bunch of jokes, but more visual jokes than we had in *Lucky Pierre*. We had a very good time shooting it, and it was made for next to nothing." Nothing new there.

Instead of submitting *Miss Nymphet's Zap-In* to the MPAA for a rating, Lewis self-imposed an X on the film. "I knew if it were rated, the picture would get no worse than an R," he said. "We didn't have frontal nudity; there were breasts shown, but that was about it." Then as now, many movie houses would not play an X (or NC-17) rated movie, but Herschell felt that the self-applied X would help lure the thrill-seeking adult crowd.

But, as occasionally happened with some of the pictures he made for other producers, *Miss Nymphet's Zap-In* could not get played — anywhere. Although *Rowan and Martin's Laugh-In* was still a popular CBS-TV staple, its Nielsen ratings were on a downswing, and film exhibitors were aware of this. Eventually, Lewis and his production partners stopped giving *Zap-In* the hard sell, and chalked it up as a loser. Why waste more time, money, and effort on something that obviously no one wanted to see?

Funnily enough, when *Laugh-In* hit its nadir in popularity, eventually plummeting to the bottom of the Nielsen ratings, theaters suddenly became interested in *Miss Nymphet's Zap-In*. "There was an incredible backlash," confirmed Lewis. "By 1971 or '72, I couldn't keep enough prints in circulation. It was evolution in reverse!"

Although the film finally made money for Lewis and the Sandys, their partnership was drawing to a close. Herschell recalled, "Fred Sandy — whether because of advancing age, increased testiness, general cussedness, dissatisfaction with me, dissatisfaction with the world, or something else entirely, I don't know — had become a very difficult partner to work with." So difficult, in fact, that Herschell's last film with the Mayflower Pictures group became one of the most unpleasant he ever worked on. Its title was *The Wizard of Gore*— the picture that actually made at least one ticket purchaser sick to her stomach.

It would be a proud moment for Herschell Gordon Lewis.

Chapter 17

Here Comes Mr. Wizard

> I was displeased with the effects because I didn't get to use any carcasses. I wanted to use *dimension* on this film. I wanted a girl in two pieces. I never got a girl in two pieces; what I got was a girl with a bunch of blood and gore on her. That is not a girl in two pieces.
>
> — Herschell Gordon Lewis

"*The Wizard of Gore* is interesting. It's about a magician whose horrible tricks actually work. When he cuts a woman in half, she is cut in half. When he sticks a sword down her throat, there is a sword down her throat. And yet, to his audience, the illusion is merely an illusion. Of course, 30 minutes after the show's over, these girls fall into 14 different pieces." That's how Lewis summed up his latest gore extravaganza.

Filmed in 1969 but not released until 1970, *The Wizard of Gore* has the distinction of being one Herschell Gordon Lewis film that literally made somebody sick to her stomach. (I was there; I saw it happen. Well, I didn't *see* it actually happen, but I did see her run to the lobby with a hand clamped over her mouth. Maybe *this* was the picture for which Lewis should have dispensed stomach-distress bags.)

Herschell acknowledged that *The Wizard of Gore* went far beyond the bounds of good taste. (It even went beyond the bounds of *bad* taste.) He said, "After *Blood Feast* and *Two Thousand Maniacs!* were released, a sophistication/erosion process set in. Motion picture audiences were delightfully childlike in their early 1960s reactions to these films, especially compared to the brutally critical evaluation they make today. As producers, it's our fault — if we can call it a fault — because we have generated this reaction ourselves. We recognized that, having seen a certain effect before, the theatergoer will demand a greater excess from us in order to get shocked again."

Lewis had what he termed a "psychological rule" in mind when he made his later gore films: Sophistication increases in direct proportion to what the individual has seen before. He elaborated, "It's as though I spend years developing an act in which I stack 18 delicate cocktail glasses atop one another, then somehow balance myself upside down as a finial to the thin glass tower; while I'm standing on my head, I play the third movement of Beethoven's violin concerto and juggle a dozen balls with my feet. The audience goes wild — but the next time I do it, they say, 'Ah, I've seen this before.' It's like a person who uses drugs, who requires larger and larger doses in order to attain that 'high' that they're after. Our target audience developed a tolerance for gore, so to speak, and so we had to serve up greater and greater dosages. It was hardly sensitive of us, but it was sensible [from a business standpoint]."

Once again, A. Louise Downe jumped on board Lewis's latest pulse-pounder. Together, she and Lewis designed all the gore effects, just as they had seven years before on *Blood Feast*. Herschell's son, Robert, also contributed to the effects, and in fact, Robert was the one who sometimes physically handled the animal viscera — especially when an actor was reluctant to get involved, which began to happen more often in Lewis's final two gore films. This was partly due to effects involving eyeballs. Nobody wanted to handle an eyeball — which is certainly understandable, since Lewis employed, as always, the real thing. In the railroad spike sequence, for example, which comes about a third of the way through *The Wizard of Gore*, it was Robert Lewis who handled the eyeball. He repeated a very similar scene for *The Gore-Gore Girls*, which also involved handling and squeezing an eyeball. (A good example of a son's devotion to his father.)

Although the screenplay was attributed to the fictitious persona of Allen Kahn, it was HG who wrote *The Wizard of Gore*, using as his springboard the classic feats of magic. "I didn't want to repeat myself, and that's why I had turned *The Gruesome Twosome* into a comedy," Lewis said. "For *The Wizard of Gore*, the script relied on illusion, or the pretense of illusion. It wasn't a straightforward gore film, in my opinion. I didn't think of it when I was writing it, but afterward I realized it was almost an occult piece."

The Wizard of Gore was filled with new faces, in front of as well as behind the camera. Ray Sager was more or less drafted into the role of the maniacal magician.

One of the most horrific images in the entire Herschell Gordon Lewis catalog crowns this ad mat from *The Wizard of Gore*. When Lewis intimated that certain scenes were almost beyond description, he wasn't kidding. (Note the "R" rating, applied prior to the film's review by the MPAA. While Lewis anticipated getting an "R," *The Wizard of Gore* was released unrated after the Association threatened to give it an "X" rating.

Although Sager claimed to be an actor in films made in Canada (none of which Lewis had ever seen), he joined *The Wizard of Gore* as a crew member. "Ray might be a good actor," Lewis commented, "but he was only going to work crew on this picture. I had found an actor to play the magician in *The Wizard of Gore*, and he was ready; he had learned his lines and was set to go. Then in walked Fred Sandy, who began to argue with this fellow. I can't even recall what it was they were arguing about. But Fred Sandy had become so testy by this point, he argued with everybody. Eventually, our actor walked off the set and never returned! So I was stuck." Thanks to

Sandy, Sager inadvertently got the lead role in the film.

Sager had a good look: He was believable as an evil magician with occult powers, as long as he didn't open his mouth to say anything. He wasn't quite so bad as to be labeled a female counterpart to Connie Mason, but he definitely did not challenge the acting expertise of other Lewis movie talents. It was almost as if Sager was a student of the Vincent Price school of overacting. He tried so hard to be good, he overdid it.

Lewis agreed that Sager was not a world-beater when it came to acting. "The thing that Ray did best was drop props on the floor," Lewis noted. "He was quite good at that. We used to joke about giving out the Ray Sager Manual Dexterity Award." (Lewis might have thought about setting up a "battle of the movie props" event with Ray Sager and Scott Hall as the contestants. He could even have offered a $1,000 prize, secure in the knowledge that neither man would ever win the event, because Sager would drop all the props, and Hall would forget them all.)

Sager had played one of the young punks in *Just for the Hell of It*, and was serious about the art of acting. In fact, he occasionally became upset with HG and others on the crew who joked about the movies they were making. "Ray Sager almost became part of our permanent staff," said Lewis. "The funny thing was, he was a serious actor. I was rather surprised when he told me he resented some of the kidding we were doing about the films we were making. He took the craft very, very seriously." That's obvious from his Montag the Magnificent portrayal, but he was the only one who could take himself seriously; everybody else was too busy laughing. In other featured roles were Judy Cler, Wayne Ratay and Phil Laurenson. The remainder of the roles were victims, theater patrons, restaurant customers, and stagehands. The film boasted Lewis's largest cast since *Two Thousand Maniacs!* Besides the principals, there were also Jim Rau, Don Alexander, John Elliot, Karin Alexana, Corinne Kirkin, Sally Brody, Karen Burke, Eric Kelner Raynard, Sheldon Reis, Julie Yager, Charlotte Bell, David Atlas, Kathy La Du, Stephen Field, and Ali Amer — a pseudonym adopted by cameraman Alex Ameripoor whenever he stepped in front of his own equipment.

Conspicuous by his absence was Thomas Wood (Bill Kerwin), who had been in three out of five of Lewis's gore pictures, and the film certainly would have benefited from his acting ability. Pictorially, *The Wizard of Gore* suffered from a preponderance of medium shots. More close-ups would have elevated the drama of the story. In addition, the acting by Don Alexander as Detective Kramer was terribly stilted. In comparison, *The Gruesome Twosome*— which also had its share of poor acting — was a much livelier picture.

The action begins in a small theater dominated by a huge prop guillotine at least eight feet high. (Either that, or Ray Sager was only a little over four feet tall.) Appearing from stage left is Montag the Magnificent, resplendent is his classic magician's top hat, black tuxedo, and cape. Montag's first trick takes place between displays of the film credits. At a snap of his fingers, the magician's assistants step forward and move the guillotine to center stage. (Unlike other magicians, whose assistants are usually curvaceous cuties wearing the kind of glittery, skimpy outfits seen on Las Vegas chorus line dancers, Montag's assistants are a couple of guys who look like they would be more comfortable hauling garbage than picking up after Montag.)

The illusionist then delivers an eloquent soliloquy that touches on the very nature of self and reality. (Pretty heady stuff for a gorror movie.) The monologue is well-written; it's just delivered in an overblown manner. Speaking to his captive audience (which appears to be about sixteen people sitting in one of the smallest auditoriums ever constructed), Montag introduces himself: "I ... am ... Montag! Master of illusion! Defier of the laws of reason! A 'magician,' if you will. But, then, what *is* a magician? A person who tears asunder your rules of logic and crumbles your world of reality, so that you can go home and say, 'Oh, what a clever trickster he is! What a sly deceiver,' and go to sleep in the security of your own *real* world! How do you know that at this second you aren't asleep in your bed, dreaming that you are here in this very theater!?" (There's more, but you get the idea.)

Gleefully placing his head in the guillotine stocks, Montag releases the blade. A moment later, his head tumbles into the waiting basket with a thud, and Lewis takes this opportunity to treat viewers to the film's first gore effect: a medium close shot of Montag's exposed neck, still locked in place in the guillotine stocks. Blood bubbles up between shorn chunks of flesh and an exposed windpipe (which, incidentally, appears to be placed too far to the left, rather than in the center of the neck, where it should be). Streams of blood cascade down the front of the guillotine and pool in the bottom of the basket. Then, unexpectedly, an arm reaches out and tips over the basket, dumping out one of the worst fake heads ever seen in a motion picture. It's so stiff and non-lifelike, it could even be mistaken for one of the "talking wig holders" from the opening of *The Gruesome Twosome*! (Hey, you don't suppose...?)

After Montag pulls himself together, the audience realizes that this guy is no Lance Burton. Having wowed the paying customers with a state-of-the-art decapitation, the master of deception follows up with another stupendous illusion: pouring liquid from one hand-held vessel into another, until — with a deft twist of the wrist — the liquid "vanishes." (Well, it was *supposed* to be a deft twist of the wrist, but Ray Sager's ability to handle props sort of gives away the gimmick. Revolving the container 180 degrees before turning it upside down lets the liquid run into a hidden compartment, keeping it from spilling all over the floor.)

Is any audience who just witnessed a startling decapitation complete with protruding trachea and gushing blood going to be impressed with this $5.98 conjuror's trick? Not likely. Apparently able to "read" his audience, Montag decides he'd better pull out all the stops, so for his next illusion he promises to saw a woman in half. The audience groans. Not *that* old trick.

The janitors — er, that is, Montag's assistants — wheel out a gurney and Montag calls on a volunteer from the audience. Nobody raises a hand, so, using his uncanny mental powers, Montag wills a young woman to step onto the stage. When she is strapped to the table with locks and stocks, the magician then pulls out his saw. His chainsaw, that is. Years before director Tobe Hooper made a little movie called *The Texas Chainsaw Massacre* (1974), H. G. Lewis had stumbled on the idea of using a gas-powered chainsaw in one of his gore films. Lewis recalled, "When you make these kinds of pictures, you're always thinking of different scenes, different effects, different ways you could do them. The chainsaw, I felt, was such a wonderful tool to use, because it had never been done before, and it just fit the story we were telling. It just seemed a natural progression." Hopefully, Lewis had the teeth removed from the chainsaw before handing it to Ray Sager, who might drop it at any moment.

Gunning his chainsaw, Montag eyes his audience expectantly. "You were expecting a mere hand saw and a covered, wooden casket?" he teases. "Oh, no! That's the old-fashioned way of sawing people in half. Today, magicians are mechanized, too, and nothing will be concealed from your view!" With maniacal glee, Montag raises the churning chainsaw and brings it down, holding it against his volunteer's stomach. It is at this point that *The Wizard of Gore* crosses the boundary that separates reality from illusion and illusion from surrealism.

As the audience watches the performance on stage, they see a chainsaw seeming to sink through a woman's body without doing any damage. Their reality consists of a universe in which a magic trick magically works. But on the stage, Montag and his victim are living in another universe entirely. In their reality, he is actually killing her. The trick doesn't work; the saw blade does what a saw blade would really do to a human body. She screams horribly as the blade bites into her abdomen, shredding flesh uncontrollably. Lewis immediately cuts to an extreme close-up of the gutted girl, the whirling chainsaw pressing into a pile of *very* realistic-looking intestines. (Of course they look real; they were real animal intestines.) The victim cries out as blood sprays onto her face. In one of the film's grossest moments, she turns her head and actually spits out a piece of her own intestine. Then she passes out of this world into the next. (This was the scene that did it for my friend.)

But all is quiet in the audience. No one has died. There is no blood. There is no gore. And when the "illusion" has been completed, the two realities join together again. Montag's volunteer walks off the stage and reclaims her seat in the audience, apparently unharmed. Montag takes his bows, and the curtain descends. Who can say what has really just happened?

Lewis's script seems to suggest that the power of this magician goes far beyond the norm. He can hypnotize; he can do a real trick (the $5.98 tumbler trick); and he can somehow circumvent the laws of real-world physics. *The Wizard of Gore* is probably HG's most interesting story, because there is much food for thought available to anyone who makes it all the way through the film. The story's ending is as bewildering as anything that has gone before, and forces a change in perspective that turns everything preceding it on its head. But the real trick with *The Wizard of Gore* is finding the patience to sit through it. Like portions of Lewis's *A Taste of Blood*, the film can be ponderous at times.

In the scene that follows the chainsaw illusion, the volunteer from the audience walks to a local restaurant where she is seated by the maître d'. She seems still to be in a trance of some sort. As other diners are led to tables on either side of her, the girl snaps out of her trance—and at that moment reality catches up to her: She tumbles to the floor in the same condition that Montag had reduced her to onstage—completely gutted, pieces of her intestines draped across her thighs, blood everywhere. Yup, she's dead for sure this time.

Despite the intensity of the film's "chainsaw trick," Lewis was not pleased with the way many of the film's effects turned out. "I just didn't like the effects in *The Wizard of Gore*," he confided. "For the scene where [Montag] saws the woman in half, I wanted to show a woman separated into two pieces. I never got a girl in two pieces, what I got was a girl with a bunch of blood and gore. That was *not* a girl in two pieces! But it wasn't anyone's fault. That I was unhappy doesn't mean we didn't give it a go." When the effect didn't work as HG had envisioned, he was forced to substitute the gore close-up. The scene is still shocking, but perhaps not in the fashion Lewis had intended. He knew from the beginning exactly what he wanted, but the particular image he intended to capture on film just wouldn't materialize.

"The disadvantage of the extreme close-up, which I had to substitute in *The Wizard of Gore*, is that you lose your orientation," Lewis explained. "There is a disadvantage to a long-shot as well, because usually you can't tell what's happening. Normally, a gore effect has to be shot in medium close-up. And while the audience is going along with what is generally referred to as a 'willing suspension of disbelief,' they are still challenging you all the time they're watching the film. They're looking for the way you did it. So normally I want the medium close-up. Sometimes I'll shoot it with two or three cameras, to provide whatever number of angles I want. But in general, the medium close-up is the best shot for a gore effect."

The restaurant scene was, again, a compromise. "It could have been done so much better," Lewis commented. "I really felt let down on this one, but we were shooting in a restaurant and, obviously, I could not cut a hole in their floor to have the girl in two separate pieces. I would have used a platform, except that it would have had to cover the entire floor and we had such a tight time frame. I could have cut to another close-up, but you don't get that cosmic effect when you have nothing but a tight close-up. Every time I see that in a film, I feel cheated. With the tight close-up shot, which we had already used once as a substitution, you get the gore, but no positioning, no frame. You can shoot gore close up, but you can't 'die' there. You can show it close up, but then you have to show what it means. We showed close-ups of hands dribbling in it, but then you've got to back off so that people can really become horrified. When you get too close it doesn't mean anything." Although he had to compromise on the picture's second gore scene, and had used a substandard head for the decapitation scene, there was still more terror on tap in *The Wizard of Gore*.

After the first victim tumbles into a pile of grue in the restaurant, the audience is introduced to the film's nominal hero and heroine, Jack Ward and Sherry Carson. She's a television personality with her own show, *Housewife's Coffee Break*. He's a reporter and general snoop. On their way home they happen to walk by the restaurant where Victim Number One died, and as the body is taken to a waiting ambulance, Sherry's hand accidentally brushes up against the dead girl and is smeared with blood. She quickly wipes it off, but apparently she has been "marked."

Sherry visits Montag backstage, where she asks him to do an interview for her television show. The magician coldly turns her away — until he magically sees the smear of blood on Sherry's hand, which has suddenly reappeared. Promising to reconsider, he invites Sherry to see his next show for free.

The next evening Sherry drags Jack back to the theater to watch Montag's performance, which is exactly the same as before, except for the grand finale. Instead of sawing a woman in half, this time he promises to drive a steel spike through her head. The audience abruptly falls silent. "Come now, my skeptical friends," Montag intones. "A moment ago you were tired of my 'old' tricks. Don't tell me you're afraid of me now." He wills a blonde to join him on stage and locks her into place on an upright gurney.

The Wizard of Gore's spike segment is one of the most revolting gore scenes in the entire Lewis catalog. Viewers who watched the brains ripped out of the beach bunny in *Blood Feast* saw approximately 40 seconds of gore. By contrast, the spike killing runs a full 2:01 from the first pounding of the spike until the effect is over. Of that 2:01, there is 1:54 of nonstop gore. The scene unravels like this: The spike is pounded into the girl's left temple and when she screams, blood gushes from her mouth. (No intestines were vomited up this time, though.) Laughing maniacally, the evil magician works the spike in and out the side of her head, until he has made a large enough hole that he can insert his fingers and dig out a chunk of gray matter. (Except this gray matter is red matter.) Satisfied that she has now become a "dumb blonde," he puts the spike back in place and continues pounding until it emerges from the opposite side. By now, Lewis has gone from using an actress (with hair long enough to conceal chunks of gore) to a false head. Unlike the excruciatingly bad head that was used to represent Montag's self-decapitation during the film's opening titles, the materials used in the spike scene appeared much more realistic.

Whereas in his previous films HG would certainly have concluded the gore scene by this point, the gory stuff in *The Wizard of Gore* just goes on and on. The magician now reaches up and presses his thumb into the right eye socket, dislodging the eyeball so that it is pushed out of place to one side. He then puts his index finger into the eye socket and begins tugging on the gristle behind it. Because Lewis was utilizing a rubber face mask for this effect, the "skin" seems to stretch and pull realistically. It looks exactly like what you would imagine such a sight to look like in real life. (Kids, don't try this at home!)

But wait — there's more! Montag now opts to pop the left eyeball. In goes the thumb, wriggling around sickeningly. A whitish slime squeezes out from under the eyelid as the eyeball is ruptured. Then — it's back to the right eye to do some *more* damage. This time he rolls it around in the socket, pinching it with thumb and index finger so that it bulges outward (the "eyelids" even crumple inward realistically). He stops just short of ripping the eye completely out of its socket. This unbelievable scene finally ends — and not a moment too soon for the majority of viewers, I'm sure. (It would be interesting to know how many people walked out of the movie at this point.) "That eyeball effect was interesting," Herschell noted. "People find the idea of doing something to somebody's eyeball absolutely repulsive; they can't stand it. Ray Sager would not do the scene. He would handle all the other viscera — and we even used a calf's brain in that scene — but he would not touch the eyes, which we had set into place behind the mask on the actress's face. So, my son, Robert, did the scene. Those are his hands in there, pulling and twisting on the eyeballs. He did the same thing in *The Gore-Gore Girls*, which we made after *The Wizard of Gore*. That film had a similar scene, and, again, it was Robert who handled the eyeball."

To the theater audience — that is, the audience *in* the film — the woman on stage appears completely undamaged. There is a spike through her head, but not a single drop of blood is spilled anywhere. Montag pulls the spike out to thunderous applause, and the girl reclaims her seat. The show is over.

Jack and Sherry go backstage to confer with Montag. The magician still refuses to be interviewed on *Housewife's Coffee Break*, but agrees to do one "special" trick for her audience in the very near future. Jack takes the opportunity to tell Montag that the woman who volunteered for his sawing-the-lady-in-half illusion was found cut in two pieces at a nearby restaurant later that same night. Montag is regretful but can hardly be held responsible. The cops believe a copycat murderer is on the loose — someone who has come to the magician's shows and stalked the volunteers, then performed the gruesome tricks for real.

It is interesting to note that Jack's dialogue in this scene specifically states that the girl in the restaurant was found in two pieces. That is the effect that H. G. Lewis intended to film, but couldn't. Obviously, when Lewis made *The Wizard of Gore*, the dialogue scenes were filmed first. It's too bad Lewis couldn't go back to re-dub the dialogue so that Jack said the girl was found "a bloody mess," or something equally nondescript. But that would have cost money — a step HG was unwilling to take. (In another dialogue scene further along in the story, the same thing happens: A character talks about the condition of a body which doesn't at all match what the audience has seen. In the latter case, the problem is more significant because several characters all describe the same thing.)

At the local morgue, an attendant is interrupted by the unexpected appearance of Montag. The magician's sudden appearance is apparently supposed to suggest that he entered the room "magically," but instead of relying on a double-exposure or superimposition to suggest this, Lewis simply had Ray Sager crouch below the level of the camera lens and stand up suddenly. Such mystery! The attendant turns to Montag and says — unbelievably — "May I help you?" (Not "What are you doing here?" or "How did you get in here?" as might be expected.) As Montag steps forward menacingly, the attendant throws up both hands and exclaims, "Get ouuu —!" His voice is cut off in mid-shout as Montag's mental power overwhelms him. (A moment later the attendant has only one hand in the air; the other is held at his side, and he keeps opening and closing his fist. HG either didn't notice the actor doing this, or didn't care.) Montag steals the corpse of his latest victim and carries it off to a cemetery, where he deposits it in an open vault. (He does this with all his victims, incidentally, but the movie never explains why he does it. Oh, well.)

For his performance the following evening, Montag's show-closing illusion involves the use of a mechanical punch press. "This is used to stamp pots out of solid metal," Montag boasts. "Tonight we've made a little modification for this performance ... a stock to keep the young lady from flinching when the punch press comes crashing down on her body!" With those words he commands yet another pretty woman to join him on stage and straps her to the table underneath the punch press. Flipping a switch, Montag grins as the machine rumbles to life and the cylinder begins spinning. As he turns a guiding wheel, the enormous steel cylinder descends to the girl's bared stomach. A moment later the theater is filled with screams as the cutting metal forces its way into the girl's writhing body.

HG included an interesting shot from Montag's point of view as the cylindrical tower tears into the girl's flesh. Instead of a side view, or straightforward top view, the angle used here helps accentuate the gruesomeness of the scene. The actress wriggles her body as blood gushes everywhere, for a very realistic effect. With her insides fully exposed, Montag reaches down and begins pulling out pieces of intestine, liver, and other organs. As usual, Montag's audience hears no screaming, sees no gushing gore. When the trick is finally over, the girl appears to be fine. She returns to her theater seat as Montag takes his bows.

Later that evening, however, the girl's body is discovered, a hole punched through her stomach. Descriptions by the film's characters about the state in which the body has been found differ radically from the scene shown to the film's viewers. While it is obvious to us that Montag punch-pressed the girl one time in one spot, Jack informs a colleague, "This time he punch-pressed a woman from head to foot." A police investigation also relates a different story. One of the officers reports, "A woman heard a man screaming in the apartment next to her. She ran in and found her neighbor lying on the bedroom floor, holding his wife's head. The rest of her body was about five feet away. She looked like she'd been run over by a threshing machine." Even Jack revises his opinion: "Another psycho murder — this time a woman completely mashed to a pulp!" What is going on here?

What was going on, of course, was a series of gore-scene compromises. While Lewis wanted the effects in *The Wizard of Gore* to really go over the top, he was forced to take a number of shortcuts that ended up shortchanging the very images he was after.

Montag steals the body of his latest victim from the morgue and carts it off to the mysterious vault. Lewis's script is very foggy on what was supposed to be happening in these scenes. Was Montag trying to collect a specific number of bodies? Why? Did he plan to use the corpses for some kind of magical rite? Was the vault a gateway to another dimension? That the scenes represent something otherworldly is obvious, if for no other reason than that Herschell employed a red lens filter when photographing them.

Joining Montag on stage the following night are two "volunteers" who will assist in a new version of the age-old sword-swallowing trick. Montag brandishes both swords, advising his audience, "Imagine — no calories! An excellent way to get your iron. The only problem with swallowing a sword is that if you wiggle around too much, it may interfere with your digestive tract." He then rams a sword down each girl's throat and the screen runs red with gore. Although there is plenty of blood running out of the mouths of both women, along with chunks of something fleshy, which could be bits of tongues, tonsils, or plain old esophagus shavings (remember HG's comment about cranberry mix?), it's the least disturbing gore scene in the picture.

Two cops are in attendance that evening, but, like everyone else in the auditorium, they see nothing amiss. To them, swallowing a sword is just a trick. Once the show is over, the cops split up, each following one of the women in an effort to nab the copycat killer they think is committing the murders. In both cases, though, something happens that prevents the cops from being able to clearly determine what is going on. (For example, one of the girls stops at a red light, but continues to let her car idle after the traffic light turns green. When the cop walks up to investigate, he discovers she is dead, bleeding profusely from the mouth.)

Sherry receives a telephone call from Jack's police contact, who reports, "Both girls were found with their insides completely torn apart!"— another instance of script-versus-film ambiguity. Lewis commented, "That was just one more instance of being restricted by unforeseen circumstances, which made the gore effects defective, I felt."

The following day, Montag appears at the television studio to perform the "special" illusion he had agreed to do for Sherry's *Housewife's Coffee Break* viewers. It is at this point that *The Wizard of Gore* graduates from a sadistic horror film to a full-fledged exercise in surrealism. With the tape rolling and the studio's television cameras trained full on Montag's mug, the magician implores his audience to concentrate ... concentrate and lock their minds with his ... construct a mental passageway between their minds and his....

At the newspaper reporters' office, everyone is staring into the television screen — everyone except Jack, who somehow wills himself not to look. He jumps up and rushes to the television studio to confront Montag, who has built a raging fire on the studio floor and is leading Sherry and everyone else toward it. They have become somnambulists — easy prey for Montag, who is trying to kill as many people as possible with this one last "trick." But when Jack bursts into the studio unexpectedly, Montag's power over the others is broken. During the ensuing struggle, Montag is pushed backward into the fire, becoming his own final victim. The corpse is burned to a crisp; the wizard lives no more.

That's not quite the end, however. Over drinks at Sherry's place, Jack begins talking about Montag and his powers. Sherry admits that there are so many unanswered questions, she doesn't know what to think. (Ditto for the audience.) Then Jack does something very strange: He begins peeling away his own skin. As Sherry watches in disbelief, Jack pulls off the mask he has been wearing, to reveal Montag's hideous visage! "You fool," he hisses, "what makes you think you know what reality is?" He knocks Sherry onto her back and begins clawing at her exposed stomach. With diabolical strength, he actually rips open her flesh, exposing her ribcage and the organs beneath, and Lewis focuses his camera on the dissection in progress.

Laughing hysterically, Sherry reaches into *her own body* and begins tearing out the organs. A horrified Montag suddenly stops in his tracks — obviously, something has gone terribly wrong with this "trick." Sherry smiles up at him. "Do you think you're the *only* one?" she says sardonically. "You are *my* illusion!"

As his resolve dissolves, the magician whimpers, "But ... but I ... I ... am ... Montag...."

Then, more forcefully, he intones, "I am Montag!" And suddenly we find ourselves back in the little theater, watching Montag the Magnificent perform his illusions. In the audience sit Sherry and Jack. She leans over to Jack and whispers, "I think he's just a big phony."

Again, Lewis's original vision for the climactic gore effect differed significantly from what ended up being used in the film. "I knew exactly what I wanted to do," he said. "I had a perfect mental picture of it. Some years earlier, for *A Taste of Blood*, I had envisioned a man walking outside with dogs howling and photographing it using a blue light on his face. I knew that's what I wanted and I wouldn't have slept in my grave if I hadn't made that shot, which I did. At the climax of *The Wizard of Gore*, the magician is supposed to pull the girl to *pieces*. It had never been done. It would have been a great effect, where a body is literally pulled to pieces. I couldn't even have thought of this effect when we shot *Blood Feast*, but we had come a long way in this business.

"I knew exactly what I needed for this scene," continued Lewis. "I needed a goat's carcass. My intention was to cover the goat carcass with either chicken skin or pig skin, and fleshed out with mortician's wax. I knew it could be done, because it had been done already on a much smaller scale [as in the thumb removal scene in *Two Thousand Maniacs!*]. There would be pockets of stage blood strategically placed to further camouflage the differences between a goat and a human carcass. When they were broken open, the pockets of stage blood would spill around so the mortician's wax would not be exposed as mortician's wax. On top would be a face mask of the actress, and we would have the face mask pulsate, using an inflatable balloon behind it."

Once he had the goat carcass prepared, the scene would be set up to focus on the actor's hands, thus allowing Lewis's son, Robert, to become the "stunt goreman," if necessary. "The actor's hands would penetrate the carcass, which would have been perforated beforehand," Lewis explained. "We were going to have this thing prepared so everything could be done by hand — no knife. I was going to have the carcass slit in key places and the bones pre-broken, so you'd be able to *rip* it open, the ribs would snap and you'd see bone ends and all the stuff you should see inside a body. Then the actor would reach in, on-camera, and pull out a jagged piece of bone, with stage blood and meat and gristle dribbling off of it. Then he reaches in and breaks another bone and pulls it out, along with the other stuff. I felt that this would be the ultimate gore effect, where we just tore a carcass to pieces, with real bones and viscera. But the entire effect got derailed. We didn't do it for a very stupid reason. We shot that scene in someone's living room. The fellow whose house we were using was afraid we were going to get glop on his carpet, even though we had a big piece of plastic under the twelve-dollar 9' × 12' rug that we had already put on top of his carpet to protect it. So we did not get to tear a goat carcass down to the bone."

Shucks.

Audiences did seem to like what made it into that final scene, however. "What we ended up doing instead," said Herschell, "was taking a certain amount of blood and gore and viscera and placing it on top of the girl, and then it was peeled away. The audience liked it, but I didn't. They didn't know what we might have done!"

The Wizard of Gore, as grotesque and disturbing as it was, became weighted down by an overly serious presentation. Lewis agreed that the film was a letdown in some respects. Although it enjoyed a longer shooting schedule than many of his gore pictures — principal photography was completed in 14 days — the film seemed rushed. "That picture was really a bunch of compromises," Lewis reflected. "It just wasn't the film I had envisioned. It's artless, but it has a certain charm to it. And in a sense it's funny." Herschell would be much more satisfied with *The Gore-Gore Girls*, which was still two years and several gallons of stage blood away.

Although most audiences seemed properly shocked by what they saw onscreen, Lewis opined, "I thought [the effects] were a little too stagy." Despite Herschell's dissatisfaction, the effects seemed to work fine for most viewers who saw the film. At a showing in Richmond, Virginia, the entire audience started yelling, throwing popcorn boxes, and stomping their feet every time blood splattered or viscera exploded on-screen. Some viewers were yelling, "Montag for President! Montag for President!" (And it wasn't even an election year.) "I thought Montag sounded like a pretty good name for the magician," commented Lewis, "but it means absolutely nothing. It's the German word for Monday, that's all." Such irreverence.

Besides his general dissatisfaction with the picture's special effects, HG also considered it one of the most difficult projects he had ever worked on. "*The Wizard of Gore* was shot in Chicago, but it was a tough picture to make," he conceded. "I made an error on that picture I hadn't made before. My two sons had worked with me on *The Gruesome Twosome* and *Just for the Hell of It*, but that was the extent of my involving family. I had a cousin named Roger Strauss, and my Aunt Jane called me and asked if I could use Roger on a picture, so I put him to work on the crew. I also used my brother's son, Barry, on the crew. The result was disastrous! Roger was working electricity. Now, that was second nature to me, but Roger didn't really know how to do it. We had made arrangements to shoot some scenes at this man's apartment. He had a very lavish apartment. We had a bull clamp which we could attach to a person's electric box and get all the power we needed before it circulated throughout the building; that way it wouldn't short out anyone's TV picture, or shut off the air conditioning, and so forth. Somehow, when Roger attached the bull clamp to the man's electric box, it burned out the whole building; everything went dark! Then the box caught on fire. He threw water on it, which is the worst thing you can do for an electrical fire. We finally were able to put out the fire, but the box was a charred mess. It cost us about $800 to replace. Naturally, the guy threw us out of his apartment. This was the same guy, incidentally, who wouldn't let us bring in the goat carcass for that final gore scene. And to top everything off, we lost an entire day's shooting."

The Wizard of Gore was put together using two cinematographers, an unusual circumstance for any professional film production. Primary photography was handled by Herschell's longtime associate, Alex Ameripoor (receiving on-screen credit here as Alex Ameri), assisted by a newcomer to the Lewis troupe, Daniel Krogh. (Krogh would go on to write the first-ever book about H. G. Lewis, *The Amazing Herschell Gordon Lewis and His World of Exploitation Films*.) Allison Louise Downe, besides receiving co-credit for the gore effects, was also listed as the film's assistant director. Lewis took credit as the film's producer and director, and also threw in a pseudonymous credit: Special Technical Effects by Sheldon Seymour.

Once principal photography was completed, Lewis arranged for the film's music scoring and editing. He turned to his longtime composer, Larry Wellington, to write the music for the film. Instead of editing the film himself, Herschell turned the picture over to Alex Ameripoor. While Ameripoor was occupied with editing tasks, Lewis busied himself working up the advertising campaign, which he built around the tag line, "The Maniac Magician Whose Tricks Really Work!" (Or don't work, as the case may be.)

As horrifying as some viewers considered the film, others found *The Wizard of Gore* inexplicably amusing. But as most film directors and writers who work in the horror genre will point out, inappropriate laughter, or laughter in the "wrong" spots, is often an involuntary response to visual stimuli that someone finds disturbing. Females will usually scream at scenes of horror; males simply do not respond that way. The same phenomenon occurs at amusement parks. A couple riding a roller coaster offers a prime example. The woman screams at the top of her lungs, while the man she's with laughs. It's partially a response conditioned by society. Tradition suggests that the male is the protector (as well as the predator) in a relationship. Because these ideas are ingrained deep in our psyches, our emotional responses to certain situations are predetermined at the subconscious level. When confronted by a stimulus that is shocking in nature — even when that stimulus is one that we consciously recognize as a fake, such as a scene in a motion picture — the human condition dictates a specific response. Thus, women scream; men laugh.

The release of *The Wizard of Gore* sealed the fate of Mayflower Pictures. Fred and Jerry Sandy took with them the rights to *She-Devils on Wheels, Just for the Hell of It,* and *The Wizard of Gore*. Lewis retained the rights to *Miss Nymphet's Zap-In*. Why did the Sandys get all the good stuff? Lewis's feeling was that it was better to walk off with cold, hard cash as opposed to accepting the rights to a few movies that had already enjoyed their first-run release. At that time, the prospect of home video was so far in the future it wasn't even a consideration. In HG's eyes, it was the cash that counted.

And who would ever try to argue that point with H. G. Lewis?

CHAPTER 18

What a Bunch of Yahoos!

> We had a couple of minor gore effects there.... A gun explodes in somebody's face. We did that with a little bit of dynamite. It didn't work very well but we used it anyway.... It just kind of went "bloop." I wanted a lot of glump coming out, and it didn't happen.
>
> — Herschell Gordon Lewis

After turning everyone's stomach with *The Wizard of Gore* (including, probably, his own), Herschell Lewis took time out to put together a couple of non-gore projects. He invited Mr. Wizard himself, Ray Sager, to join the jolly good fun of his newest production, *This Stuff'll Kill Ya!* The picture combined diluted elements of *Moonshine Mountain* and *Two Thousand Maniacs!* and added to the mix elements of con-artist games, (dis)organized religion, and country-tinged music — all wrapped up nice 'n' purty with a promotional campaign that stressed the drama of the film.

For Midwesterners who liked their cinema stories plain and simple, *This Stuff'll Kill Ya!* must have had great appeal. "We shot [it] in Oklahoma City in 1969," Herschell said. "I used Taalkius Blank as the preacher, Reverend Boone. The picture ran 100 minutes, which was long for us, but part of that was because of the number of songs we had." All the songs were credited to the writing talents of Sheldon Seymour, which meant that HG wrote them. The story, a solo job by Lewis, revolved around Reverend Boone, a boisterous, Bible-thumping, backwoods con-artist who rattles off biblical phrases in between soliloquies on free love and moonshine whiskey. "*This Stuff'll Kill Ya!* was almost a modernized version of *Moonshine Mountain*," Lewis admitted. "We had the whiskey, we had the federal agents, we had the threat of violence against somebody who opposed the likker-makers. We also had a couple of mild gore effects in that one." (What more could one possibly want?)

Alex Ameripoor, working once more with Lewis, was overjoyed when he found out that one of his favorite movie actors, Tim Holt, was going to appear in *This Stuff'll Kill Ya!* (In fact, this was Holt's last picture.) "Tim Holt apparently had a sad career," said Lewis. "He never quite achieved stardom, although he was one of the featured players in *The Treasure of the Sierra Madre*. His costars in that picture were Walter Huston and Humphrey Bogart. Alex Ameripoor was a student of motion pictures, and he felt *The Treasure of the Sierra Madre* was one of the finest films ever made. He was exhilarated when he found out Tim Holt was going to do our picture."

Holt had been living in Oklahoma City for some years, selling television and radio spot advertising for a local company — just as Lewis had done when he was trying to break into films early in his career. When Lewis offered him a role in *This Stuff'll Kill Ya!* he gladly accepted — but Holt's best days were plainly in the past. He had left his acting career somewhere in the dust that settled on the roadway behind him. "When we had our first run-through I asked Alex if he had met Tim Holt yet," recalled Lewis. Ameripoor nodded his head slowly and responded, "I met the wreckage that was Tim Holt."

Herschell acknowledged, "He looked beat up, his teeth were black, and he was no longer the boyish, good-looking fellow that everybody remembered so fondly from his films. But it was perfectly clear that Tim Holt was still a professional when it came to acting. His part was not large, but he was a pleasure to work with. I brought along Ray Sager, who played the part of a character named Grady in the film. Ray also was the assistant director under his real name, which was Raymond Szegho." The rest of the cast, which included Eric Bradly, Gloria King, Larry Drake, and Terence McCarthy, were locals from the Oklahoma City area. "Many of them were students at the University of Oklahoma at Norman, or members of little theater groups from the area," Herschell said.

With a plotline that included several murders, HG had the opportunity to try out a couple of minor gore effects. "In our story, there is a little town tucked away on a back road, and that road leads to a strange congregation," Lewis elaborated. "The church is really a front for a moonshine ring. This may sound rather blasphemous, but it wasn't filmed that way. The minister of the church is also the head of the moonshine ring. They are selling moonshine all around the county, and eventually word leaks out about what's going on. Federal agents come in and try to arrest the gang, but the moonshiners get the agents drunk, then pose them in compromising positions and take photographs. So the agents are forced to leave.

"Then murders begin to occur in a biblical way," Lewis continued. "We had a couple of mild gore effects there. One of the girls in the congregation has objected to the way these agents are treated, and ultimately she is stoned to death. Two other girls who have stumbled onto evidence of what is going on are crucified on wooden crosses. That wasn't a true gore effect; they are simply found there in the morning. We 'discover' them. Somebody else is burned to death when his car goes over a cliff. Later on, a gun explodes in somebody's face. We did that with a little bit of dynamite. It didn't really work very well but we used it anyway. For that scene we used a face mask over a stick of dynamite, but it just kind of went 'bloop.' I wanted a lot of glump coming out, and it didn't happen." It's disheartening when a directors wants glump but just gets bloop.

One minor gore effect that did turn out well in *This Stuff'll Kill Ya!* was the "stoning" scene, in which a woman is stoned to death. Lewis had originally wanted to use such an effect in *Two Thousand Maniacs!* but the difficulty involved in pulling off such a stunt realistically prevented it from ever reaching the screen. "We tried a stoning effect in *Two Thousand Maniacs!* short-range, and it didn't work," recalled Lewis. Part of the reason the effect didn't pan out was that HG was trying to film it in broad daylight. Ultimately he and David Friedman substituted the "Teetering Rock" boulder smash instead — which probably made

Two Thousand Maniacs! a better picture in the long run.

The revised effect involved a combination of low-level lighting and a specially textured stone. Lewis stated, "We got the stoning effect to work on *This Stuff'll Kill Ya!* because we shot it at night, not in the daytime, so some of the problems we might have had didn't crop up. We used a textured stone peppered with stage blood which, when it hit our actress in the face, looked for all the world as if it had scraped her skin and bruised the living daylights out of her. *That* worked! It made up for the scene where we blew the man's head off." (This is "mild" gore?)

This Stuff'll Kill Ya! made a profit for Lewis, but it could never be considered one of his outstanding successes. He followed it up with another film that barely managed to turn a profit, *Year of the Yahoo* (1972). "That one was a complete dud," proclaimed Herschell. "We had Claude King in the lead role. Claude King was a fairly well-known country-western singer who'd had a hit record called 'Wolverton Mountain.'" The film also featured performances from a long list of no-names, including Terrell Cass, Tom Lytel, Leslie Slater, Robert Jolly, and Robert Swain. Taalkius Blank, who had starred in *This Stuff'll Kill Ya!*, returned to the Lewis stable for *Year of the Yahoo*, as did Ray Sager, who once more pulled double duty as actor and assistant director.

Year of the Yahoo was terribly ordinary. "The title comes from Jonathan Swift's *Gulliver's Travels*," pointed out Lewis. The script was written by Allen Kahn; Lewis produced and directed the film. It was made in San Antonio, Texas, and concerned a country-western singer who decides to run for the U.S. Senate. "I think it might have performed better if another picture called *The Candidate* had not come out so soon after it," said Herschell. "*The Candidate* was a Robert Redford picture, and except for the music, in my opinion it was almost a direct lift from *Year of the Yahoo*." The only thing that helped make Lewis feel better is that the Redford picture flopped almost as badly as had *Year of the Yahoo*.

Once again, Lewis composed the music for the film, crediting himself as Sheldon Seymour. "I used that name because I didn't want people to think this was a one-man gang," said Lewis. "I didn't want people to think I could do a lot of things, none of them well — which is the conclusion you draw when somebody does it all. It just doesn't look good."

After the release of *Year of the Yahoo*, things began to wind down on the motion picture front for Herschell Gordon Lewis. He had been on his own the past couple of years — ever since the break up of Mayflower Pictures. As a one-man operation, HG headed up Lewis Motion Picture Enterprises, which at least sounded good. "I went drifting along until 1971, when I was approached by a fellow named Bob Smith," recalled Herschell. "Bob Smith was the owner of a Baskin-Robbins ice cream store, and somehow he had gotten the money together to get a picture made. So he wanted to know if I would direct a film he wanted to make, which was a black sex film. Again, this was soft-core. I had no interest in doing hard-core pornography. I wasn't doing anything else at the time, so I agreed to direct the picture for Bob. The crew was very thin — there were only three people behind the camera — but it was immensely successful, because it came along at a time when the black exploitation market was heating up."

The finished picture was titled *Black Love*. It was released in 1972, the year that Lewis said goodbye to gore.

CHAPTER 19

Gore Smorgasbord

> We came across the pulling out of the eyeball quite by accident. My son, Bob, was the only one who would do that. Everybody else, knowing it was a dead animal's eyeball, refused to touch it. We had to stand around waiting until he came in because it was the only way to get the scene finished.
>
> — *Herschell Gordon Lewis*

As the years slipped by, so did Herschell Lewis's stranglehold on the gore movie market. By the early 1970s everyone, it seemed, was investigating the genre. Fanfare, American International, Crown International, and Hallmark Pictures were the most notable independent production companies to invade the domain, but there were others. Even the majors were adopting some of the hard-hitting stylistic touches of rebel filmmakers like H. G. Lewis. The director commented, "There finally came a time when blood actually became respectable. Even viscera became respectable to a degree. I'll never forget when I went to see *Catch 22*: Here's intestines falling out, and *I* wasn't the one who had to do it. Somebody else actually did it! But you have to wonder if that scene would have been in that multi-million dollar picture if we hadn't made our little $24,000 *Blood Feast*."

The new decade ushered in a new era of permissiveness in motion pictures. Hard-core sex films, previously relegated to play in areas like Manhattan's 42nd Street and Washington's 14th Street corridor, had begun unreeling at neighborhood cinemas. Change was everywhere. Britain's Hammer Films began pumping up the sexual quotient of their gothic horror films with *Lust for a Vampire*, *Dr. Jekyll and Sister Hyde*, and other features similarly entrenched in the R category.

Other film companies saw great opportunities to exploit the era's new permissiveness. Titles like *Slaughter Hotel* and *Whirlpool*, promoted as daring adult horror films, relied on sex as much as or more than horror, pushing R ratings as far as they could go. As the decade progressed, so did film producers' willingness to dump poorly photographed and poorly dubbed foreign products on the U.S. market, sometimes doctoring their acquisitions with new English-language footage to increase audience appeal. Such subterfuge culminated in the release of a movie entitled *Snuff*, which was sold to the exploitation market as an *actual* "snuff film." In reality, *Snuff* was a nondescript South American action import to which was appended a U.S.–filmed climax of an "on-camera murder." The murder was nothing more than a typical H. G. Lewis–style gore sequence, obvious to anyone who had the slightest knowledge of film effects.

It was becoming ever more difficult for Lewis to compete effectively in a business where even the major film companies were releasing pictures that boasted buckets of bloodletting. The writing was on the wall, and it became clearer with each passing day. "I wasn't even going to make *The Gore-Gore Girls*," Herschell confided. "I had another idea in mind for a light sex-comedy called *Galaxy Girls*." But the way things worked out, *Galaxy Girls* was the picture that didn't get made.

"The only reason *The Gore-Gore Girls* went into production was a fellow named Bob Dachman," recalled HG. "He told me he had a son, Alan, who was interested in writing a screenplay. I told him that *everybody* had a son who wanted to write a screenplay." Dachman responded by offering to put up the money to make the picture, *if* Herschell would produce and direct it. It was such an easy way to make a movie, Lewis couldn't afford to turn down the offer. After all, nobody was asking him to risk his own capital for this venture.

"Alan's screenplay wasn't too bad," allowed Herschell. "We made a lot of changes to it, but overall it was a solid effort." In fact, the script was one of the most formulaic of any that Herschell filmed. It certainly couldn't boast the originality of *The Wizard of Gore* or *Blood Feast*, nor could it compete with the twisted humor of *The Gruesome Twosome* or *Two Thousand Maniacs!* In many ways, it was a precursor to the stalk-and-slash films that dominated the horror genre in the 1980s. In that sense, *The Gore-Gore Girls* is the least original of H. G. Lewis's gorror films, but it is the most extreme in terms of horrific imagery. It went further than anything Lewis had done before, although the comedic tone of the film lessened the emotional impact of the effects on the audience—or so Lewis claimed. "By the time we made that film, we were beginning to parody ourselves," he noted. "It was intentionally done that way, but whether it was done out of boredom with gore effects, or whether I thought we had done it all before and needed to do something new and different, I can't say."

In what would become de rigeur for films in the Italian *giallo* tradition popularized by Mario Bava with *Blood and Black Lace* and Dario Argento with *Deep Red* and others, the killer in *The Gore-Gore Girls* is dressed head to toe in black leather and is never without black leather gloves. In a pre-credits "quickie" kill that's almost a throwaway, a young beauty, Suzy Creampuff (Corlee Bew), admires herself in a tabletop mirror. Abruptly, a black-gloved hand grabs her hair from behind and pushes her face repeatedly into the mirror. As Suzy's body tumbles to the floor, a quick medium shot reveals all that's left of the girl's face. Lewis then cuts immediately to the credits, backed by a terribly out of place jazz score. (Herschell said he used plenty of canned music for *The Gore-Gore Girls*, but this is canned music that should have remained in the can.) Although the pre-credits murder doesn't take your breath away in the same way that *Blood Feast*'s LEGS CUT OFF! scene did for 1963 audiences, it does get a significant point across to the viewer: *The Gore-Gore Girls* intends to live up to its title.

Unlike earlier Lewis horror films in which the killer's identity is disclosed in the opening reel (*Blood Feast*, *The Gruesome Twosome*, *Color Me Blood Red*, etc.), *The Gore-Gore Girls* can be classified as a bona fide mystery. Not until the story's denouement is the killing culprit exposed.

"Alan Dachman wrote the basic screenplay, but he did not write the gore effects for the film," Herschell pointed out.

"The effects were my own." The movie's gore sequences were choreographed and staged by Lewis and longtime pulmonary partner Allison Louise Downe, who acted as the film's assistant director. Unlike the killings in *Two Thousand Maniacs!* and other Lewis horrors, the gore sequences here almost invariably focus on disfigurement. There are no hacked-off limbs or gutted abdomens on display; instead, there is a preponderance of facial mutilations. There is a significant reason for that, admittedly — as the story line will reveal — but *The Gore-Gore Girls* goes beyond mere gore, into the realm of cinematic sadism.

Following the (mirror) shattering opening murder and the film's requisite credit crawl, Dachman's story downshifts into low gear as we are introduced to private detective Abraham Gentry (Frank Kress, super sharp in his early '70s duds). A combination of Sherlock Holmes and James Bond, this is the kind of cool cat that couldn't possibly exist outside of a scriptwriter's imagination. Such a character would have seemed totally out of place in *Blood Feast*, but he fits right into the warped world of *The Gore-Gore Girls*. Spouting witticisms at every opportunity on whatever subject is close at hand, from girls to gore, Gentry comes off as an anemic version of the Roger Moore version of 007 — lame puns and all.

Somewhat better is Amy Farrell as Nancy Weston, crime-scene reporter for a local paper. Farrell overplays her part, but hers is the more likable role, and it's easy to embrace her performance while forgiving the shortcomings of her characterization. Taking the initiative in their newfound business relationship, Weston baits Gentry with a high-priced offer from her employer: If he can identify the killer of the go-go dancers, the paper will pay him $25,000. Solve the case, and he'll earn another 25Gs. Gentry's acceptance of the offer ensures that reporter Weston will remain on hand to complicate matters at every turn — a crucial plot contrivance when it comes down to matters climactic, with Weston unintentionally risking her life to uncover the murderer's identity. (What viewer could possibly miss seeing this coming?)

Gentry embarks on a crash-course study of the city's T&A bars, which are all owned by a fast-talking shyster kook named Marzdone Mobile (Henny Youngman). At a club called Marz's Heaven, Gentry keeps a watchful eye on the clientele as well as the dancers. Barney the bartender (played by Ray Sager, who is much better here than in *The Wizard of Gore*) tips Gentry to a weirdo named Grout (Frank Rice) who likes to draw faces on squash, tomatoes, melons, etc., and smash them to smithereens with his fist. Grout is trying to re-create his favorite pastime — smashing in the heads of the Vietcong during his tour of duty in 'Nam. Naturally, Grout ends up becoming a prime suspect in the go-go murders. A secondary suspect is women's libber Mary McIlhenny (Emily Mason), who believes strippers are setting back women's rights by twenty years. McIlhenny and her supporters periodically stage violent pickets at Marzdone's strip joints and threaten to do in the dancers, prompting police intervention on a regular basis. What a bunch of pests.

The picture's second killing takes place while another of the strippers, Candy Cane (Lena Bousman), is at home, admiring herself in a mirror. In one of the unintentionally funniest scenes in a Lewis gore film, Candy's throat is slit with a large, gimmicked knife that springs a leak. Like the weapons in *The Gruesome Twosome*, this prop knife was rigged with a concealed tube and squeeze bulb to allow stage blood to be pumped into the blade point. As it is drawn across the actress's neck, a red slash appears just as it is supposed to do, but stage blood also starts running out the handle end of the knife! Lewis, of course, decided not to re-shoot the scene, figuring that his audience would be looking at the blade end of the knife, not the handle. (How could the director guess that gorehounds would be examining this movie frame by frame on their VCRs decades later?)

Following the phony neck slash, the killer begins work in earnest, demolishing the dancer's face by hacking away with a meat cleaver and twisting large chunks of facial flesh almost inside-out in an effort to make as much of a gooey mess as possible. Lewis augmented the gore with crackling, bubbling sound effects that are queasily appropriate. Although bone-crunching, flesh-ripping, eyeball-squirting sound effects can easily be overused or overdone if the director is not careful, Lewis did a pretty fair job of maintaining a level of realism with sound effects for *The Gore-Gore Girls*. He managed this by *underplaying* the effects. "It was my own dereliction, but we didn't have enough sound effects when we started out goring people," Herschell confessed. Indeed, there are portions of *Color Me Blood Red* and *Blood Feast* where the hacking and cutting of limbs and other body parts are played out in almost total pantomime. There were literally no "gore sounds" accompanying the death sequences of these pictures.

That wasn't the case with *The Gore-Gore Girls*. "I eventually learned that if you're going to have entrails [falling out of a body], you need a gooey sound effect [to match the image]," said Lewis. "Squeezing a bunch of tomatoes will give you that sound. Cabbage is good, too. In fact, I think a head of cabbage is the best for gore sound effects. If you pull a head of cabbage apart, it sounds like a body being pulled apart." (You have to wonder how the man knows this.)

As happens to many of the victims in *The Gore-Gore Girls*, the maniac's latest victim also has her eyes plucked from their sockets. With another whack from the cleaver blade, one of the orbs is sliced wide open, and the killer dangles it from the end of the cleaver. (You almost expect the maniac to inaugurate a game of paddle-eyeball.)

Not long afterward, a team of investigators turns up at the house, led by the incompetent Lieutenant Anderson (Russ Badger). Taking dozens of unnecessary photographs of the crime scene from every conceivable angle, the police photographers continually get in Anderson's way as they bumble back and forth, blinding him with flashbulbs and tripping over his feet. It's an amusing comment on police procedure.

To gather clues about the two murders, Gentry interviews hot-trotting stripper Lola Prize (Nora Alexis), a friend of the girls who were killed. Lola offers the detective a lot more than just information, but being a private dick, Gentry keeps it zipped. After he leaves, Lola is visited by a tall, dark figure caped in black. A quick knife slice across the throat sends Lola sprawling across a table, and while she's busy coughing up blood, the killer grabs a meat tenderizer and literally beats her buttocks into pulp. When the flesh has been properly tenderized, the maniac opens a container of salt and pours it into the wounds. (Like, ouch.)

But the killer doesn't stop there, no siree bob. In what is probably the most extreme scene in the entire H. G. Lewis catalog, Lola's body is now turned face up

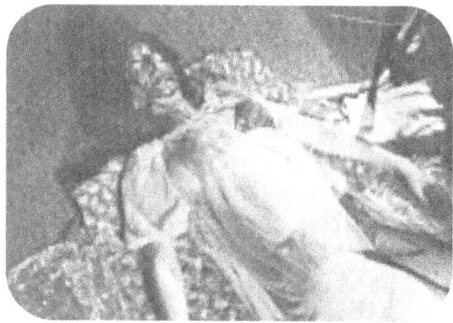

The Gore-Gore Girls, from top: early victim loses face; reporter Nancy Weston (Amy Farrell, center) eyes super-sleuth Abraham Gentry (Frank Kress, right); weirdo Grout (Frank Rice) says no; some scenes were filmed at a strip club.

and the murderer's fingers pray out the girl's eyes. The killer's coup de grâce comes just a moment later. Lewis noted that most viewers were left aghast by what they saw on-screen: "The two best results we had from the viewpoint of audience reaction," HG said, "were the tongue scene in *Blood Feast* and the eyeball burst in *The Gore-Gore Girls*. In that scene the maniac pulls the eyeball out of a girl's head and *squeezes*. You see the knuckles tighten around the eyeball, and you see the eyeball the entire time; we didn't cut away. Finally, it bursts, and this inky, black glop squirts out all over the place. I have seen people faint, vomit, turn green, leave the auditorium, and go to the washroom because of that scene." (What an epitaph this would make.)

And that, unbelievably, is *still* not all. With one eyeball popped and the other yanked, twisted, and mashed into a gelatinous mess, the killer now takes a two-pronged fork and jams it into the empty eye socket, not once, not twice, but thrice. (This is what's known in the trade as "bonus" gore.) It's one sick scene.

The Lola Prize death scene is disturbingly similar to the real-life deconstruction of Mary Kelly, one of the victims to suffer Jack the Ripper's murderous frenzy in nineteenth century London. Kelly was the final Ripper victim, and surviving photographs show a corpse that looks like a prop from a Herschell Gordon Lewis movie. In particular, Kelly's face was so savagely sliced up (the nose was removed entirely), she truly looked like one of the victims in *The Gore-Gore Girls*.

The actress in the burst eyeball scene, Nora Alexis, was drenched in stage blood and animal tripe, looking somewhat less than human. She took everything in good stride, though. "Some actors and actresses didn't mind getting gore on them because we took it so casually," remarked Lewis. "It was a step-by-step process. 'In this scene you kiss this guy. In this scene you walk down the street. In this scene you have gore on you.' It was just another shot in the picture. *But*— when it came to squeezing eyeballs, they balked. Animal intestines didn't matter, or didn't matter too much, but there was something about the eyeballs. In fact, that's what caused me to put it in *The Gore-Gore Girls*. My son, Bob, on the set of *The Wizard of Gore*, was fooling around with that head and he pulled the eyeball out, and people on the *set* were screaming. These were people who had seen us set the whole thing up! I thought, if they're that disturbed by that one scene in *The Wizard of Gore*, let's *really* give it to 'em in *The Gore-Gore Girls*." Give it to them he did. And how.

To return to the plotline, however. To make sure the field remains open so he can conduct his own investigation into the killings, Gentry suggests to the police that the recent murders are the work of a religious maniac, sending the gullible Lieutenant Anderson on a wild goose chase for a Bible with Lola Prize's fingerprints.

Meanwhile, Gentry marches onward with his own investigation, the police (and the killer) seemingly one step behind. Marlene (Hedda Lubin), a waitress at one of Marzdone's clubs, threatens to quit if Gentry keeps sniffing around the strip joints, prompting the dapper detective to add another suspect to the mix.

We then look in on victims three and four—a double murder. Breaking into the home of Linda (Marina Salli), another of Mobile's strippers, the killer slices open the girl's throat (the prop knife works correctly this time), then uses a hot iron to disfigure her face. The flesh sizzles and bubbles as it is cooked by the heat of the iron, eventually turning into a crisp, blackened

The Gore-Gore Girls: Mob boss Henny Youngman; Nora Alexis as stripper Lola Prize; in a scene either cut or lost, Lola hitches a ride; Abraham Gentry (Frank Kress, right) plays it cool before Lieutenant Anderson (Russ Badger); two extras cram an archway to get into the shot.

mass. By now the viewer surely figures there's more to come, and there is: The killer tears open Linda's blouse and, using a *big* pair of scissors, snips off the tip of one nipple. (It's a very realistic nipple, by the way.) Certainly this scene will make some viewers wince — especially those of the female gender — but Lewis lightens the macabre mood by including a shot of milk jetting out of the torn tittie, which the killer catches in a martini glass. Then the other nipple is cut open — and *chocolate* milk fountains out! "I had many arguments about that particular scene," said Lewis. "To me, that is an obvious fantasy, but some people don't view it as fantasy. I thought it was hilarious. How can you *not* take that scene as a joke? But even as we were shooting that scene with the milk shooting through the tube, people on the crew didn't understand exactly what I was doing, or why. So I thought, I'd better have chocolate milk coming from the second nipple so people will *know* it's meant as an outrageous joke. So help me, they *still* didn't get it! When I told the crew, 'Let's blow chocolate milk through that second tube,' they didn't understand why I would want to do that. I guess too many people took it seriously, but it certainly wasn't intended to be serious." With two flavors of breast milk in the glasses, the killer clinks the glasses together and the comedic interlude ends — and the gore begins again.

Linda's roommate (Menda MacPhail) walks into the apartment and steps directly into the killer's clutches. Struggling ineffectually, the stripper is led to a huge, clear bowl of French fries which have been left cooking on the stove. The maniac shoves the girl's face into the roiling liquid, which boils the flesh off the skull. Tilting back the victim's head, the killer sees that chunks of flesh have fallen into the vat of fries, along with both eyes, which have been dissolved by the intense heat. (There's the eyeball motif again.) Satisfied at last, the killer dumps the body on the floor, grabs a ladle, and begins stirring the contents of the bowl on the stove. It now appears to contain a virtual hodgepodge of edibles: greasy French fries, gobs of filleted flesh, hard-boiled eyes, and even scaly patches of scalp. (Hey — a bonus!)

"It's a funny thing," Lewis mused, "but there's something about that double-murder scene that really gets to people. I hadn't realized when we shot the scene where the girl gets her face ironed that it would make such an impact on audiences, but that particular effect really terrifies some people. I screened it for a couple of friends and they couldn't watch it; they literally could not look at the iron being pressed into the girl's face. I like the part where the girl's face is pushed into the vat of French fries. That's *my* kind of effect, because you can see pieces of glop coming off [the face] and dropping into the bowl."

The police turn up a women's lib pin at each of the murder sites, but Gentry manages to convince the lamebrain lieutenant that they have been planted by the killer to throw everyone off the trail of the real killer, who must be a Bible-thumping madman. With the cops once more on a wild goose chase, Gentry has a clear field for scoping out the real murderer and claiming the reward money from Nancy Weston's employer. He meets with Marzdone Mobile to set up a strip contest at Mobile's biggest club, Marz's Heaven.

Mobile was played by the most unlikely celebrity ever to appear in a Herschell Gordon Lewis film — Henny Youngman. "Henny was a friend of Bob Dachman," revealed Lewis. "I wasn't trying to get Henny Youngman into the film, but Dachman *insisted* that I have this man in the film. Henny Youngman speaks very rapidly, especially when he is nervous or excited, and only by threatening to put English subtitles under his lines was I able to get him to slow down."

At least Youngman knew his lines, which was more than Lewis sometimes expected from the people who showed up to be in his films. "Henny was extremely cooperative," Herschell said, "and he was on time and he knew his lines, and where I come from, that is the kingdom of heaven relative to an actor. I'm sure he knew what the nature of the film was. Unlike some of the latter-day saints of film production, we weren't interested in hiding our plotlines from the cast and giving them only the pages that had their lines and actions on them. Henny Youngman had a full script in front of him, so there was never any question of what we did or planned to do. In fact, at one point I saw him examining a pressbook on one of the other films, so he obviously knew where our reputation lay."

Gentry has a plan to uncover the murderer's identity. The striptease contest at Marz's Heaven is advertised in Nancy's newspaper. Gentry makes sure that the randy reporter at his side takes part in the sultry shenanigans on stage that night. Stuffed to the gills with enough four-shot zombies, she willingly gets into the act, out-stripping the strippers. Unknowingly, Nancy is feeding the killer's frenzy until it short-circuits on overload.

Using the reporter as bait, Gentry leads her to his place, where she crashes on the couch. Gentry ducks into a hiding place and watches the door. Sure enough, before long the killer breaks in, poised to disfigure the newsgirl-stripper with a bottle marked *Acid—Made in Poland*. (There's a joke there, somewhere.) At the last moment, Gentry steps out to rescue Nancy from the evil clutches of the maniac—Marzdone Mobile's head waitress, Marlene. Gentry reveals to the audience that Marlene was once married to Marzdone, but when her head and chest were severely disfigured in an accidental fire, Mobile abandoned her for his strippers. Since then, Marlene has been taking revenge by disfiguring the girls Mobile likes the most. Marlene attempts to escape, but stumbles out a second-story window and crashes onto the pavement below, splitting her head wide open. The overkill factor comes into play a moment later when a car runs over what's left of her head. "What a character," muses Gentry. "That's Marlene—all over."

The Gore-Gore Girls, as a whole, is a more competent piece of filmmaking than *Blood Feast* or *The Gruesome Twosome*, but then, that's to be expected of the last motion picture Lewis made. The director had applied all the tricks of the trade he had acquired over the years. By this time, Lewis had a solid technical crew behind him who knew how to make specialty pictures with a minimum of fuss and bother. Ray Sager was helping out behind the scenes as the second unit director, and Daniel Krogh was hired as the second unit cameraman. Main production unit photography was being handled by ever-dependable Alex Ameripoor. Herschell had other familiar faces on board the production as well, including A. Louise Downe as Assistant Director and Larry Wellington as Music Coordinator—not to mention the fellow who contributed musical backgrounds to the picture, the indefatigable Sheldon Seymour!

"I thought *The Gore-Gore Girls* was by far the most hip and certainly the most whimsical of the gore films," proclaimed Lewis. "In many areas, it's funny. It's a comedy with gore. That may be difficult to visualize, but it was done very much upbeat, an obvious fantasy." Obvious to Herschell, maybe; to others, the picture was an exercise in extremes of human cruelty. There are huge amounts of jaw-snapping, flesh-ripping, bone-breaking, eye-gouging, throat-slashing gore on display in the film. Although it is true that the gore is tempered by inserts of black humor throughout the picture (for example, the shot of the maniac catching two flavors of breast milk in martini glasses), the gore is so abundant, and so extreme, that it overwhelms everything else — including the lighter moments of Dachman's script, which in many places is genuinely amusing.

Not surprisingly, the film's extreme brutality ensured that *The Gore-Gore Girls* would be tagged with an X rating. Lewis objected strenuously to the rating, partly because he saw the film as a fantasy, partly because he felt the gore was offset by the script's humor. "Despite the fact that we deliberately made them in a world of fantasy, a film like *The Gore-Gore Girls* is automatically rated X [or NC-17]," Herschell complained.

In contrast, other horror films released around the same time often scored PG ratings, although there were always a few that were rated R, such as *Theater of Blood*, a popular Vincent Price vehicle. Lewis was adamant, however, that the MPAA often played favorites, and routinely showed leniency toward pictures produced by major film companies. He pointed out, "The major companies very seldom made an X picture. When they have gore in a film, it is not substantial enough to warrant an X rating, only an R. Whenever the majors did make an X picture, they made one with maximum audience appeal." Two X titles from major companies that saw release about the same

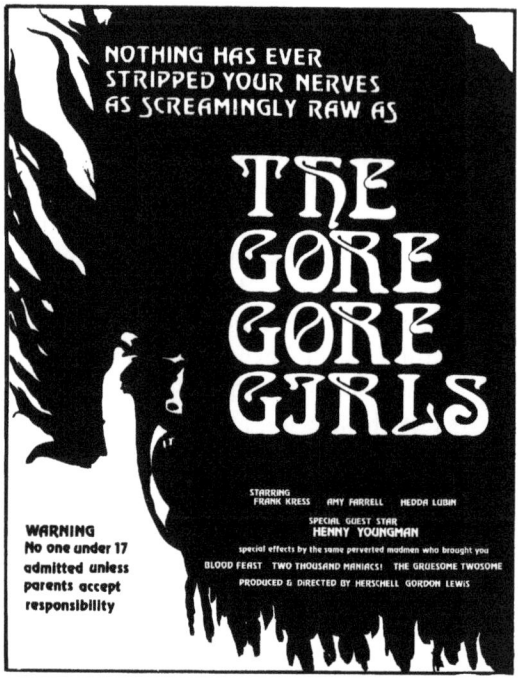

One of Lewis's most impressive ad campaigns. Simple, effective, eye-gouging. Er, eye-catching.

time as *The Gore-Gore Girls* were *Last Tango in Paris* and Stanley Kubrick's *A Clockwork Orange*. Both earned X ratings because of scenes featuring nudity, although the Kubrick picture was steeped in violence, as well.

"*A Clockwork Orange* was subsequently cut down to an R," Lewis pointed out, "and they [the producers] were required to make only two cuts to get that R rating. When [the MPAA] gave *The Gore-Gore Girls* an X, I immediately appealed it. But registering an appeal costs money — that's where the independent gets trapped. I appealed their rating on the grounds of some of the other types of pictures they had rated R and even PG. I felt it was a disservice to give *The Gore-Gore Girls* an X — not a disservice to the world in general, but to *me*. I felt they were giving it an X because it was a low-budget film. I had already prepared our promotional campaign, which had the R designation all over it. I was certain we would get an R. To my mind, there was nothing in *The Gore-Gore Girls* that justified an X rating. Well, the Appeals Board met in New York, so I went to New York to give my argument, which took about half an hour. Aaron Stern was representing the MPAA, and Stern made his argument, which took 20 seconds: He simply asked them to confirm [the original rating] and they confirmed it." So much for Lewis's marketing strategy to get *The Gore-Gore Girls* a saturation playoff.

Herschell admitted he could have made concessions to the MPAA to have the picture re-rated, but artistic integrity prevailed. "I had a chance there, I suppose, to get an R rating by emasculating the film," Lewis conceded. "But again, I cannot believe that I'd have had any picture if I did that." (What could you call *The Gore-Gore Girls* without the gore?)

The rating debacle undoubtedly helped to shape HG's opinion that the MPAA does more harm than good for the motion picture industry. "I don't think the MPAA is a particularly wise organization," Lewis stressed. "They are subject to pressure, as many political organizations are. I still remember when MGM threatened to resign unless [the MPAA] changed their rating on *Ryan's Daughter*—which they then did. Well, at that point, the MPAA lost all credibility for film producers because they felt that the ratings could be manipulated."

What was true at the time of the release of *The Gore-Gore Girls* holds true today. "Today it's very popular to go for an R rating," said Lewis, "and if they give you an NC-17, you agree to cut two scenes and they then give you the R and everyone has saved face. You go to see the R-rated film and the theater is full of 13-year-olds! This seems to be a universal circumstance. If a picture gets an X, or NC-17, the nature of that rating can be misleading, especially in the case of a gore film, because what we have is a difference of percentages rather than a difference of graphics. A triple-X rating, which is the same thing as an X rating, or now an NC-17, when it pertains to the sexual act is very clear: It means that the explicitness has gone beyond an R. But it's not the explicitness of the gore in a gore film that differs, it's the quantity that differentiates an X from an R. Many R-rated films give you two- or three-second bursts of gore. We would linger on it. It could be exactly the same shot [of someone's intestines hanging out], but we gave them ten seconds instead of two, or thirty seconds instead of five, or whatever the number might be, and that's what I think [the MPAA] found objectionable. I find that reaction not consistent with the yardstick applied anywhere else in the industry. If I have two people kissing, they can kiss for four minutes and that will not change the PG rating of a film. If, while they are kissing, a breast is exposed and some four-letter words are uttered, that will change the picture to an R — or it used to; now, it might stay a PG. But the picture could not change to an X, regardless of the amount of hugging, kissing, or fondling, unless the *nature* of the shot changed."

Though almost ten years had passed since the release of *Blood Feast*, HG heard through the grapevine that his latest gore epic was stirring up almost as much controversy as his first. *The Gore-Gore Girls* became a victim of self-appointed local theater censors (usually the projectionists, but sometimes the theater owners), who decided that their clientele needed to be protected from the bloody images Lewis was foisting on an unsuspecting public. Even with the X rating, some theaters were cutting the film's more outrageous moments (the eyeball burst was, naturally, the scene most often trimmed) before letting it play. "I sometimes think we had more mutilations *of* our films than we had *in* our films," Herschell commented. "Local censors would take scenes out and then decide it was too much trouble to put them back in." The result often was that prints came back to Lewis's headquarters in constituent pieces which had to be reassembled in running order.

The reasons for local municipalities, theater owners, or projectionists to "censor" a product which had already been "censored" (or restricted) by virtue of an X rating were entirely personal. It certainly wasn't fair to the filmmaker or the distributor (which, in the case of *The Gore-Gore Girls*, was the same person), because the product was not being allowed to reach its intended audience unmolested. Adult viewers who paid adult admission prices intending to see a motion picture made for adults were being ripped off. "Why these people think gore films would adversely affect the viewer is something I cannot fathom," said Lewis. "It couldn't adversely affect anyone any more than the creators of Walt Disney comic books feel that showing a dog stretched out adversely affects the viewer of their comic books, or any more than the writer of a novel feels that his words adversely affect his readers. I certainly don't think that when Warner Bros. made *The Maltese Falcon*, or when Metro made *Ben-Hur*, they expected the viewers to go out and ape what was shown on the screen. I don't think that the viewers of the Muppets reacted to some of the senseless violence that they saw on that show — and it was one of my favorite programs, by the way! — no, I've heard that old saw for years. In fact, I heard it long before I was in the business, and the concept of motion pictures or any art form generating a response is nonsense. What it *might* do is expose a response, but it certainly won't create that response. If people were so weak-minded that they could be proselytized or brainwashed by film, the medium would have gone a lot further than it has." Just think of the government applications alone.

After the hubbub over *The Gore-Gore Girls*' rating had died down, Herschell directed his attention to the problem of getting the picture into theaters. "We had a terrible time getting that film played," he revealed. "It had, in my opinion, pretty good production values, it had a sense of humor, it was wry, and overall I felt it was a good picture and it had a good campaign. But it wasn't performing well."

That's no surprise when one takes into account the things some local censors were doing to the film. Using *Blood Feast* as a yardstick, HG said, "That picture was also emasculated in certain situations, but where it played uncut, audiences generally went into the theater and came out *not pleased* — but they were simply *astounded* enough to talk the picture up. Invariably we would open on a Friday night and business would be so-so. Saturday would be good, but — and this is unusual in the film business — Sunday would out-pull Saturday. That meant word of mouth was spreading around. Obviously, that word of mouth wasn't damning us; it was somebody saying, 'my gosh, you can't imagine what they're showing on the screen. Why, this fellow reaches into a girl's mouth and pulls out her tongue!' It became an 'in' thing to go and see that picture." This never happened with *The Gore-Gore Girls*, because the severity of the gore sequences prompted more local editing of the picture than had occurred before. Who was going to talk up a motion picture that was missing the "good stuff"?

But there was another reason that *The Gore-Gore Girls* failed to perform well: Some territories were turned off by the title. "There were some distributors in what were then my best territories in the South, who suggested that some theater owners were afraid of the go-go girl image," Lewis related. "There was a crackdown in some towns on go-go joints, and they felt that a more straightforward title with the word *blood* in it would work [better]. Film distributors tend to run on tracks, and the word *blood* works in one title, so [they think] it's going to work in another. To them, it's titles — not content — that matter. They aren't entirely correct, but they aren't entirely incorrect, either. So I was perfectly willing [to change the title]. We retitled it *Blood Orgy* on some prints, and we made up a new campaign, but it didn't do that much for the film."

Lewis was reluctant to change much of the campaign simply because he believed the material couldn't be bettered. "We were in love with our own copy," he confided. "We wrote no new copy for *Blood Orgy*. One reason we never changed it was that exhibitors were also in love with our copy. If we'd come back with any suggestion of being uncertain of our ground, it would have damaged our image. They knew our films made money, and that was a big, big key."

But the problem with *The Gore-Gore Girls* wasn't the copy; it was the picture itself, which many saw as too extreme, despite the inclusion of comedic flourishes. "There were a few theater owners who wouldn't play it," affirmed Lewis.

"But *The Gore-Gore Girls* situation wasn't unique. We had half a dozen circumstances where a film was pulled after it opened because of pressure within the community, but invariably it was reopened elsewhere, and sometimes in a multiple, where it drew no bad publicity at all. It's as though someone had vented his spleen and then, having taken it out on some poor theater owner who had to withdraw the picture, crawled back into the woodwork."

Although Lewis had a few more movie ideas planned for production after *The Gore-Gore Girls*— including two more gore titles — this was his final film. His science-fiction parody, *Galaxy Girls*, made it only as far as script form. There was also an idea for a really far-out gore film entitled *Mr. Bruce and the Gore Machine*, and some years after that, HG thought about making a picture called *Herschell Gordon Lewis's Grim Fairy Tales*. The latter title made it as far as a draft script, but was never finalized.

"There were several reasons why I got out of the film business," said Lewis, "but one of the main reasons was the sheer witlessness that began to predominate the production end of the business in the 1970s. I became appalled by some of the people who were coming into it. My philosophy of life had always been to enjoy what I do to the max without damaging anybody else. Some of the people getting into the business seemed not to care who they damaged." Maybe it was time to get out while the getting was still good.

CHAPTER 20

Life After Gore

> In a French magazine called *Cahiers du Cinéma*, I was classified as a subject for further research — but they say the same thing about cancer.
>
> — *Herschell Gordon Lewis*

With *The Gore-Gore Girls* behind him, Lewis began working on the script for *Galaxy Girls*, a lighthearted sex comedy with a science-fiction twist. "*Galaxy Girls* was going to be a different kind of picture altogether," Lewis said. "The story was about some girls who came from a planet where sex is food — that is, they must have sex to live; it's their nourishment. But the men on their planet look like suitcases." Already, one can imagine the possibilities.

"The alien girls are beamed to Earth, but they don't have any idea what human men look like," continued Lewis. "They think a suitcase is a man. I designed the story as a comedy in the vein of Woody Allen's *Sleeper*. Had we ever made that picture, I imagine it would have gotten a PG rating. There wasn't going to be any nudity in it; it wasn't designed at all to have any prurient appeal." The *Galaxy Girls* script eventually made its way to Canada, where Ray Sager attempted to launch it as an independent production, but was never able to get the picture off the ground.

Around the same time that Lewis composed the *Galaxy Girls* script, he also began work on a project tentatively titled *Mr. Bruce and the Gore Machine*. "That was something I came up with when it looked like *Galaxy Girls* was not going to get made," recalled Lewis. "I was not tiring of gore films, but I felt after *The Gore-Gore Girls* that something like *Galaxy Girls* would be able to get a broader playoff. A producer's integrity is tempered by what he can get played in theaters, after all."

The plot of *Mr. Bruce and the Gore Machine* was ingenious because its simplicity and its originality allowed for the generation of spectacular gore sequences that required little or no setup. The story's modus operandi enabled Lewis to come up with virtually any kind of gore sequence he liked, without having to tie it in to the action or specific events of the story. It was almost analogous to a "gore dream machine."

This time, the story line wasn't built around an Egyptian caterer or an artist who liked to paint with blood or a killer who was only interested in disfiguring faces, drinking blood, or scalping women — all of which required gore of a specific bent. The central element of *Mr. Bruce and the Gore Machine* was the *machine*, which mangled its victims in various and sundry ways. "This was widely divergent from anything I had done before," noted Lewis. "I think it's laughable that people who are trying to recall a movie they saw two days ago can't recall the title of it because it was so much like a movie they saw four days ago. Our films had disparity of plot, which was as wide as we could make it." The plotline of *Mr. Bruce and the Gore Machine* focused on a man who owns and operates a health parlor equipped with all the latest exercise apparatus. He also has a very special piece of equipment reserved for those "special" guests who want to lose weight in a hurry. "The idea for this project was based on an old joke," said Lewis. "The joke was: My wife went down to the exercise parlor and lost 37 pounds. One of the machines tore off her leg. Based on that joke, my son Bob and I came up with the script."

The story's potential for versatility of gore effects delighted its writers. Lewis thought it had the potential to be one of his best horror pictures, because so many people were joining health spas where there were gadgets aplenty for exercising every muscle in the human body, except possibly the sphincter. "The machine in this exercise parlor would pull something off of you," Lewis continued. "It might be your head, it might be your arm, it might be your leg, it might be one half of your rear end. It might even be something substantially more personal!" Herschell planned to film *Mr. Bruce* in the style of *The Gore-Gore Girls*: extreme in its effects, but full of black humor to temper the gore. "It was going to be in that black-comedy style, but it would have been much more camp," HG suggested, "because *The Gore-Gore Girls* is on the far end of possibility. The events of *Mr. Bruce and the Gore Machine* just couldn't be possible."

Herschell had other projects in mind as well, although none came as close to fruition as *Mr. Bruce and the Gore Machine*.

"I had synopses of several other [gore films] that I had developed over the years," he confirmed. "It never would cross my mind to tread a piece of ground twice. There's no need to, unless you are imaginatively sterile — which, unfortunately, some of these [modern scriptwriters] seem to be. They set up a pseudo-psychological circumstance for their lunatic, and that circumstance doesn't vary at all from film to film, or for that matter from producer to producer! Similarly, the person they have as the heavy always kills in a specific pattern — that is, he'll kill everyone who comes to swim or row on a lake. He will kill off a descendant of a specific individual. He will kill off those who tried to kill him off ten years before. We didn't do that; to me, that lets the audience down. Any amount of suspense is gone. Suspense is inconsequential to a gore film, I'll grant you that, but there's no reason to take the position that you have contempt for suspense."

The kinds of effects Lewis envisioned for his unmade gorror projects were just as shocking and ambitious as anything he had committed to film in the past. "I never had problems coming up with new ways to kill off victims," he laughed. "As a matter of fact, I have a *bank* of ways to kill off movie victims. One lies in bed at night, giggling and laughing and grinning at one's inventiveness, most of which, unfortunately, will never make it to the screen."

Besides his films, Herschell had been involved with doing a bit of live theater now and then. That may come as a shock to some until they find out what kind of theater Lewis was doing. In fact, "dead theater" might be a better term than "live theater." Lewis owned three Chicago cinemas, known as the Lewis-Andrews Theatres. He opened one theatre in the Old Town district of Chicago, christening it the Blood

Shed. (Get it?) Later, HG changed its name to The Cinema Bizarre. Besides showing some of his own films, Lewis also booked older (read: cheaper) horror classics like Karloff's *Frankenstein* and Lugosi's *Dracula*, neither of which had been seen in a theater setting in years, except on rare occasions in revival houses.

Besides playing horror films at the Blood Shed, Herschell set up stage shows and audience-participation stunts. It wasn't quite "dinner theater," it certainly wasn't Broadway, but it was fun, nevertheless. "We had live 'monsters' in the theater who would put on a 'gore show' during the intermissions between movies," recalled Lewis. "A girl would come out screaming with a monster chasing her. We had a guy we called Irving Vampire. He would chase her up and down in front of the screen, and finally he would catch her and slit her throat. We used the knife with the tube and stage blood in a squeeze bulb which he held in his hand, and he would slit her throat quite nicely. Sometimes the blood would shoot across the stage! In fact, they once got stage blood on the screen, which didn't please me at all."

The live shows were quite popular, especially with kids who invariably turned up at Saturday matinees. Unfortunately, the Blood Shed did not enjoy a particularly long life. "After the 1968 political conventions [which led to inner-city rioting], nobody would go into Old Town anymore," said Lewis. "They were afraid. It was almost as if a switch had been turned off—and that was the end of the theater."

With the Blood Shed closed for good, Lewis turned his attention back to horror cinema with a vengeance, ramping up the gore to bolder extremes than ever before in his final two gore productions. Although neither *The Wizard of Gore* nor *The Gore-Gore Girls* matched the profits of his earlier titles, both eventually joined *Blood Feast* on the shelves of independently owned video stores, rattling a new generation of film fans. "I'm quite convinced that part of the reason for the rebirth of gore films [has been] video cassettes and cable television, which allowed for the screening of specialty products," Lewis remarked. There is, in fact, an entirely new subculture of gore films, produced by amateurs owning their own camcorders, distributed via mail order through advertisements in genre magazines like *Videoscope* and *Filmfax*.

In earlier decades, fans made 8mm and Super-8mm silent home horror movies; a lucky few made 16mm sound home movies—but almost none got shown outside of the filmmaker's circle of friends and associates. By the 1990s, all of that changed. No one spent money on expensive film and skyrocketing developing costs anymore—not when a two-hour blank video cassette costing $2.99 could take its place, simplifying the photographic process and allowing the results to be gauged immediately. Amateur auteurs sprang up like triffids, oppressive and unrelenting, churning out horrors by the hundreds—fantasy fodder for an ever-growing subterranean market.

The kind of simplified gore effects seen in such amateur videos are reminiscent of the pioneering pulse-pounders of H. G. Lewis ("LEGS CUT OFF!"), but there are fans whose talent for emulating Hollywood-style tricks of the trade is nothing to wheeze at. Serious students of shock cinema studied the makeup techniques of artists like Rob Bottin, Tom Savini, and John Carl Beuchler, who had themselves studied the work of John Chambers and Dick Smith and, yes, even H. G. Lewis. Advances in makeup and effect technology enabled modern-era artists to depict everything from ghosts and ghouls to guts and gore. Even Lewis admitted that the stylized gore effects seen in later horror films like *Re-Animator* and *Dead-Alive* were repulsively realistic. "The latter-day techniques of killing people one sees in some of the gore films made in the 1980s and '90s are certainly technically superior to the stuff that we did," Lewis acknowledged. "In a sense, we were primitives in our era; we were the D. W. Griffiths of gore. But I don't think [later generations of filmmakers] have the fun that we had, and I don't think that they are all that inventive. If an effect can't be done with [established] procedures, as with paste-on effects or exploding clothing, they'll go elsewhere. The idea of sticking a pool cue into somebody's gut and having the blood gush out is simply foreign to their thinking in terms of production. They have too much committee-think and too many people around to take the entrepreneurial or auteur point of view toward gore effects."

Although HG never made a picture of the caliber of Jacques Tourneur's *Curse of the Demon*, Terence Fisher's *Horror of Dracula*, Mario Bava's *Black Sunday*, Wes Craven's *A Nightmare on Elm Street*, George Romero's *Night of the Living Dead*, John Carpenter's *Halloween*, or even Sean Cunningham's *Friday the 13th*, there can be little argument that Lewis's contribution to the genre, as vile and bilious as it was, had an impact on the future of modern horror. In fact, gore started to become a genre staple as early as the mid–1970s, when Italian macabre maestros Mario Bava and Dario Argento used bloody stunts to unnerving effect in *Twitch of the Death-Nerve* (a.k.a. *Bay of Blood*) and *Suspiria*. In rapid succession, the genre produced *Friday the 13th*, Romero's *Dawn of the Dead*, David Cronenberg's *Shivers* (a.k.a. *They Came from Within*), Lucio Fulci's *Zombie*, and numerous others, nearly all breaking new ground with blood-and-guts galore — not to forget William Friedkin's *The Exorcist*, which caused a fantastic furor when it debuted in 1973.

Numerous imitators of Lewis's style sprang up over the years. Pictures like *Bloodsucking Freaks, I Drink Your Blood, The Undertaker and His Pals*, and dozens of others owed a great debt to *Blood Feast*. In an interview that appeared in the 1975 book *Kings of the B's*, Lewis noted, "Just as [there were filmmakers who] followed us into the nudies, [there are those who] follow us into gore. I read with interest a remark made at the convention of the Adult Filmmaker's Association that, to separate themselves from the 16mm producers, they were going to go into horror films. They've heard from the distributors [that] the pictures make money. But it's a more complex business than aiming a camera and firing. Yes, they can go to California and hire special effects men ... whereas I deal with my own ragtag legion that I've dealt with for years. What they cannot do is recognize what we have done in the past already.

"I see films every day being ground out," continued Lewis. "Some of these people come to work on our crew for free, to learn how to make horror films. Which is like saying to a golf pro, 'Will you teach my friend how to play golf today? I learned yesterday.' You can't do it that way. One learns this business from sitting in an audience and watching a public reaction, and what you thought was a great effect, they laugh at. Something you threw away, they are horrified at, and you say, 'Oh, why didn't I spend more time with that?' But there are many people now who are, if not making gore films, including gore sequences [in their films]. There are people who are trying to combine gore and sex in the films, and I think that's a tactical error [*Kings of the B's*, ed. by Todd McCarthy and Charles Flynn (New York: Dutton, 1975), p. 359]." Lewis couldn't have been more correct, because sex-horror films generally turn off both types of audiences, those who came to see the sex and those who came to see the horror; neither side enjoys the films and the box office suffers as a result.

Lewis felt that his films were not made for a specific audience, although they seemed to play more frequently in the South. "We did not gear our films to any particular audience," he stressed. "We *created* an audience. There was no demographic composition to the group before we came in. I know that some film companies aim their product, and the promotion of that product, at the 12 to 21 age range. We didn't do that. We didn't care whether the individual coming into the theater was 91 or 11.

"I think our pictures went over better in the southern regions simply because the distribution was better [in the South]," Lewis remarked. "In those days, independent product had a better chance of getting played in the South. I don't think it had much to do with whether it played at a drive-in or a conventional theater, or whether it was a big town or a small town. I think it had to do with the acceptable nature of our product among film distributors rather than among audiences. I've heard many times that these pictures will play well in the South; it's almost a way of apologizing for a picture that doesn't get played often in the North. But with a picture such as *She-Devils on Wheels*—which was a classic compared to some of the biker pictures I've seen—we did get a big playoff in the North, the picture did well, the theaters that showed it did well. So the type of product is, I think, not the answer, and the type of audience is not the answer; it's the type of distribution [that matters]."

Had it been possible, Lewis would have made different kinds of pictures more often, but the economics of independent low-budget filmmaking virtually dictated the type of picture to make. As Lewis often noted, he and David Friedman had to do something different to get noticed. Other independents, such as American International, were making pictures in categories in which Lewis couldn't hope to compete. At the time that HG was about to break the macabre-movie mold with *Blood Feast*, AIP was making its series of Edgar Allan Poe pictures and beach party comedies. "AIP's beach pictures were, I felt, not the kind of picture an independent could or should make well," Lewis commented. "Such a picture required Frankie Avalon or Annette Funicello, it required a mindlessness with gloss, and the one area in which we had no possible means of competing was one of gloss. We were using our own money, largely, and there wasn't a lot of 'fat' in the budget—not that that's a factor; but what is a factor is being able to make a picture that competes. I could not have made a *Beach Blanket Bingo* picture for less than several hundred thousand dollars, and even then I would have [had] just another picture in that same area." This, then, is the reason Lewis never attempted to compete with American International or other companies in different areas of exploitation: Beach pictures had gloss and Frankie Avalon; Poe pictures had gloss and Vincent Price; but gore pictures needed little more than gore.

But as HG frequently pointed out, his filmmaking entourage offered more than gore—at least on occasion. "We introduced such things as the banjo music background [used in *Two Thousand Maniacs!*]

for which *Bonnie and Clyde* was lionized some years later," he said. "We introduced the use of short scenes as transitions between major scenes [in *The Adventures of Lucky Pierre*]. I'm not the least bit irritated, outraged, annoyed, or chagrined that others are reaping the benefits of what we started. This isn't a case, I must admit, of some dedicated scientist discovering the secret of faster-than-light propulsion, and then dying intestate so that others can come along behind him and get the glory for what he did. We were in the *film* business! I enjoyed every minute of it, and I have no regrets except that perhaps I might have collected more film rentals from some of the scoundrels in that business. It bothers me not at all that others are carrying this torch which may be burning brighter now than it did before."

As the gore genre that Lewis pioneered was cautiously adopted by filmmakers who saw *Blood Feast* and *Two Thousand Maniacs!* in their formative years, as "splatter" began to matter with the mega-success of later independent productions like *Friday the 13th*, it finally became acceptable for familiar faces to join the casts of genre productions. "I always did think a gore film would work just as well if it featured 'name' actors," Lewis maintained. "I'm not talking about 'legitimizing' the genre, I'm talking about adding a factor which forces whoever is making that film to pay more attention all the way up the line to the realism of the effects and the plotline. But you couldn't use just anybody; it would have to be the right actor. For example, Burt Reynolds would *not* be a good choice because Burt Reynolds is a 'good ol' boy.' Christopher Lee is not a good example either, because everybody expects him to act that way. But Jack Lemmon would be a perfect person to either tear apart [a victim], or be torn apart himself, or be witness to such an activity."

Herschell may never have had Jack Lemmon in one of his productions, but given the types of pictures he made, he didn't bat a bad average when it came to promoting some recognizable names in his casts. Karen Black, Tim Holt, Henny Youngman, and Harvey Korman are names with which most movie and television fans will be familiar. And William/Bill/Rooney Kerwin, a.k.a. Thomas Wood, was at least a star player in Lewis's own unique universe. (And let's not forget Scott Hall and Connie Mason — although HG might like to.)

A variety of circumstances encouraged HG to consider leaving the world of feature filmmaking. At the top of his personal list of pet peeves was the difficulty he often encountered when trying to collect film rentals for his pictures. In John McCarty's *The Sleaze Merchants* (New York: St. Martin's, 1995), Lewis explained, "I got tired of dealing with so many flimflam distributors. The fun had gone out of [making movies]. I had no position. I couldn't say to a distributor, 'If you play this picture, I'll also give you this one.' Universal can say, 'If you play this picture, I'll give you *Jurassic Park* second run.' So I had no carrots to dangle in front of the jackasses. Beyond this, there were just so many other pitfalls. For example, the producer gets last count. Let's suppose a theater in Joplin, Missouri, is playing my picture. How do I know how much money is coming into the box office? Today, the [theater] chains prevent much of that just by the very nature of the bookkeeping they have to have. The automation is such that cheating becomes almost impossible. It wasn't that way when I was in the business. Most theaters that we played in were individually owned, so you had to trust that whatever grosses might be reported were what they said they were. They were reported to the subdistributor, who had the second count. I, as producer, got third count. So Lord knows what the actual film rentals might have been [*The Sleaze Merchants*, p. 49]."

There were other reasons that HG got out of the film business, however. In the August 7, 1974, edition of the film industry bible, *Variety*, a startling report appeared bearing the headline, "Herschell Lewis Has 'Fraud' Woes." The report cited a story in the Chicago *Tribune* for July 28th of that year which said that Lewis had declared personal bankruptcy in mid–May following a federal investigation for "intent to defraud investors in various franchise schemes." The *Tribune* story said that "scores of investors" had told the newspaper they had been "defrauded [by Lewis] in car rental, gas-saving device, and abortion referral service swindles." A Flint, Michigan, judge charged Lewis with having "bilked a Michigan couple out of $4,000 in a bogus abortion referral service," and an auto-rental franchise won a judgment of $22,000 against him, "clearing the way for more than 300 other investors to file suit to recover funds amounting to $500,000."

Would a person holding a master's degree in journalism as well as a Ph.D. in psychology, who had taught at Roosevelt University, who had produced and directed numerous 35mm motion pictures, whose expertise in advertising led him to top-line his own agency (Lewis, Nelson, Kahn), and who was a sought-after guest lecturer in the advertising field, really try to "bilk" a couple out of $4,000? Would a professor of psychology think it wise to set up a "bogus abortion referral service?" Who was kidding whom?

Herschell hid nothing when he attempted to explain how he got caught up in the litigation surrounding the charges that appeared in the Chicago *Tribune* and *Variety*. "There was some difficulty," he admitted. "I had made some most unwise investments, which is not unusual for someone who has cash and becomes impressed by the amount of cash he has. That particular problem will not recur."

The bottom line was that, through investments in a variety of businesses, Lewis became the principal stockholder of those businesses. As the principal stockholder, it was he who was ultimately held responsible for the indiscretions of others. The buck stopped with him. Herschell elaborated on the situation that had been reported in *Variety*: "I bought a bunch of theaters and I invested in a whole bunch of different businesses. I had a lot of money in those days. Anyway, one of the businesses I went into was an automobile-rental place that went belly-up. I was actually still in advertising at Lewis, Nelson, Kahn, and [the auto business] didn't have anything to do with my source of income, except that the businesses were all cross-collateralized. Basically, that means you use the assets of one business to build the assets of another. The bank accepted the movies as part of the collateral, which I found astonishing, because I thought they had run their course and weren't really commercially viable anymore.

"When the auto-rental thing went under, a lot of the evils were brought back onto my shoulders," Lewis continued. "And that business tore everything else down: the films, the theaters, my agency, *everything*. I ended up in a little office with four people in it, including me. At the time I said, 'How unfair this is — a lifetime of building up, torn down so fast.' But I expect if all that hadn't happened, I wouldn't be where I am today."

Where Lewis is today, he enjoys a warm climate, lives in a big home, owns nice automobiles, has a very respectable income, and enjoys plenty of free time to pursue the pastimes that give him the greatest pleasure. His principal money-making activities today involve writing. "That whole fiasco with the car-rental business forced me to go back to the typewriter to earn my living," he said. "After everything went belly-up I was sitting on the sidelines looking at what used to be my own businesses, and the fellow who was the manager of one of my theaters refused to honor passes to that theater which I had given to some friends. To me, that was the unkindest cut of all." Herschell was determined not to be left forlorn and forgotten by those who took advantage of him in the aftermath of the court case. "I still had the Mitchell camera, I still had all the [movie-making] equipment, and there were some people who still believed I could make films," HG recalled. "But film is not like advertising, which is a day-to-day business. So I began over, using my typewriter instead of a movie camera. And slowly I worked my way into dominance with direct-response writing."

About a year after the court case was behind him, Herschell became involved with a company known as The Bradford Exchange, for which he wrote a lot of direct-marketing advertising copy. In short order he was made the company's Director of Development. Not long after that, a firm known as the Calhoun Collector's Society, based in Minneapolis, got in touch with Lewis. They invited him to join their staff as the Director of Advertising and Development. Although he wasn't all that keen on the cold climate, Lewis accepted Calhoun's offer, relocating to Minneapolis in 1976. Within a year the company boosted Lewis into a top management slot, as a vice-president of marketing. His V-P activities brought him into contact with other companies and individuals in the advertising field, and Lewis eventually began getting offers for speaking engagements and seminar appearances. "Other companies began saying to me, 'Gee, if only you were free, we could do a lot of business,'" recalled Lewis. Figuring he could write advertising copy from any geographic location, HG decided he'd rather be warm than cold, and opted to forgo the frigid Minneapolis winters for more pleasant environs. "In October of 1979 I resigned from Calhoun," he said. "I had one seminar to do in Wisconsin in January of 1980, and after that I just kept driving until I got to Florida." And there he stayed.

In the years since his southerly relocation, Lewis has remained active in the advertising and writing fields. "Now I write direct response campaigns and I write books," he said. There are a large number of specialty publications sporting Lewis's byline, including *Copywriting Secrets and Tactics* (Dartnell), *Direct Marketing Strategies and Tactics* (Dartnell), *Big Profits from Small Budget Advertising* (Dartnell), *Herschell Gordon Lewis on the Art of Writing Copy* (Prentice Hall; two editions), *Direct Mail Copy That Sells* (Prentice Hall), *More Than You Ever Wanted to Know About Mail Order Advertising* (Prentice Hall), *How to Make Your Advertising Twice as Effective at Half the Cost* (Bonus Books), *Open Me Now!* (Bonus Books), *Sales Letters That Sizzle* (National Textbook Company), *Silver Linings–Selling to the Expanding Mature Market* (Bonus Books), *The Businessman's Guide to Advertising and Sales Promotion* (McGraw-Hill), *How to Write Powerful Fund Raising Letters* (Pluribus Press), *How to Write Powerful Catalog Copy* (Bonus

Books), *Selling on the Net* (co-authored with his son, Robert [NTC]), *The World's Greatest Direct Mail Sales Letters* (co-edited with Carol Nelson [NTC]), *Catalog Copy That Sizzles* (NTC), *The Complete Advertising and Marketing Handbook* (Bonus Books), *Cybertalk That Sells* (co-authored with Jamie Murphy [NTC]), *The Advertising Age Handbook of Advertising* (co-authored with Carol Nelson [NTC]), and *How to Handle Your Own Public Relations* (Burnham). With his wife, Margo, Herschell also wrote *Everybody's Guide to Plate Collecting* — not exactly the sort of thing one would expect from the man who invented on-screen spleen-rupturing. And if that's not enough to flip your *Gruesome Twosome* wig, take note that Herschell is also the co-author of *Symbol of America: Norman Rockwell*. Who would've thunk.

The closest HG has come to getting his filmmaking hands dirtied again was when he, Ian Kennedy, and Jerry Reitman produced a video entitled *100 of the Greatest Direct Response Television Commercials*. It's not the kind of eerie epitaph his gorehound fans expected, certainly; but as Herschell pointedly remarks, the direct-response market has been extremely kind to him. "Frankly, I've never worked less or made more money than I do right now." he enthused. "I lead the good life, I sit by my pool and smoke good cigars, and I play tennis every day." With his small but distinctive place in horror film history secure, there's little incentive for Herschell to return to the world of independent budget filmmaking.

"Making a feature film is brutally hard work," Lewis said, "especially when you get into every facet of filmmaking, as I used to: directing, producing, writing, running the camera, doing the music, doing the effects, hiring the cast and crew, and so forth. Now, if I get tired of hitting the keys on my computer keyboard, I can walk outside and sit by the pool for an hour. It's difficult to reconcile this lifestyle, which I love, with going back to filmmaking bedlam."

It took quite a few years, but Lewis eventually became a darling of the new generation of horror fans weaned on magazines like *Fangoria* that celebrated movie special effects, often to the exclusion of motion picture writers, actors, producers, or directors. Within the first two years of the magazine's debut, a total of three articles appeared on Lewis. Subsequently, other genre film publications began writing about the man who rendered gold from gore. By the early 1980s, there was a sort of Lewis renaissance on video cassette. In rapid succession, *Blood Feast*, *Two Thousand Maniacs!* and *Color Me Blood Red* turned up on tape, followed by *The Wizard of Gore* and some of Lewis's non-gore subjects. Difficulty tracking down the rights to other Lewis titles such as *A Taste of Blood* has kept a few of his films off the market — but it's merely a matter of time before his entire catalog is made available to modern fright fans.

"I suppose I was the first with gore as a byway of film," Lewis mused, "but I had no idea that the type of film I made still had any consequence in the public mind. Now it appears that it will go on forever. Maybe fifty years from now someone will say, 'Ah! This is the kind of film that Lewis originated.' But it's certainly not a major achievement. I made a change to horror films — people now die with their eyes open — but it's not like discovering nuclear fission." No Nobel Prize for Herschell so far.

HG may think his contributions to the horror film genre inconsequential; nevertheless, the study of the gospel of gore continues unabated. Special-effects master Tom Savini has upped the ante for hard-core gore with his incredibly realistic exsanguinations of living bodies in such films as *Day of the Dead, Friday the 13th Parts I* and *IV*, and *Maniac*; and even Savini's effects have been trumped in recent years by others who grew up with gore as a mainstay of the macabre.

Although Lewis has remained aloof from the film industry of the 1990s, several potential projects have been suggested as appropriately violent vehicles to return him to the director's chair. "It has been brought to my attention that I might continue to make films," said Herschell, "but nobody has ever come up with a solid deal. Meanwhile, in the area of direct response, I have achieved some position, and I'm doing very well at it, to be quite candid. So I'm not interested in fronting a new picture. I would only go back into the film business if someone were to arrive at my doorstep with a pre-packaged production agreement and to say, 'Here, use our money, we'll give you X amount of dollars and a percentage of the gross.'" As a matter of fact, in the late 1980s an independent filmmaker was making the rounds of producers in Hollywood, trying to drum up interest in making a picture entitled *Gore Feast*, a proposed semi-sequel to *Blood Feast*. Although HG never got to see the script, he did hear about the project through the gore grapevine — but a final deal was never hammered out.

In another instance there was a bona fide script written "on spec" under the title *Blood Feast Part 2*. But again, a film deal never materialized. Lewis himself eventually talked to David Friedman about making a sequel to their most famous film. "Dave Friedman and I have talked about doing *Blood Feast 2*," Lewis admitted, "but, again, I'm not going to put my money into it. I'm perfectly willing to direct such a picture, but it's got to be financed totally by someone else." Producers, take note.

Although *Blood Feast 2* is just an idea that has been kicking around for a while, Herschell does have a fully scripted gore film ready and waiting to go — *Herschell Gordon Lewis's Grim Fairy Tales*. The title is an exploitation natural. Made inexpensively, such a film would certainly do well in the video and cable markets. But again, Lewis is only interested in writing and directing. If it ever happens, well and good; and if it doesn't happen, that's all right, too.

Herschell has few regrets when it comes to his motion picture career. He still winces when he thinks about the goat-carcass effect he let slip away during the making of *The Wizard of Gore*, and there are a few other effects he wanted to do but was never able to pull off. "I simply couldn't afford to do some of the gore effects I had in mind," he noted. "For instance, I always wanted to have a picture where I had a body blow up. I wanted a stick of dynamite inside a human being, and I wanted to have that body literally explode. I could have done it, but with the expense involved and the costs of setting it up, it would have cost as much as the entire budget for *Blood Feast*. And no effect, no matter how wonderful, is worth that kind of expense in my book."

The ripples from that $24,500 production are still being felt in modern horror films. Whether he realized it at the time or not, H. G. Lewis carved out a niche in the fantasy film world with his unflinching look at what lay beneath the surface of human horror. When the masked killer of Wes Craven's *Scream* tells guest star Drew Barrymore, "I want to see what your insides look like," she might have saved everyone a lot of bother by referring him to the films of Herschell Gordon Lewis.

They didn't call him the Godfather of Gore for nothing.

Filmography

The Adventures of Lucky Pierre (1961). Also known as ***Lucky Pierre***. Written by David F. Friedman and Herschell Gordon Lewis; directed by Herschell Gordon Lewis. Running time: 70 minutes.

Cast: Lawrence J. Aberwood, Linda Cotton, William Kerwin, Billy Falbo (Lucky Pierre).

Alley Tramp (1966). Also known as ***Alley Tramps; I Am a Woman; Pleasure Me, Master***. Written by Allison Louise Downe and Paul Gordone; directed by Herschell Gordon Lewis. Running time: 68 minutes.

Cast: Lamone Baimu, Lisa Bourdon-Annette Courset, Marie Delmonde, Jean Lamee, Jacques Sette, Annette Souvet.

Bell, Bare and Beautiful (1963). Written by Leroy C. Griffith; directed by Herschell Gordon Lewis. Running time: 75 minutes.

Cast: Virginia Bell (Gina), Sunny Dare (Elsa), Jerome Eden, David F. Friedman (Barney), Joy Hodges (Betty), William Kerwin (Rick).

Black Love (1972). Directed by Herschell Gordon Lewis. Running time: 72 minutes.

Blast-Off Girls (1967). Written and directed by Herschell Gordon Lewis. Running time: 83 minutes.

Cast: Julia Ames (Barbara), Sharon Camille (Maxine), Dan Conway (Boojie Baker), Sarasue Gleiss (Laurie), Barbara Harrison (Angel), Ann Heath (Harriet), Sherri Lane (Kim), Ray Sager (Gordie), Harland Sanders (Himself), Sally Tenerelli (Sally); Dennis Hickey, Tom Liace, Ralph Mullin, Tom Tyrell, Chris Wolsky (Members of "The Big Blast").

Blood Feast (1963). Written by A. Louise Downe; produced by David F. Friedman; directed by Herschell Gordon Lewis. Running time: 63 minutes.

Cast: Mal Arnold (Fuad Ramses), Lyn Bolton (Mrs. Fremont), Toni Calvert (Trudy), Gene Courtier (Tony), Jerome Eden (High Priest), Al Golden (Dr. Flanders), Scott H. Hall (Police Captain), Louise Kamp (Victim), Thomas Wood [William Kerwin] (Pete Thornton), Ashlyn Martin (Marcy), Connie Mason (Suzette Fremont), Craig Maudslay, Jr. (Garbage Scow Driver), Astrid Olsen (Victim), Sandra Sinclair (Pat Tracey), Hal Rich.

Blood Orgy see ***The Gore-Gore Girls***

Boin-n-g! (1963). Produced by David F. Friedman; directed by Herschell Gordon Lewis. Running time: 75 minutes.

Cast: Lawrence J. Aberwood, Linda Cotton.

Color Me Blood Red (1965). Also known as ***Model Massacre***. Produced by David F. Friedman; written and directed by Herschell Gordon Lewis. Running time: 79 minutes.

Cast: Cathy Collins (Mitzi), Candi Conder (April), Jerome Eden (Rolf), Scott H. Hall (Farnsworth), William Harris (Gregorovich), James Jackel (Jack), Don Joseph [Gordon Oas-heim] (Adam Sorg), Patricia Lee (Sydney), Iris Marshall (Mrs. Carter), Elyn Warner (Gigi).

Copenhagen Psychic Love see ***The Psychic***

Daughter of the Sun (1962). Written by David F. Friedman and Herschell Gordon Lewis; produced by David F. Friedman;

directed by Herschell Gordon Lewis. Black-and-white with color inserts. Running time: 60 minutes.

Cast: Rusty Allen (Pamela Walker), Jerome Eden (School Board Member), Elsie Kerbin, Pearl Krohn.

Destruction, Inc. see ***Just for the Hell of It***

The Devil's Camera see ***Scum of the Earth***

The Ecstasies of Women (1969). Produced by Tom Dowd; directed by Herschell Gordon Lewis.

The Girl, the Boy, and the Pill (1967). Also known as ***The Girl, the Body, and the Pill; The Pill.*** Written by Allison Louise Downe; directed by Herschell Gordon Lewis. Running time: 73 minutes.

Cast: George Brown (Brad Martin), Roy Collodi (Pike Grover), Todd Harris (Charlie), Valedia Hill (Irene Hunt), James Nelson (Roy Stanton), Nancy Lee Noble (Randy Hunt), Sue Puccinelli (Nancy Foster), Pamela Rhae (Marcia Barrington), Bill Rogers (Wesley Nichols), Kay Ross (Alice Nichols), Ray Sager [Ray Szegho] (Tony), Otto Schlessinger (Mr. Price), Pat Tenerelli (Freddy), Eleanor Valli (Grace Nichols).

Goldilocks and the Three Bares (1963). Also known as ***Goldilocks' Three Chicks.*** Produced by David F. Friedman; directed by Herschell Gordon Lewis. Running time: 70 minutes.

Cast: Mal Arnold, Allison Louise Downe (Allison Edwards), William Kerwin (Tommy), Netta Mallina (Myrna), Rex Marlow (Eddie), Craig Maudslay, Jr., Joey Maxim (Himself), Delores Mooney, Judy Parsons, Maria Stinger, Toni Toomey.

Goldilocks' Three Chicks see ***Goldilocks and the Three Bares***

The Gore-Gore Girls (1972). Also known as ***Blood Orgy.*** Written by Alan J. Dachman; produced and directed by Herschell Gordon Lewis. Running time: 84 minutes.

Cast: Nora Alexis, Russ Badger (Police Lieutenant), Amy Farrell (Nancy Weston), Frank Kress (Abraham Gentry), Phil Laurenson, Heddy Lubin, Frank Rice (Grout), Ray Sager [Ray Szegho], Henny Youngman (Mobile).

The Gruesome Twosome (1967). Written by Allison Louise Downe; produced and directed by Herschell Gordon Lewis. Running time: 80 minutes.

Cast: Andrea Barr, Rodney Bedell, Marcelle Bichette, Tom Brent, Ronnie Cass, Elizabeth Davis, C. A. Dukes, Chris Martell, Dianne Raymond, Sherry Robinson, Karl Stoeber, Mike Todd, Barrie Walton, Gretchen Wells, Dianne Wilhite.

Hell Kitten see ***The Prime Time***

How to Make a Doll (1968). Written by Bert Ray and Herschell Gordon Lewis; directed by Herschell Gordon Lewis. Running time: 81 minutes.

Cast: Patricia Rhea, Jim Vance, Bobbi West, Robert Wood (Percy Corly).

I Am a Woman see ***Alley Tramp***

Jimmy, the Boy Wonder (1966). Also known as ***Jimmy, the Wonder Boy.*** Directed by Herschell Gordon Lewis. Running time: 69 minutes.

Cast: Nancy Berg (Aurora).

Jimmy, the Wonder Boy see ***Jimmy, the Boy Wonder***

Just for the Hell of It (1968). Also known as ***Destruction, Inc.*** Written and directed by Herschell Gordon Lewis. Running time: 85 minutes.

Cast: Rodney Bedell, Agi Gynes, Nancy Lee Noble, Ray Sager [Ray Szegho], Steve White.

Linda and Abilene (1969). Directed by Herschell Gordon Lewis.

Living Venus (1960). Also known as ***The Devil's Camera.*** Directed by Herschell Gordon Lewis. Running time: 74 minutes.

Cast: Lawrence J. Aberwood, Linne Ahlstrand, Robert Bell, Danica D'Hondt (Peggy Brandon), Billy Falbo, William Kerwin (Jack Norwall), Harvey Korman (Ken Carter), Jeanette Leahy.

Lucky Pierre see *The Adventures of Lucky Pierre*

The Magic Land of Mother Goose (1967). Also known as *Santa Visits the Magic Land of Mother Goose*. Directed by Herschell Gordon Lewis.

Miss Nymphet's Zap-In (1970). Also known as *Zap-In*. Written and directed by Herschell Gordon Lewis.

Model Massacre see *Color Me Blood Red*

Monster A' Go-Go (1965). Also known as *Terror at Halfday*. Directed by Bill Rebane; uncredited writing and direction by Herschell Gordon Lewis; additional dialogue by Lewis (as Sheldon Seymour). Running time: 70 minutes.
 Cast: Lois Brooks, Del Clark, Aviva Crane, Leonard Gelstein, Barry Hopkins, Phil Morton, George Perri, Lori Perri, Art Scott, Robert Simons, Rork Stevens, Stu Taylor, Peter Thompson, Dean Tompis, June Travis.

Moonshine Mountain (1964). Also known as *White Trash on Moonshine Mountain*. Written by Charles Glore; directed by Herschell Gordon Lewis. Running time: 90 minutes.
 Cast: Jeffrey Allen [Taalkius Blank], Mark Douglas, Charles Glore (Doug Martin), Bonnie Hinson, Ben Moore, J. G. Patterson, Jr., Adam Sorg, [Gordon Oas-heim], Carmen Sotir.

Nature's Playmates (1962). Written by Bentley Williams; directed by Herschell Gordon Lewis. Running time: 62 minutes.
 Cast: Ingrun Albert, Allison Louise Downe (Diana), Al Glick (Camp Director), Fred Gordon (Camp Director), Warrene Gray, Shirley Gresham, Peter Lathrop (Ellsworth Elliott), Craig Maudslay, Jr., Marsha Monnet, Amy O'Donnell, Scott Osborne (Russ Harper), Judy Parsons, Elaine Roberts, Teri Stevens (Mrs. Elliott), Doris Wishman.

The Pill see *The Girl, the Boy, and the Pill*

Pleasure Me, Master see *Alley Tramp*

The Prime Time (1960). Also known as *Hell Kitten*. Written by Robert Abel; produced by Herschell Gordon Lewis; directed by Gordon Weisenborn; cinematography by Andrew M. Costikyan; editing by Elsie Kerbin. A Mid-Continent Films production. Running time: 76 minutes.
 Cast: Karen Black (Painted Woman), James Brooks (Tony), Ray Gronwold (The Beard), Jo Ann LeCompte (Jean), Robert Major (Shorty), Maria Pavelle (Gloria), Frank Roche (McKeen), Betty Senter (Ruthie).

The Psychic (1968). Also known as *Copenhagen Psychic Love*. Produced and directed by James F. Hurley and Herschell Gordon Lewis. Running time: 90 minutes.
 Cast: Dick Genola, Robin Guest, Carol Saenz, Bobbi Spencer.

Santa Visits the Magic Land of Mother Goose see *The Magic Land of Mother Goose*

Scum of the Earth (1963). Also known as *The Devil's Camera*. Produced and directed by Herschell Gordon Lewis. Running time: 71 minutes.
 Cast: Mal Arnold (Larry), Toni Calvert (Marie), Allison Louise Downe (Kim), William Kerwin (Harmon), Edward Mann (Mr. Sherwood), Craig Maudslay, Jr. (Ajax), Sandra Sinclair (Sandy), Lawrence Wood (Lang).

The Secret of Dr. Alucard see *A Taste of Blood.*

She-Devils on Wheels (1968). Written by Allison Louise Downe; produced by Jerry Sandy; directed by Herschell Gordon Lewis. Running time: 83 minutes.
 Cast: Rodney Bedell (Ted), John Chaffin (Police Officer), Roy Collodi (Bartender), Betty Connell (Queen), David Harris (Bill), Joani Kramer (Russian), Nancy Lee Noble (Honey-Pot), Laura Platz (Supergirl), Pat Posten (Whitey), John Shackleford (Police Officer), Donna Stelzer (Mac), Donna Testa (Poodle), Ruby Tuesday (Terry), Christie Wagner (Karen), John Weymer (Joe-Boy), Steve White (Doodie), Rick Williams (Outlaw).

Sin, Suffer, and Repent (1965). Directed by Herschell Gordon Lewis.

Something Weird (1967). Written by James F. Hurley; directed by Herschell Gordon Lewis. Running time: 80 minutes.

Cast: Lawrence J. Aberwood, Lee Ahsmann, Jeffrey Allen [Taalkius Blank], Mudite Arums, William Brooker, Daniel Carrington, Janet Charlton, Roy Collodi, Stan Dale, Dick Gaffield, Ted Heil, Kathleen Koenig (The Apparition), Elizabeth Lee, Norm Lenet, Tony McCabe, Louis Newman, Richard Nilsson, Roger Papsch, Carolyn Smith, Larry Wellington.

Suburban Roulette (1967). Written by Herschell Gordon Lewis, Jim McGinn, and James Thomas III; directed by Herschell Gordon Lewis. Running time: 91 minutes.

Cast: Allison Louise Downe (Margo Elston), Debbie Grant (Cindy Fisher), William Kerwin (Marty Conley), Tony McCabe (Ron Elston), Ben Moore (Bert Fisher), Richard Mark Oliver (Conley Child), Ione Rolnick (Fran Conley), Bob Roth (Card Buyer), Michael Shallop (Conley Child), Joseph Trucco (Conley Child), Elizabeth Wilkinson (Ilene Fisher), Ray Woods (Police Chief).

A Taste of Blood (1968). Also known as *The Secret of Dr. Alucard*. Written by Donald Stanford; produced by Sidney J. Reich; directed by Herschell Gordon Lewis. Running time: 117 minutes.

Cast: Dolores Carlos (Sherri Morris), Gail Janis (Vivian), William Kerwin (Dr. Hank Tyson), Sheldon Seymour [Herschell Gordon Lewis] (British Seaman), Sidney J. Reich (Lawyer), Bill Rogers (John Stone), Ted Schell (Lord Gold), Otto Schlessinger (Dr. Howard Helsing), Lawrence Tobin (Detective Crane), Eleanor Valli (Hester), Elizabeth Wilkinson (Helene Stone).

Terror at Halfday see *Monster A' Go-Go*

This Stuff 'll Kill Ya! (1971). Written and directed by Herschell Gordon Lewis. Running time: 75 minutes.

Cast: Jeffrey Allen [Taalkius Blank] (Reverend Boone), Eric Bradly, Larry Drake, Tim Holt, Gloria King, Terence McCarthy.

Two Thousand Maniacs! (1964). Produced by David F. Friedman; written and directed by Herschell Gordon Lewis. Running time: 87 minutes.

Cast: Jeffrey Allen [Taalkius Blank] (Mayor Buckman), Gary Bakeman (Rufe), Linda Cochran (Betsy), Mark Douglas (Harper), Jerome Eden (John Miller), Yvonne Gilbert (Beverly Wells), Thomas Wood [William Kerwin] (Tom White), Michael Korb (David Wells), Shelby Livingston (Bea Miller), Connie Mason (Terry Adams), Ben Moore (Lester), Vincent Santo (Billy), Andy Wilson (Police Officer).

White Trash on Moonshine Mountain see *Moonshine Mountain*

The Wizard of Gore (1968; released 1970). Produced by Jerry Sandy; written by Allen Kahn; directed by Herschell Gordon Lewis. Running time: 96 minutes.

Cast: Don Alexander (Detective Kramer), Judy Cler (Sherry Carson), John Elliot (Detective Harlan), Phil Laurenson (Greg), Wayne Ratay (Jack), Jim Rau (Steve), Ray Sager [Ray Szegho] (Montag).

Year of the Yahoo (1972). Directed by Herschell Gordon Lewis. Running time: 80 minutes.

Cast: Jeffrey Allen [Taalkius Blank], Terrell Cass, Robert Jolly, Claude King, Tom Lytel, Ronna Riddle, Ray Sager [Ray Szegho], Leslie Slater, Robert Swain.

Zap-In see *Miss Nymphet's Zap-In*

Index

Abbott and Costello Meet the Mummy 40
Abel, Robert 15, 16
Aberman, Lawrence (a.k.a. Lawrence J. Aberwood) 35, 107
Aberwood, Lawrence J. 35; see also Aberman, Lawrence
Adler, Allen 16
Adult Filmmaker's Association 175
The Adventures of Lucky Pierre 10, 19, 22–26, 27, 31, 36, 100, 101, 102, 104, 122, 129, 143, 177, 182
Advertising Age 8
Afraid of the Dark 67
The African Queen 11
Ahsmann, Lee 107
Alexana, Karin 146
Alexander, Don 146
Alexis, Nora 163, 164, 165
Allen, Rusty 27, 28, 29, 30
Allen, Woody 172
Alley Tramp 107, 182
The Alligator People 14
Alone in the Dark 67
The Amazing Herschell Gordon Lewis and His World of Exploitation Films (book) 155
Ameri, Ali 146; see also Ameripoor, Alex
American International Pictures 5, 7, 9, 11, 15, 40, 66, 69, 109, 132, 134, 136, 139, 140, 160, 176
American Medical Association 23
American Sunbathing Association 23
Ameripoor, Alex (a.k.a Alex Ameri) 146, 155, 157, 158, 167
Angels from Hell 136
April Fool's Day 67
Argento, Dario 161, 175
Arkoff, Samuel Z. 9, 139, 140
Armstrong, Michael 63
Arnold, Mal 32, 33, 43, 51, 53, 56, 57
Arums, Mudite 107
Ashley, John 62
Atlas, David 146
Avalon, Frankie 176
Babb, Kroger 3
Badger, Russ 163, 165

Bakeman, Gary 70, 71, 74, 75, 76
Barfred Laboratories 39
Barrymore, Drew 181
Bates, Kathy 106
Bava, Mario 161, 175
Bay of Blood 175
Beach Blanket Bingo 176
The Beatles 117
Bedell, Rodney 134, 138
Bell, Charlotte 146
Bell, Virginia 27, 36
Bell, Bare and Beautiful 7, 36, 37, 43, 182
Ben-Hur 81, 170
Berg, Hal 105, 106
Berg, Nancy 106
Beuchler, John Carl 174
The Beverly Hillbillies 81
Bew, Corlee 161
Bibo, Walter 23
Birth of a Baby 32
Black Christmas 67
Black Love 159, 182
Black Sunday 175
Black, Karen 16, 19, 49, 177
Blank, Taalkius (a.k.a. Jeffrey Allen) 70, 74, 75, 157, 159
Blast-Off Girls 110, 116–117, 118, 182
The Blob 14
Blood and Black Lace 161
Blood Feast 1, 2, 5, 7, 10, 12, 19, 32, 33, 37, 38–65, 66, 67, 69, 70, 71, 80, 81, 84, 85, 89, 91, 92, 93, 94, 98, 102, 104, 107, 109, 114, 119, 122, 129, 134, 135, 140, 141, 144, 145, 150, 154, 160, 161, 162, 163, 164, 167, 169, 170, 174, 175, 176, 177, 180, 181, 182
Blood Feast Part 2 2, 8, 181
Blood from the Mummy's Tomb 5
Blood Orgy see The Gore-Gore Girls
Blood Shed Theatre 174
Blood Sisters 67
Bloodsucking Freaks 175
Bloody Birthday 67
Bogart, Humphrey 157

187

Bogdanovich, Peter 12
Boin-n-g! 35, 36, 129, 134, 182
Bolton, Lyn 43
Bonnie and Clyde 81, 177
Bora Bora 140
Born Losers 136, 140
Bottin, Rob 174
Bousman, Lena 162
The Bradford Exchange 179
Bradly, Eric 158
Brain Dead 41
Brando, Marlon 44
Brides of Blood 62
Brinkman, Richard 129
Brody, Sally 146
Brooker, William 107
Brooks, James 16
Brooks, Lois 101
Brown, George 118
Burke, Karen 146
Burnette, Carol 19
The Burning 67
Burton, Lance 147

A Clockwork Orange 168
Calhoun Collector's Society 179
Camera Equipment Company 79
The Candidate 159
Carlos, Dolores 125, 126, 127
Carnival Story 18
Carpenter, John 79, 175
Cass, Terrell 159
Cassavettes, John 136
Castle, William 43
Castle of Frankenstein (magazine) 39
Catch-22 160
Cat-Women of the Moon 102
CBS Television 135, 143
Chambers, John 174
Chaney, Lon, Jr. 122
Channing, Carol 46
Chopping Mall 67
Chrysler Motors 18
Chudnow, David 119, 133
Chudnow, Rosamond 133
The Cinema Bizarre 174
Cinemation Pictures 139
Clark, Del 101
Clark, Dick 136
Cler, Judy 146
Clinton, Bill 64
Cochran, Linda 70, 71, 77
Cohen, Herman 14, 60
Collodi, Roy 118, 129, 137, 138
Colonial Motel 49, 50
Color Me Blood Red 2, 42, 58, 83–96, 97, 102, 104, 107, 114, 124, 125, 161, 163, 180, 183

Color Service Laboratory 22
Columbia Pictures 81
Conder, Candi 86, 90
Connell, Betty 137
The Conqueror Worm 107
Conway, Tom 11
Copenhagen Psychic Love see *The Psychic*
Corman, Roger 5, 14, 22, 23, 24, 49, 83, 120, 136, 140
Costikyan, Andrew M. 17
Cotton Council of Memphis 8
Courtier, Gene 49
Craven, Wes 175, 181
Cronenberg, David 175
Crown International Pictures 136, 160
Cunningham, Sean 175
The Curse of Frankenstein 9, 11, 41, 60
Curse of the Demon 175
Curtin, Jack 22
Cushing, Peter 11, 40
The Cycle Savages 136
Cyrano de Bergerac 105

Dachman, Alan J. 161, 162, 168
Dachman, Bob 161, 166
Daughter of the Sun 5, 27–31, 36, 182, 183
Davis, Sammy, Jr. 121, 122
Dawn of the Dead 175
Day of the Dead 181
The Day of the Teenie-Boppers 132
Dead-Alive 41, 175
The Deadly Mantis 14
Deep Red 161
The Del-Tones 114
Dern, Bruce 19, 136
Destruction, Inc. see *Just for the Hell of It*
Devil's Angels 136
Disney, Walt 170
Don't Answer the Phone 67
Don't Go in the House 67
Don't Open Till Christmas 67
Don't Raise the Bridge, Lower the River 130
Douglas, Mark 70, 72, 74
Dowd, Tom 25, 32, 36, 107, 142
Downe, Allison Louise (a.k.a Vickie Miles) 32, 33, 37, 39, 40, 41, 53, 54, 107, 109, 115, 119, 128, 136, 137, 138, 145, 155, 161, 167
Dr. Jekyll and Sister Hyde 160
Dracula 174
Dragstrip Riot 9
Drake, Larry 158
The Devil's Camera see *Scum of the Earth*

Eastwood, Clint 10
The Ecstasies of Women 142, 183
Eden, Jerome 47, 53, 54, 70, 76, 84, 86
Elliot, John 146

The Erotic Adventures of Zorro 105
Esquire (magazine) 81
Exchange National Bank of Chicago 92, 93
The Exorcist 14, 81, 175
An Eye for an Eye 106

F & B Ceco 79
Fairchild, Morgan 48
Falbo, Billy 19, 24, 25, 31
Family Plot 19
Famous Monsters of Filmland (magazine) 39
Fanfare Pictures 7, 136, 160
Fangoria (magazine) 180
Farrell, Amy 162
Ferrer, Jose 105
Field, Stephen 146
Filmfax (magazine) 174
Filmgroup 140
Fisher, Terence 43, 175
Flipper 37
Flynn, Charles 176
Fonda, Peter 136
Foreign Correspondent 91
Forrest, Steve 18
Forsythe, Cecil 57
Frankenstein 174
Frenzy 91
Friday the 13th 8, 40, 42, 46, 57, 67, 175, 177, 181
Friday the 13th Part IV, The Final Chapter 42, 181
Friedkin, William 175
Friedman, Carol 22
Friedman, David F. 1, 3, 4, 17, 21, 22, 23, 24, 25, 27, 29, 31, 32, 33, 34, 35, 36, 37, 39, 43, 47, 48, 50, 52, 53, 57, 58, 59, 60, 61, 62, 63, 65, 67, 68, 69, 77, 79, 80, 82, 83, 84, 86, 92, 93, 94, 95, 97, 99, 104, 105, 122, 129, 133, 138, 139, 158, 176, 181
Fulci, Lucio 175
Funicello, Annette 176

Garden of Eden 23
Galaxy Girls 161, 171, 172
The Giant Behemoth (a.k.a. *Behemoth, the Sea Monster*) 16
Gilbert, Yvonne 70, 78
The Girl, the Body, and the Pill see *The Girl, the Boy, and the Pill*
The Girl, the Boy, and the Pill 116, 117, 183
Girls' School Screamers 67
Glick, Al 32
Glore, Chuck 86, 97
The Glory Stompers 134, 136
Golden, Al 44, 45, 135
Goldilocks and the Three Bares 32, 36, 183
Goldilocks' Three Chicks see *Goldilocks and the Three Bares*

Gordon, Alex 11
Gordon, Lewis H. (HGL pseudonym) 101
Gordone, Paul 107
Gore Feast 181
The Gore-Gore Girls 2, 8, 12, 41, 42, 43, 49, 58, 76, 96, 145, 150, 154, 160–171, 172, 173, 174, 183
Graduation Day 67
Green Acres 81
Gresham, Shirley 32
Griffith, D. W. 175
Griffith, Leroy 35, 36
Gross, Jerry 139
The Gruesome Twosome 2, 12, 42, 43, 58, 109–115, 121, 128, 133, 134, 145, 146, 147, 155, 161, 162, 167, 180, 183
Gulliver's Travels 159
Gynes, Agi 134, 135, 136

Hall, Scott F. 43, 44, 52, 55, 56, 84, 85, 88, 128, 146, 177
Hallmark Films 63, 160
Halloween 8, 14, 40, 42, 67, 175
Halloween 5 42
Hammer Films 5, 9, 11, 40, 41, 62, 160
The Hand (1960) 60
Hansen, Mark (HGL pseudonym) 101
Happy Birthday to Me 67
A Hard Day's Night 117
Harris, Bill 92
Hawks, Howard 7, 12, 14
He Knows You're Alone 67
Hefner, Hugh 18, 47
Hell Kitten see *The Prime Time*
Hell Night 67
Hell's Angels on Wheels 7, 136
The Hellcats 136
Hemisphere Pictures 62
Hendrix, Jimi 103
Herman, Adolf 34, 35
Herschell Gordon Lewis's Grim Fairy Tales 171, 181
Hide and Go Shriek 67
Hill, Valedia 118
Hitchcock, Alfred 7, 12, 19, 82
Hite, Henry 101, 102
Hollywood Chainsaw Hookers 67
Holt, Tim 49, 157, 158, 177
Hooper, Tobe 147
Hopkins, Barry 101
Hopper, Dennis 136
Horror of Dracula 9, 11, 41, 175
The Horror of Party Beach 114
Hot Rod Girl 14
How to Make a Doll 110, 133–134, 135, 183
How to Make a Monster 133
How to Marry a Millionaire 133

How to Murder Your Wife 133
How to Stuff a Wild Bikini 133
How to Succeed in Business Without Really Trying 133
Hunter, Tab 47, 49
Hurley, James 103, 107, 109, 141, 142
Huston, Walter 157
Hyatt, Daniel 16

I Am a Woman see *Alley Tramp*
I Drink Your Blood 175
I Know What You Did Last Summer 67
I Was a Teenage Frankenstein 60
I Was a Teenage Werewolf 9, 14
Image et Son 82
The Immoral Mr. Teas 23
The Incredible Shrinking Man 14
The Incredibly Strange Creatures Who Stopped Living and Became the Mixed-Up Zombies 102

Jack the Ripper 64, 164
Jackson, Eli 35, 36
Jackson, Michael 1
Jacqueline Kay Corp. 92, 102
Jaekel, James 86
Janis, Gail 125
Jaws 14
Jaye, Sidney 128, 129
Jimmy, the Boy Wonder 105, 183
Jimmy, the Wonder Boy see *Jimmy, the Boy Wonder*
Johnson, Bill 29
Jolly, Robert 159
Joseph, Don 85; *see also* Oas-heim, Gordon
Joseph, Erwin 17, 18, 19, 20, 21, 22, 23
Jurassic Park 81, 105, 177
Just for the Hell of It 7, 110, 134–135, 138, 146, 155, 156, 183

Kaaber, Bent 122
Kahn, Allen 145, 159
Kamp, Louise 54
Karloff, Boris 40, 174
Kelly, Mary 164
Kennedy, Ian 180
Kennedy, Robert 103
Koenig, Kathleen 107
Kerbin, Elsie 17
Kerr, Harry 97, 98, 99, 103
Kerwin, Barbara 115
Kerwin, Kim 115
Kerwin, William (a.k.a. Thomas Wood, Rooney Kerwin) 11, 19, 24, 32, 33, 35, 38, 40, 43, 45, 47, 48, 55, 63, 68, 119, 120, 124, 128, 146, 177
King, Claude 159
King, Gloria 158
King, Stephen 12

King Solomon's Mines 11
Kings of the B's 175, 176
Kirkin, Corinne 146
Klein, Bill 20, 21, 23, 24
Kohlberg, Stanford 34, 35, 36, 37, 59, 60, 65, 69, 84, 92, 93, 94, 95, 97, 102, 104, 130, 142
Korb, Michael 70, 77
Korman, Harvey 19, 49, 177
Kress, Frank 162, 165
Krogh, Daniel 155, 167
Kubrick, Stanley 168

LaDu, Kathy 146
Lamour, Dorothy 49
Lang, Fritz 7
Last Tango in Paris 168
Laughlin, Tom 136, 140
Laurenson, Phil 146
Leary, Timothy 103
LeCompte, Jo Ann 16
Lee, Christopher 11, 40, 122, 177
Lee, Patricia 86
The Leech Woman 14
The Legacy 107
Lemmon, Jack 177
Leone, Sergio 10
Lewis, Barry 155
Lewis, Jerry 130, 131
Lewis, Margo 180
Lewis, Michael 115
Lewis, Robert 76, 115, 145, 150, 154, 160, 165, 173, 180
Lewis-Andrews Theaters 173
Lewis, Nelson, Kahn Advertising Agency 178
Lewis and Martin Films 13, 20, 29
Lewis Motion Picture Enterprises 159
Li'l Abner 99, 101
Linda and Abilene 66, 141, 142–143, 183
Link Belt Company 13
The Little Shop of Horrors 23
Living Venus 18–20, 21, 22, 31, 39, 49, 102, 119, 183
Livingston, Shelby 70, 71, 72, 74, 75
Lorre, Peter 40
"Louie, Louie" 114
Lourie, Eugene 16
Love Camp #7 105
Lubin, Hedda 165
Lucas, George 46
Lucky Pierre see *The Adventures of Lucky Pierre*
Lugosi, Bela 174
Lust for a Vampire 160
Lytel, Tom 159

MacPhail, Menda 166
The Mad Doctor of Blood Island 62
The Magic Land of Mother Goose 33, 183, 184

The Maltese Falcon 170
Maniac (1980) 67, 181
Manson, Charles 142
Mark of the Devil 63
Marshall, Brian 106
Martin, Ashlyn 49
Mason, Connie 43, 45, 46, 47, 48, 49, 52, 56, 58, 67, 68, 70, 73, 79, 83, 92, 126, 146, 177
Mason, Emily 162
Max Factor 39
Maxim, Joey 32
Maximum Overdrive 12
Mayflower Pictures 109, 115, 121, 139, 143, 156, 159
McCabe, Tony 119
McCarthy, Terence 158
McCarthy, Todd 176
McCarty, John 105, 177
McGinn, Jim (a.k.a James Thomas) 18, 119, 120
Metro-Goldwyn-Mayer Pictures 169, 170
Meyer, Russ 3, 23
Microwave Massacre 67
Mid-Continent Films 15, 16, 17, 18, 19, 20, 21
Miles, Vickie 136; *see also* Downe, Allison Louise
Mimic 56
The Mini-Skirt Mob 136
Miss Nymphet's Zap-In 143, 156, 184
Mississippi State 8
Model Massacre see *Color Me Blood Red*
Modern Film Distributors 3, 17, 18, 19
Mom and Dad 17
Monroe, Marilyn 49, 68
Monster A' Go-Go 5, 100–102, 104, 105, 109, 184
The Monster That Challenged the World 14
Mooney, Delores 32
Moonshine Mountain 67, 81, 94, 95, 96, 97–99, 102, 104, 105, 119, 129, 157, 184
Moore, Ben 67, 70, 71, 74, 75, 76, 77, 97, 119, 120
Moore, Roger 162
Morlock Advertising Agency 21
Morton, Phil 101
Mother's Day 67
Motion Picture Association of America 10, 63, 118–119, 145, 168, 169
Mr. Bruce and the Gore Machine 171, 172–173
The Mummy (1932) 40
The Mummy (1959) 9
The Mummy's Curse 40
The Mummy's Ghost 40
The Mummy's Hand 40
The Mummy's Tomb 40
The Muppets 170
Murphy, Jamie 180
My Bloody Valentine 67

Nature's Playmates 32, 36, 184
Neimark, Paul 61
Nelson, Carol 180
New Year's Evil 67
Newman, Paul 11
Newsweek (magazine) 81
Nicholson, Jack 136
Nicholson, James H. 9, 66
Night of the Living Dead 175
Night School 67
Nightmare (1981) 67
A Nightmare on Elm Street 8, 42, 175
Niles, Fred 15, 16
Nixon, Richard 103
Noble, Nancy Lee 118, 138
Northwestern University 8, 9
Novel Books 61, 67

Oas-heim, Gordon (a.k.a Don Joseph) 84, 85, 86, 87, 90, 91, 93, 98
L'Observateur 82
O'Donnell, Amy 32
Oedipus Rex 64
Olsen, Astrid 51, 53
The Omen 107

Parades, George (HGL pseudonym) 101
Paramount Pictures 3, 17, 81, 99
Parsons, Judy 32
Patterson, L. G. "Pat" 97, 129
Pays, Armand (HGL pseudonym) 101
Peckinpah, Sam 12, 41
Perry, George 101
Pfeiffer, Frank 101
Pickman, Jerry 3
The Pill see *The Girl, the Boy, and the Pill*
Playboy (magazine) 47, 48, 49, 52
The Pleasant Valley Boys 81
Pleasure Me, Master see *Alley Tramp*
Poe, Edgar Allan 40, 176
Polanski, Roman 82
Posner, Bill 132
Price, Vincent 40, 146, 168, 176
The Prime Time 15–18, 19, 21, 22, 31, 49, 102, 106, 108, 184
Prom Night 67
The Prowler 67
The Psychic 141–142
Psycho (1960) 82, 91

Ratay, Wayne 146
Rau, Jim 146
Raymond, Dianne 112
Raynard, Eric Kelner 146
Reagan, Ronald 1, 60
The Re-Animator 41, 175
Rebane, Bill 100, 101, 102

Redford, Robert 159
Reefer Madness 17
Reich, Sid 37, 92, 93, 102, 103, 107, 121, 122, 125, 129, 132, 133
Reis, Sheldon 146
Reitman, Jerry 180
Reynolds, Burt 69, 177
Rhea, Patricia 133
Rice, Frank 162, 164
Ringling Bros. and Barnum & Bailey Circus 91, 93
Riot on Sunset Strip 7
Roche, Frank 16
Rocky 8
Rogers, Bill 118, 122, 123, 125
Rolnick, Ione 119
Romanoff, Andy 78, 127, 129, 137
Romero, George 175
Rooney, Mickey 46
Ross, Eddie 25
Ross, Kay 118
Rowan and Martin's Laugh-In 24, 135, 143
Ryan's Daughter 169

Sack, Al 21, 22, 107
Sager, Ray (a.k.a. Ray Szegho) 115, 118, 134, 145, 146, 147, 148, 150, 151, 157, 158, 159, 162, 167, 172
Salli, Marina 165
San Diego Union 70
Sandy, Fred 103, 109, 110, 115, 133, 139, 140, 143, 145, 146, 156
Sandy, Jerry 109, 110, 139, 143, 156
Santa Claus Visits the Magic Land of Mother Goose see *The Magic Land of Mother Goose*
Santo, Vincent 76, 79
The Savage Seven 136
Savini, Tom 174, 180
Schell, Ted 124, 125
Schlessinger, Otto 118, 127
Schmidhofer, Martin 13, 24
Schwartz, Abbott 133
Scott, Chuck 81, 97
Scream 67, 181
Screen Actors Guild 15, 16, 19
Scum of the Earth 33, 102, 184
The Secret of Dr. Alucard see *A Taste of Blood*
The Sender 107
The Sensitive see *Something Weird*
Senter, Betty 16
Seymour, Sheldon (HGL pseudonym) 101
Shakespeare, William 44
The She-Creature 11
She-Devils on Wheels 5, 7, 110, 135–140, 143, 156, 176, 184
She-Freak 105
Sheldon, Seymour (HGL pseudonym) 101
Sherman, General William T. 70
Shivers 175
Shrine Circus 49
Signal 30 13
Silent Night, Deadly Night 67
Simons, Robert 101
Sin, Suffer, and Repent 32–33, 184
Sinatra, Frank 68, 121, 122
Sinatra, Nancy 136
Sinclair, Sandra 33, 42
Sinise, Bob 95
Slater, Leslie 159
Slaughter High 67
Slaughter Hotel 160
The Sleaze Merchants (book) 105, 177, 178
Sleeper 172
Slumber Party Massacre 67
The Smash-In see *Just for the Hell of It*
Smith, Bob 159
Smith, Dick 174
Smith, Jeff 101
Smith, R. L. (HGL pseudonym) 101
Snuff 160
Soderblom, Kenny 25
Something Weird 67, 107, 108, 109, 110, 115, 122, 141, 184, 185
Son of Dracula 122
Sonney, Dan 3, 95
Sonney Amusement Enterprises 95
Sophocles 64
Sorority House Massacre 67
Spahn, George 141
Spahn Movie Ranch 141, 142, 143
Spartan Tropical Gardens 27, 28, 29, 36, 38
Spielberg, Steven 46
Stanford, Donald "Dok" 101, 121, 122
Star Wars 42
Stern, Aaron 169
Stern, Tom 136
Stevens, Rork 101
Stinger, Maria 32
Stoker, Bram 123
Strasberg, Lee 48
Strauss, Roger 155
Streisand, Barbra 46
Suburban Roulette 66, 67, 110, 118–120, 127, 185
Suez Motel 45, 48, 49, 50, 52
Suspiria 175
Swain, Robert 159
Sweet, Tony 28
Sweetwood, Thomas (a.k.a. William Kerwin) 33
Swift, Jonathan 159
Szegho, Raymond 158; see also Ray Sager

Tadie, Alan 129
Tamiroff, Akim 119

A Taste of Blood 2, 12, 61, 103, 107, 110, 118, 120, 121–131, 132, 133, 148, 153, 180, 185
Taste the Blood of Dracula 62
Taylor, Elizabeth 68
Taylor, Rod 49
Taylor, Stu 101
Teenage Rebellion 140
Teen-Age Strangler 123, 127, 132
Teenage Zombies 14
The Terror 5
Terror at Halfday see *Monster A' Go-Go*
Terror from the Year 5000 14
Terror Train 67
Teton, Al 94
The Texas Chainsaw Massacre 67, 147
Thar She Blows! 105
Theater of Blood 168
They Came from Within 175
The Thing (1982) 79
This Stuff'll Kill Ya! 49, 67, 157–159, 185
Thomas, James 118; *see also* McGinn, Jim
Thompson, Peter 101
Thunder Road 97
Time (magazine) 81
Tobin, Lawrence 127
Toomey, Toni 32
Torquemada 64
Trans-America Films 140
Travis, June 101
Treasure of the Sierra Madre 157
The Trip 7
Triton College 107, 141
Trucks 12
Tuesday, Ruby 138
Twentieth Century–Fox Pictures Corp. 9, 14, 81
Twitch of the Death-Nerve 175
Two Thousand Maniacs! 1, 2, 12, 19, 38, 42, 46, 48, 56, 58, 66–82, 83, 84, 85, 91, 92, 93, 94, 97, 98, 99, 102, 104, 105, 107, 109, 122, 139, 140, 144, 154, 157, 158, 159, 161, 162, 176, 177, 180, 185

The Undead 15
The Undertaker and His Pals 175
United Artists Pictures 69
United Film and Recording Studio 20, 21, 22, 23
Universal Pictures 14, 81, 122, 177
Vance, Jim 133

Variety 178
The Vengeance of She 107
Vercruse, Bob 128
Videoscope (magazine) 174
Voodoo Woman 15
The Vulture 119

Warner Bros. Pictures 9, 14, 81, 170
Warner, Elyn 85, 87, 89
WCOJ Radio 8, 9
Weisenborn, Gordon 16
Welles, Orson 7, 14
Wellington, Larry 25, 107, 129, 139, 167
Wells, Gretchen 112
West, Bobbi 133
Which Way to the Front? 130
Whirlpool 160
White Trash on Moonshine Mountain see *Moonshine Mountain*
Whitman, Walt 7
The Wild Angels 134, 136
The Wild Bunch 41
Wilkinson, Elizabeth 119, 123, 127
William Morris Agency 31
Williams, Bentley 32
Wilson, Andy 79
Wise, Robert 12
Wishman, Doris 32
The Wizard of Gore 2, 13, 38, 41, 58, 78, 103, 105, 109, 115, 118, 125, 134, 143, 144–156, 157, 161, 162, 165, 174, 180, 181, 185
WKY-TV 9
Wood, Edward D., Jr. 14, 120
Wood, Robert 133
Wood, Thomas 19, 24, 68, 70, 177; *see also* Kerwin, William
WRAC Radio 9

Yager, Julie 146
Year of the Yahoo 67, 159, 185
Youngman, Henny 49, 162, 165, 166, 167, 177

Zanuck, Darryl F. 61
The Zap-In see *Miss Nymphet's Zap-In*
Zolotareff, Seymour 18
Zombie 175
Zombie High 67

www.ingramcontent.com/pod-product-compliance
Ingram Content Group UK Ltd.
Pitfield, Milton Keynes, MK11 3LW, UK
UKHW050524150426
5217IPUK00026B/1794